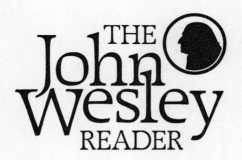

THE John Wesley READER

Also by Al Bryant

LoveSongs: Daily Meditations for Married Couples
Daily Meditations with F. B. Meyer
Near the Sun: A Sourcebook of Daily Meditations
  from Charles Haddon Spurgeon
Keep in Touch: 366 Day Starters for Young Adults
Today, Lord, I Will: A Daily Devotional

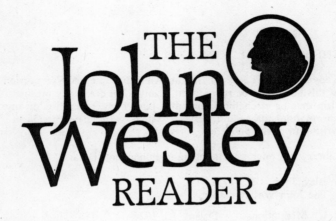

THE John Wesley READER

Compiled by Al Bryant

Foreword by Dr. Charles L. Allen

WORD BOOKS
PUBLISHER
WACO, TEXAS

A DIVISION OF
WORD, INCORPORATED

THE JOHN WESLEY READER

Library of Congress Cataloging in Publication Data:

Wesley, John, 1703–1791.
   The John Wesley reader.

   1.   Meditations. I.   Bryant, Al, 1926–   . II.   Title.
BX8217.W54B788   1983   242   83–16759

Unless otherwise indicated, Scripture quotations are taken
from the King James Version, that edition of the Holy Scriptures
known and loved by John Wesley. Scriptures marked RSV are from the
Revised Standard Version of the Bible, copyrighted 1946, 1952, ©
1971 and 1973 by the Division of Christian Education of the National
Council of the Churches of Christ in the U.S.A. Scriptures marked NIV
are from the New International Version of the Bible, copyrighted ©
1973 the New York Bible Society International. Scripture marked LB is
from *The Living Bible, Paraphrased* (Wheaton: Tyndale House
Publishers, 1971 and is used by permission.

Printed in the United States of America

Contents

13

Foreword

QUOREM PARS MAGNA FUI
(Of which things I was an important part)

John Wesley was born in the Epworth Church parsonage, Lincoln-shire, England, June 17, 1703—the fifteenth child in a family of nineteen.

He died on Wednesday, March 2, 1791, in a house on City Road, London.

Among his very last words were: "The best of all, God is with us." Shortly before his death, with waning strength he sat up and sang some lines from Isaac Watts' hymn:

> I'll praise my Maker while I've breath;
> And when my voice is lost in death,
> Praise shall employ my nobler powers,
> My days of praise shall ne'er be passed. . . .

Between the above two events were eighty-eight years, nine-and-a-half months, in which was lived one of the most remarkable and significant lives in all of Christian history.

John Wesley's words need to be read and read again in every generation. And to fully understand what he said, one needs to know something about him.

His father, Samuel Wesley, was the rector of the Epworth Parish. He was the son and grandson of ministers and was no ordinary man. Few priests in the Church of England were the equal of Samuel Wesley, either in intellectual acumen or moral sensitivity. He was a most worthy man.

Susannah Wesley, John's mother, was even more remarkable. In an age when women were not given the educational opportuni-ties men had, here was one woman who could have talked on most important subjects of religion and philosophy with the great-est minds of the day. She has been called "the most capable woman in England." As a theological thinker, she had no superior in her day. Mrs. Wesley gave long hours to directing the studies of her children. John Wesley's ability to understand intellectual differences and his complete intolerance of moral evils had their origin at his mother's knee.

Perhaps no experience affected Wesley's entire life more than one that occurred on February 9, 1709, when he was not quite six years old. The family home was on fire. It was thought that all of the family were safely out of the house. Then it was discovered that John was trapped in an upstairs room. He was rescued, and on the very spot—as the house was burning—his mother dedicated the child to God anew, saying he had been "plucked as a brand from the burning." From that moment on, Mrs. Wesley had a special affection for John and regarded him in a very special way.

John Wesley was no self-made man. He attended Charter House and Oxford University. Those were two of the finest schools in all the world. There, his acute mind and sensitive soul were greatly influenced by a very thorough and formal education. His father, grandfather, and great-grandfather had been Oxford men before him, and he was proud to be in the Oxford tradition. He gained a reputation for scholarship and became truly an intellectually outstanding man.

During the next nine years he served as a fellow of Lincoln College, with a brief interim as his father's assistant in the capacity of parish clergyman. Later he came to Savannah, Georgia, as a missionary, and here we see the beginning of the breakdown of Wesley's high-church religion. His ministry in Georgia was not successful. He wrote in his journal, "Why (what was least of all expected), that I, who went to America to convert others, was never myself converted to God." In Savannah, Wesley came to know a Moravian pastor by the name of Spangenberg. On shipboard going over, Wesley found himself cringing with fear in the midst of a storm, but the Moravians on board faced the peril with perfect poise. The fact that they were different from himself broke Wesley's pride. Upon his return to England, he came to know a very outstanding Moravian, Peter Bohler, who had come there from Frankfurt.

The story here must be told in Wesley's own words: "In the evening I went very unwillingly to a Society in Aldersgate-street, where one was reading Luther's preface to the Epistle to the Romans. About a quarter of nine, while he was describing the change which God works in the heart through faith in Christ, I felt my heart strangely warmed. I felt I did trust in Christ, Christ alone, for salvation; and an assurance was given me, he had taken my sins, even mine, and saved me from the law of sin and death. I began to pray with all my might for those who had in a more especial manner despitefully used me and persecuted me. I then openly testified to all there, what I now first felt in my heart." This was on Wednesday evening, May 24th, 1738. That was the rising of the sun in John Wesley's life—the sun that never set.

Today as we look back upon the eighteenth century, we see three great movements: the rise of the Anglo-Saxon nations, the rise of Methodism, and the rise of the great modern missionary movement. John Wesley might say of all of them, *Quorem pars magna fui* (Of which things I was an important part). These three converge upon a common object—the salvation of mankind. They all unite with Wesley in saying, "The world is my parish," which words he spoke in front of his own father's church at Epworth. Each of these three movements would suffer without the support of the others.

During the year following his Aldersgate experience, John Wesley made four momentous decisions, which eventually led to the founding and worldwide mission of the Methodist Church:

First, he approved field preaching. He found himself shut out of the churches, so he took to the open fields. Wesley's high-church scruples were melted away by the opportunities of evangelism. This was really the forerunner of revivalism.

Second, he approved of lay preaching. It would have been utterly impossible to get ordained ministers to carry on this new movement. To permit unordained men to preach was scandalous to high-churchmen, but John Wesley stood by that decision.

Third, Wesley decided to organize converts and give them some kind of supervision. He became a practical churchman.

Fourth, Wesley decided to house his societies, and the actual beginning of the world's first Methodist chapel was at Bristol, May 12, 1739. Later a chapel was built in London—the Foundry—and soon a second chapel was built in London. From such beginnings the housing of Methodism went on.

Was Wesley conscious of what he was doing? The answer is no. Like Abraham, the father of the faithful, he rose at the call of God and went out, knowing not whither. Men who were dedicated to God never worried about what the results would be.

This brings to mind such notables as Moses at the burning bush, Paul on the road to Damascus, and men like Martin Luther and John Calvin and John Knox. Like them, Wesley became a hero of the faith.

John Wesley never professed to discover new truths, but to restore the old faith. He was no innovator, but a renovator. As one reads the excellent collection of readings from John Wesley's sermons and journals in this volume, two errors concerning John Wesley and Methodism are completely dispelled. Some have fallen into the error of thinking that Wesley cared nothing for doctrinal truth, and that Methodism was thereby made by him a movement of doctrineless sentiment and creedless enthusiasm. Others have imagined that Wesley brought forward new and strange doctrines never known to the church before his time, and that from those dogmas Methodism arose. We easily see both of these ideas are completely in error.

Here let us sum up very briefly, the doctrines that John Wesley preached:

(1) The doctrine of the authority and inspiration of the Holy Scriptures.

(2) The doctrine of the depravity of human nature and inability of man to turn to God without the aid of the Holy Spirit.

(3) The doctrine of the atonement of Christ, made through his vicarious sacrifice for the sin of the world, which is the sole meritorious cause for man's acceptance with God.

(4) The doctrine of the universality of that atonement, whereby "whosoever believeth shall not perish, but have eternal life."

(5) The doctrine of justification by faith alone as the instrumental cause of man's salvation.

(6) The doctrine of the new birth and the absolute need of a conscientious conversion or regeneration.

(7) The doctrine of sanctification by the cleansing power of the Holy Ghost through faith in Christ.

(8) The doctrine of the witness of the Spirit, bearing witness with the spirit of a regenerated person that he is a child of God.

John Wesley met the needs of his day and generation through the masses of people who were defeated. He declared the availability of God's grace for all people—that every person is a child of God. To the churches he proclaimed a salvation that would make religion a power instead of a burden, and that would lift religion from drudgery to joyful fellowship with God. The gospel that

John Wesley preached was "good news" to the people of his day. His translation of Christ into terms which promised the man of his century salvation literally became a translation that transformed a century.

One thing further—John Wesley was concerned with the society in which he lived. For him, religion was no mere matter of an emotional experience; it was a program of action that called for a plan of attack wherever an evil was damaging the lives of people. He especially waged his fight against what he regarded as the four greatest evils of his age—poverty, war, ignorance, and disease. After more than a half century of war against these evils, one can say that the modern social conscience had been born.

Wesley believed each person is "steward" of wealth, not owner. It has been claimed that Wesley was the founder of modern philanthropy and that his attitude toward human need was far in advance of the older attitude of an almsgiving charity.

Wesley was an untiring enemy of ignorance. It was his theory that every person is entitled to the blessing of education. It may be that his theories of education were lacking at some points, but his conviction as to who should be educated gives him a place in the history of education. Green, the historian, stated, "Wesley gave the first impulse to our popular education."

Wesley was not a pacifist in the modern sense, but he believed passionately that men of reason ought to be able to settle their differences. To Wesley's mind, war was insanity. He felt there was no need to discuss war in relation to religion. War stood condemned on the basis of "common sense."

Wesley was deeply concerned with human suffering. In London he organized a group of volunteers who systematically visited the sick. London was divided into twenty-three sections, with two visitors assigned to each section. They were instructed to inquire into the spiritual state of the sick, but also to discover their trouble and to seek medical advice, to relieve them if they were in want and to render any other needed service. John Wesley believed in a practical application of Christianity.

As we read carefully selected passages from John Wesley's writings in the following pages, we are reading the words of one of the most extraordinary Christian geniuses who ever lived on this earth.

CHARLES L. ALLEN
Houston, Texas

Preface

The journals of John Wesley as well as his published sermons and letters have left with us a rich heritage of spiritual truth in the Wesleyan tradition. These are the sources from which the devotional meditations in this book have been selected. Since such a large body of modern-day believers are still following in that vigorous tradition, it is hoped that this collection will find wide acceptance and meet the devotional needs of many around the world.

As I did in similar collections from the writings of Andrew Murray, F. B. Meyer, and Charles Haddon Spurgeon, I have arranged these meditations in a daily sequence of progression. Thus, it is hoped that the book may be used not just as a daily devotional, but also as a sourcebook of choice thought on important subjects as seen through the mind and writings of one of Christianity's greatest advocates and champions.

The Methodist Episcopal Church of America was officially constituted by the Christmas Conference of 1784 under the direction of Thomas Coke, who had been appointed by John Wesley to superintend the colonial expansion of the Wesleyan movement. The bicentennial of this establishment will be celebrated in 1984, and provided the immediate impetus for bringing together this *John Wesley Reader*.

Of necessity, the meditations in this collection are but a small representation of the man, John Wesley. His indefatigable labors launched Methodism, a movement still vital and flourishing two centuries after his death. This book is dedicated to his memory and published in the interest of his ministry. Both the man and his message emerge in these selected excerpts from his journals, personal correspondence, and sermons.

AL BRYANT

1. A Place to Begin

Walking with God

And Enoch walked with God: and he was not; for God took him. . . . Noah was a just man and perfect in his generations, and Noah walked with God.
Genesis 5:24; 6:9

How different is the case, how vast the preeminence, of those who "walk by faith"! . . .

Those who *live* by faith, *walk by faith.* But what is implied in this? They regulate all their judgments concerning good and evil, not with reference to visible and temporal things, but to things invisible and eternal. They think visible things to be of small value, because they pass away like a dream; but, on the contrary, they account invisible things to be of high value, because they will never pass away. Whatever is invisible is eternal; the things that are not seen, do not perish. So the apostle: "The things that are seen are temporal; but the things that are not seen are eternal." Therefore, they who "walk by faith" do not desire the "things which are seen"; neither are they the object of their pursuit. They "set their affection on things above, not on things on the earth." . . . They weigh whatever occurs in this balance: "What influence has it on my eternal state?" They regulate all their tempers and passions, all their desires, joys, and fears, by this standard. They regulate all their thoughts and designs, all their words and actions, so as to prepare them for that invisible and eternal world to which they are shortly going. They do not *dwell* but only *sojourn* here; not looking upon earth as their home, but only

Travelling through Immanuel's ground,
To fairer worlds on high.

The Healing Creator

And the Lord said, I will destroy man whom I have
created from the face of the earth; both man, and beast,
and the creeping thing, and the fowls of the air; for
it repenteth me that I have made them.
Genesis 6:7

Can the Creator despise the work of his own hands? Surely that is impossible! Has he not then, seeing he alone is able, provided a remedy for all these evils? Yea, verily he has! And a sufficient remedy; every way adequate to the disease. He has fulfilled his word: He has given "the seed of the woman to bruise the serpent's head." "God so loved the world, that he gave his only-begotten Son, that whosoever believeth in him might not perish, but have everlasting life."

Here is a remedy provided for all our guilt: He "bore all our sins in his body on the tree." And "if any one has sinned, we have an Advocate with the Father, Jesus Christ the righteous."

And here is a remedy for all our disease, all the corruption of our nature. For God has also, through the intercession of his Son, given us his Holy Spirit, to renew us both "in knowledge," in his natural image—opening the eyes of our understanding, and enlightening us with all such knowledge as is requisite to our pleasing God—and also in his moral image, namely, "righteousness and true holiness."

And supposing this is done, we know that "all things" will "work together for our good." We know by happy experience, that all natural evils change their nature and turn to good; that sorrow, sickness, pain, will all prove medicines, to heal our spiritual sickness. They will all be to our profit; will all tend to our unspeakable advantage; making us more largely "partakers of his holiness," while we remain on earth; adding so many stars to that crown which is reserved in heaven for us.

Loving and Serving

As for me and my house, we will serve the Lord.
Joshua 24:15

We may inquire, first, what it is to "serve the Lord," not as a Jew, but as a Christian; not only with an outward service, (though some of the Jews undoubtedly went farther than this), but with inward, with the service of the heart, "worshipping him in spirit and in truth." The first thing implied in this service is faith— believing in the name of the Son of God. We cannot perform an acceptable service to God till we believe on Jesus Christ whom he has sent. Here the spiritual worship of God begins. As soon as any one has the witness in himself; as soon as he can say, "The life that I now live, I live by faith in the Son of God, who loved me, and gave himself for me"; he is able truly to "serve the Lord."

As soon as he believes, he loves God, which is another thing implied in "serving the Lord." "We love him because he first loved us"; of this faith is the evidence. The love of a pardoning God is "shed abroad in our hearts, by the Holy Ghost which is given unto us." Indeed this love may admit of a thousand degrees, but still every one, as long as he believes, may truly declare before God, " 'Lord, thou knowest that I love thee.' Thou knowest that 'my desire is unto thee, and unto the remembrance of thy name.' "

And if any man truly love God, he cannot but love his brother also. Gratitude to our Creator will surely produce benevolence to our fellow-creatures. If we love him, we cannot but love one another, as Christ loved us. We feel our souls enlarged in love toward every child of man. And toward all the children of God we put on "bowels of kindness, gentleness, longsuffering, forgiving one another," if we have a complaint against any, "even as God, for Christ's sake, hath forgiven us."

One thing more is implied in "serving the Lord," namely, obeying him; steadily walking in all his ways, doing his will from the heart. Like those, "his servants" above, "who do his pleasure, who keep his commandments, and hearken to the voice of his words"; these, his servants below, hearken unto his voice, diligently keep his commandments, carefully avoid whatever he has forbidden, and zealously do whatever he has enjoined; studying always to have a conscience void of offense toward God and toward man.

God Sees Our Hearts

[And God said:] I know thy abode, and thy going out, and thy coming in.

2 Kings 19:27

If we believe that God knows all these things about us, then we should take care not to do the least thing, not to speak the least word, not to indulge the least thought, which we would have the least reason to think would offend him. Suppose that a messenger of God, an angel, were to be standing now at your right hand, and fixing his eyes upon you, would you not take care to abstain from every word or action that you knew would offend him? Yes, suppose some of your mortal fellow-servants, suppose only a holy man, stood by you, would you not be extremely cautious how you conducted yourself, both in word and action? How much more cautious ought you to be, when you know that not only a holy man, not an angel of God, but God himself, the Holy One "that inhabiteth eternity," is inspecting your heart, your tongue, your hand, every moment! And that he himself will surely bring you to judgment for all you think, and speak, and act under the sun!

Yea, if God sees our hearts, as well as our hands, and in all places; if he understands our thoughts long before they are clothed with words, how earnestly should we urge that petition, "Search me, O God, and know my heart: try me, and know my thoughts: And see if there be any wicked way in me, and lead me in the way everlasting" (Ps. 139:23, 24). Yea, how needful is it to work together with him, in "keeping our hearts with all diligence" till he hath "cast down imaginations, evil reasonings, and every thing that exalteth itself against the knowledge of God, and brought into captivity every thought to the obedience of Christ."

Rest for the Weary

There the wicked cease from troubling; and there the weary be at rest.

Job 3:17

There, then, "the weary are at rest." The blood of the Lamb has healed all their sickness, has washed them thoroughly from their wickedness, and cleansed them from their sin. The disease of their nature is cured; they are at length made whole; they are restored to perfect soundness. They no longer mourn the "flesh lusting against the Spirit"; the "law in their members" is now at an end, and no longer "wars against the law of their mind, and brings them into captivity to the law of sin." There is no root of bitterness left; no remains even of that sin which did "so easily beset them"; no forgetfulness of "Him in whom they live, and move, and have their being"; no ingratitude to their gracious Redeemer, who poured out his soul unto death for them; no unfaithfulness to that blessed Spirit who so long bore with their infirmities. In a word, no pride, no self-will is there; so that they who are "delivered from the bondage of corruption" may indeed say one to another, and that in an emphatical sense, "Beloved, now are we the children of God; and it doth not yet appear what we shall be; but we shall be like him, for we shall see him as he is."

Treasures in the Psalms

When I consider thy heavens, the work of thy fingers,
the moon and the stars, which thou hast ordained;
What is man, that thou art mindful of him?
Psalm 8:3, 4

How often has it been observed, that the Book of Psalms is a rich treasury of devotion, which the wisdom of God has provided to supply the wants of his children in all generations! In all ages the Psalms have been of singular use to those who loved or feared God; not only to the pious Israelites, but to the children of God in all nations. And this book has been of sovereign use to the Church of God, not only while it was in its state of infancy (so beautifully described by St. Paul in the former part of the fourth chapter to the Galatians) but also since, in the fullness of time, "life and immortality were brought to light by the gospel." The Christians in every age and nation have availed themselves of this divine treasure, which has richly supplied the wants, not only of "babes in Christ," of those who were just setting out in the ways of God, but of those also who had made good progress therein; yea, of such as were swiftly advancing toward "the measure of the stature of the fullness of Christ."

What Is Man?

When I consider thy heavens, the work of thy fingers, the moon and the stars, which thou hast ordained; What is man, that thou art mindful of him? and the son of man, that thou visitest him? . . . Man is like to vanity: his days are as a shadow that passeth away.
Psalms 8:3, 4; 144:4

These are two remarkable passages. In the first (Ps. 8) man is considered as a cipher, a point, compared to immensity. The second is, "Lord, what is man, that thou hast such respect unto him? Man is like a thing of nought. His time passeth away like a shadow!" In the new translation the words are stronger still: "What is man, that thou takest knowledge of him! or the son of man, that thou makest account of him!" Here the Psalmist seems to consider the life of man as a moment, a nothing, compared to eternity. Is not the purport of the former, "How can he that filleth heaven and earth take knowledge of such an atom as man? How is it that he is not utterly lost in the immensity of God's works?" Is not the purport of the latter, "How can he that inhabiteth eternity stoop to regard the creature of a day—one whose life passeth away like a shadow?" Is not this a thought which has struck many serious minds, as well as it did David's, and created a kind of fear lest they should be forgotten before him who grasps all space and all eternity? But does not this fear arise from a kind of supposition that God is such a one as ourselves?

If we consider boundless space, or boundless duration, we shrink into nothing before it. But God is not a man. A day, and millions of ages, are the same with him. Therefore, there is the same disproportion between him and any finite being, as between him and the creature of a day. Therefore, whenever that thought recurs, whenever you are tempted to fear lest you should be forgotten before the immense, the eternal God, remember that nothing is little or great, that no duration is long or short, before him. Re-

28

member that God "presides over every individual as over the universe; and the universe, as over each individual." So that you may boldly say,

> Father, how wide thy glories shine,
> Lord of the universe—and mine!
> Thy goodness watches o'er the whole,
> As all the world were but one soul;
> Yet counts my every sacred hair,
> As I remain'd thy single care!

2. The Path to Perfection

Obeying the Creator

What is man, that thou art mindful of him? and the son of man, that thou visitest him?
Psalm 8:4

A Christian cannot think of the Author of his being without abasing himself before him; without a deep sense of the distance between a worm of earth, and the one who sits on the circle of the heavens. In his presence he sinks into the dust, knowing himself to be less than nothing in his eye; and being conscious, in a manner words cannot express, of his own littleness, ignorance, foolishness. So that he can only cry out, from the fullness of his heart, "O God! What is man? What am I?"

He has a continual sense of his dependence on the Parent of good for his being, and all the blessings that attend it. To him he refers every natural and every moral endowment; with all that is commonly ascribed either to fortune, or to the wisdom, courage, or merit of the possessor. And hence he acquiesces in whatsoever appears to be his will, not only with patience, but with thankfulness. He willingly resigns all he is, all he has, to his wise and gracious disposal. The ruling temper of his heart is the most absolute submission, and the tenderest gratitude, to his sovereign Benefactor. And this grateful love creates filial fear; an awful reverence toward him, and an earnest care not to give place to any disposition, not to admit an action, word, or thought, which might in any degree displease that indulgent Power to whom he owes his life, breath, and all things.

And as he has the strongest affection for the Fountain of all good, so he has the firmest confidence in him; a confidence which neither pleasure nor pain, neither life nor death, can shake. But yet this, far from creating sloth or indolence, pushes him on to the most vigorous industry. It causes him to put forth all his strength, in obeying him in whom he confides. So that he is never faint in his mind, never weary of doing whatever he believes to be his will. And as he knows the most acceptable worship of God is to imitate him he worships, so he is continually laboring to transcribe into himself all his imitable perfections; in particular, his justice, mercy, and truth, so eminently displayed in all his creatures.

From Death to Life

What is man, that thou art mindful of him, and the son of man that thou dost care for him?
Psalm 8:4 (RSV)

But tell me frighted nature, what is death?
Blood only stopp'd, and interrupted breath?
The utmost limit of a narrow span?
And end of motion, which with life began?

Death is properly the separation of the soul from the body. Of this we are certain. But we are not certain (at least in many cases) of the time when this separation is made. Is it when respiration ceases? According to the well-known maxim, *Nullus spiritus, nulla vita:* "Where there is no breath, there is no life." Nay, we cannot absolutely affirm this: For many instances have been known, of those whose breath was totally lost, and yet their lives have been recovered. Is it when the heart no longer beats, or when the circulation of the blood ceases? Not so. For the heart may beat anew; and the circulation of the blood, after it is quite interrupted, may begin again. Is the soul separated from the body, when the whole body is stiff and cold as a piece of ice? But there have been several instances lately, of persons who were thus cold and stiff, and had no symptoms of life remaining, who, nevertheless, upon proper application recovered both life and health. Therefore we can say no more, than that death is the separation of the soul and body; but in many cases only God can tell the moment of that separation.

But what we are much more concerned to know, and deeply to consider, is the end of life. For what end is life bestowed upon the children of men? Why were we sent into the world? For one sole end, and for no other, to prepare for eternity. For this alone we live. For this, and no other purpose, is our life either given or continued. It pleased the all-wise God, at the season which he saw best, to arise in the greatness of his strength, and create the heavens and the earth, and all things that are therein. Having prepared all things for him, he "created man in his own image, after his own likeness." And what was the end of his creation? It was one, and no other—that he might know, and love and enjoy, and serve his great Creator to all eternity.

The Making of a Man

For thou hast made him [man] a little lower than the
angels, and hast crowned him with glory and honour.
Psalm 8:5

Man, "being in honor, continued not," but became lower than even the beasts that perish. He willfully and openly rebelled against God, and cast off his allegiance to the Majesty of heaven. Hereby he instantly lost both the favor of God, and the image of God wherein he was created. As he was then incapable of obtaining happiness by the old, God established a new covenant with man; the terms of which were no longer, "Do this and live," but, "Believe, and thou shalt be saved." But still the end of man is one and the same; only it stands on another foundation. For the plain tenor of it is, "Believe in the Lord Jesus Christ, whom God hath given to be the propitiation for thy sins, and thou shalt be saved"; first, from the guilt of sin, having redemption through his blood; then from the power, which shall have no more dominion over you; and then from the root of it, into the whole image of God. And being restored both to the favor and image of God, you shall know, love, and serve him to all eternity. So that still the end of his life, the life of every man born into the world, is to know, love, and serve his great Creator.

And let it be observed, as this is the end, so it is the whole and sole end, for which every man upon the face of the earth, for which every one of *you* were brought into the world and endued with a living soul. Remember! You were born for nothing else. You live for nothing else. Your life is continued to you upon earth, for no other purpose than this, that you may know, love, and serve God on earth, and enjoy him to all eternity. Consider! You were not created to please your senses, to gratify your imagination, to gain money, or the praise of men; to seek happiness in any created good, in anything under the sun. All this is "walking in a vain shadow"; it is living a restless, miserable life, leading to a miserable eternity. On the contrary, you were created for this, and for no other purpose, by seeking and finding happiness in God on earth, to secure the glory of God in heaven. Therefore, let your heart continually say, "This one thing I do"—having one thing in view, remembering why I was born, and why I am continued in life—"I press on to the mark." I aim at the one end of my being, God; even at "God in Christ reconciling the world to himself." He shall be my God forever and ever, and my guide even unto death!

Our Gracious God and Savior

[David said] In my distress I called upon the Lord, and cried unto my God: he heard my voice out of his temple, and my cry came before him, even into his ears.
Psalm 18:6

Of the Christian it might be said: "Then they cried unto the Lord in their trouble, and he delivered them out of their distresses" (Psalm 107:6). His eyes are opened in quite another manner than before, even to see a loving, gracious God. While he is calling, "I beseech thee, show me thy glory!"—he hears a voice in his inmost soul, "I will make all my goodness pass before thee, and I will proclaim the name of the Lord: I will be gracious to whom I will be gracious, and I will show mercy to whom I will show mercy." And, it is not long before "the Lord descends in the cloud, and proclaims the name of the Lord." Then he sees, but not with eyes of flesh and blood, "The Lord, the Lord God, merciful and gracious, longsuffering, and abundant in goodness and truth; keeping mercy for thousands, and forgiving iniquities, and transgressions, and sin."

Heavenly, healing light now breaks in upon his soul. He "looks on him whom he had pierced," and "God, who out of darkness commanded light to shine, shineth in his heart." He sees the light of the glorious love of God, in the face of Jesus Christ. He has a divine "evidence of things not seen" by sense, even of "the deep things of God"; more particularly of the love of God, of his pardoning love to him that believes in Jesus. Overpowered with the sight, his whole soul cries out, "My Lord and my God!" For he sees all his iniquities laid on him, who "bare them in his own body on the tree"; he beholds the Lamb of God taking away his sins. How clearly now does he discern, that "God was in Christ reconciling the world unto himself; making him sin for us, who knew no sin, that we might be made the righteousness of God through him"—and that he himself is reconciled to God, by that blood of the covenant!

Experiencing God with Our Senses

O taste and see that the Lord is good: blessed is the man that trusteth in him.
Psalm 34:8

The moment the Spirit of the Almighty strikes the heart of him who was till then without God in the world, it breaks the hardness of his heart, and creates all things new. The Sun of Righteousness appears, and shines upon his soul, showing him the light of the glory of God in the face of Jesus Christ. He is in a new world. All things around him are become new, such as it never before entered into his heart to conceive. He sees, so far as his newly opened eyes can bear the sight,

> The opening heavens around him shine,
> With beams of sacred bliss.

He sees that he has "an advocate with the Father, Jesus Christ the righteous"; and that he has "redemption in his blood, the remission of sins." He sees "a new way that is opened into the holiest by the blood of Jesus"; and his light "shineth more and more unto the perfect day."

By the same gracious stroke, he that before had ears, but heard not, is now made capable of *hearing*. He hears the voice that raised the dead—the voice of him who is "the resurrection and the life." He is no longer deaf to his invitations or commands, to his promises or threatenings; but gladly hears every word that proceeds out of his mouth, and governs thereby all his thoughts, words, and actions.

At the same time, he receives other spiritual senses capable of discerning spiritual good and evil. He is enabled to *taste,* as well as to see, how gracious the Lord is. He enters into the holiest by the blood of Jesus, and tastes of the powers of the world to come. He finds Jesus' love far better than wine; yea, sweeter than honey or the honeycomb. He knows what that meaneth: "All thy garments smell of myrrh, aloes, and cassia." He feels the love of God shed abroad in heart by the Holy Ghost which is given unto him; or, as our Church expresses it, "feels the working of the Spirit of God in his heart." Meantime, it may easily be observed, that the substance of all these figurative expressions is comprised in that one word, faith taken in its widest sense; being enjoyed, more or less, by every one who believes in the name of the Son of God.

The Perfect Man

Mark the blameless man, and behold the upright, for there is posterity for the man of peace.
Psalm 37:37 (RSV)

But where shall you find one who answers this happy and amiable description? Wherever you find a Christian; for this, and this alone, is real, genuine Christianity. Surely you did not imagine that Christianity was no more than such a system of opinions as is vulgarly called faith; or a strict and regular attendance on any kind of external worship. O no! Were this all that it implied, Christianity were indeed a poor, empty, shallow thing; such as none but half-thinkers could admire, and all who think freely and generously must despise. But this is not the case; the spirit above described, this alone, is Christianity. And, if so, it is no wonder that even a celebrated unbeliever should make that frank declaration, "Well, after all, these Christian dogs are the happiest fellows upon earth!" Indeed they are. Nay, we may say more; they are the only truly happy men upon earth because they are the only ones who can be in a right relationship to their Creator and Heavenly Father.

The Perfect Man Described

Mark the perfect man, and behold the upright: for the end of that man is peace.
Psalm 37:37

I am, first, briefly to inquire, who is the person here spoken of, "the upright and perfect man"? In speaking on this head, I shall not endeavor to describe the character of an upright Jew, such as David himself was; or any of those holy men who lived under the Mosaic dispensation: it more nearly imports us to consider such an upright man, as are those that live under the Christian dispensation; such as have lived and died since "life and immortality have been brought to light by the gospel."

In this sense, he is a perfect and upright man who believes in the name of the Son of God: he is one in whom it has pleased the Father to reveal the Son of his love; and who, consequently, is able to declare, "The life that I now live, I live by faith in the Son of God, who loved me, and gave himself for me." . . .

This faith will, undoubtedly, work by love. Accordingly every Christian believer has "the love of God shed abroad in his heart, by the Holy Ghost which is given unto him." And, loving God, he loves his brother also: his good will extends to every child of man. By this, as well as by the fruits of love, lowliness, meekness, and resignation, he shows that there is the same "mind in him which was in Christ Jesus."

As to his outward behavior, the upright Christian believer is blameless and unreprovable. He is holy, as Christ who has called him is holy, in all manner of conversation; ever laboring to have a conscience void of offense, toward God and toward man. He not only avoids all outward sin, but "abstains from all appearance of evil." He steadily walks in all the public and private ordinances of the Lord blameless. He is zealous of good works; as he has time, doing good, in every kind and degree, to all men. And in the whole course of his life, he pursues one invariable rule—whether he eats or drinks, or whatever he does, to do all to the glory of God.

36

3. The Eternal God

Of Time and Eternity

Remember how short my time is: wherefore hast thou made all men in vain?
Psalm 89:47

What is time? It is not easy to say, as frequently as we have had the word in our mouth. We know not what it properly is. We cannot well tell how to define it. But is it not, in some sense, a fragment of eternity, broken off at both ends?—that portion of duration which commenced when the world began, which will continue as long as this world endures, and then expire forever?—that portion of it, which is at present measured by the revolution of the sun and planets; lying (so to speak) between two eternities, that which is past, and that which is to come? But as soon as the heavens and the earth flee away from the face of him who sits on the great white throne, time will be no more; but sink forever into the ocean of eternity!

By what means can a mortal man, the creature of a day, form any idea of eternity? What can we find within the compass of nature to illustrate it? With what shall we compare it? What is there that bears any resemblance to it? Does there not seem to be some sort of analogy between boundless duration and boundless space? The great Creator, the infinite Spirit, inhabits both the one and the other. This is one of his peculiar prerogatives: "Do not I fill heaven and earth, saith the Lord?"—yea, not only the utmost regions of creation, but all the expanse of boundless space! Meantime, how many of the children of men may say,

> Lo, on a narrow neck of land,
> 'Midst two unbounded seas I stand,
>   Secure, insensible!
> A point of time, a moment's space,
> Removes me to that heavenly place,
>   Or shuts me up in hell!

On the Length of Eternity

Before the mountains were brought forth, or ever thou
hadst formed the earth and the world, even from
everlasting to everlasting, thou art God.
Psalm 90:2

Are we able to form a more adequate conception of eternity to come? To do this, let us compare it with the several degrees of duration which we are acquainted with: An ephemeron fly lives six hours; from six in the evening, to twelve. This is a short life compared with that of a man, which continues threescore or fourscore years; and this itself is short, if it be compared to the 969 years of Methuselah. Yet what are these years, yea, all that have succeeded each other, from the time that the heavens and the earth were erected, to the time when the heavens shall pass away, and the earth with its works shall be burned up, if we compare it to the length of that duration which never shall have an end?

To illustrate this, a late author has repeated that striking thought of St. Cyprian: "Suppose there were a ball of sand as large as the globe of earth: suppose a grain of this sand were to be annihilated, reduced to nothing, in a thousand years; yet that whole space of duration, wherein this ball would be annihilating, at the rate of one grain in a thousand years, would bear infinitely less proportion to eternity, duration without end, than a single grain of sand would bear to all the mass!"

To fix this important point the more deeply in your mind, consider another comparison: Suppose the ocean to be so enlarged, as to include all the space between the earth and the starry heavens. Suppose a drop of this water to be annihilated once in a thousand years; yet that whole space of duration, wherein this ocean would be annihilating, at the rate of one drop in a thousand years, would be infinitely less in proportion to eternity, than one drop of water to that whole ocean.

Look then at those immortal spirits, whether they are in this or the other world. When they shall have lived thousands of thousands of years, yea, millions of millions of ages, their duration will be but just begun: They will be only upon the threshold of eternity!

38

The All-Knowing God

Before the mountains were born or you brought forth
the earth and the world, from everlasting to
everlasting you are God.
Psalm 90:2 (NIV)

The sum of all is this: the almighty, all-wise God sees and knows, from everlasting to everlasting, all that is, that was, and that is to come, through one eternal *now*. With him nothing is either past or future, but all things equally present. He has, therefore, if we speak according to the truth of things, no foreknowledge, no afterknowledge. This would be ill consistent with the apostle's words, "With him is no variableness or shadow of turning"; and with the account he gives of himself by the prophet, "I the Lord change not." Yet when he speaks to us, knowing whereof we are made, knowing the scantiness of our understanding, he lets himself down to our capacity, and speaks of himself after the manner of men. Thus, in condescension to our weakness, he speaks of his own purpose, counsel, plan, foreknowledge. Not that God has any need of counsel, of purpose, or of planning his work beforehand. Far be it from us to impute these to the Most High; to measure him by ourselves! It is merely in compassion to us that he speaks thus of himself, as foreknowing the things in heaven or earth, and as predestinating or foreordaining them. But can we possibly imagine that these expressions are to be taken literally? To one who was so gross in his conceptions might he not say, "Think you I am such a one as yourself? Not so: As the heavens are higher than the earth, so are my ways higher than your ways. I know, decree, and work in such a manner as it is not possible for you to conceive: but to give you some faint, glimmering knowledge of my ways, I use the language of men, and suit myself to your apprehensions in this your infant state of existence."

What is it, then, that we learn from this whole account? It is this, and no more—(1) God knows all believers; (2) wills that they should be saved from sin; (3) to that end, justifies them; (4) sanctifies, and; (5) takes them to glory.

O that men would praise the Lord for this his goodness; and that they would be content with this plain account of it, and not endeavor to wade into those mysteries which are too deep for angels to fathom!

Obedient Stewardship

Who will rise up for me against the evildoers? or who will stand up for me against the workers of iniquity?
Psalm 94:16

He who gives us all, must needs have a right to all: so that if we pay him anything less than all, we cannot be faithful stewards. And considering, "every man shall receive his own reward, according to his own labor"; we cannot be wise stewards, unless we labor to the uttermost of our power; not leaving anything undone, which we possibly can do, by putting forth all our strength.

Brethren, "Who is an understanding man and endued with knowledge among you?" Let him show the wisdom from above, by walking suitably to his character. If he so account of himself, as a steward to the manifold gifts of God, let him see that all his thoughts, and words, and works, be agreeable to the post God has assigned him. It is no small thing, to lay out for God all which you have received from God. It requires all your wisdom, all your resolution, all your patience, and constancy—far more than ever you had by nature; but not more than you may have by grace. For his grace is sufficient for you; and "all things," you know, "are possible to him that believeth." By faith, then, "put on the Lord Jesus Christ"; "put on the whole armour of God" . . . and you will be enabled to glorify him in all your words and works; yea, to bring every thought into captivity to the obedience of Christ!

The God Who Governs

The Lord hath prepared his throne in the heavens; and his kingdom ruleth over all.
Psalm 103:19

The true God is the Governor of all things: "His kingdom ruleth over all." The government rests upon his shoulder, throughout all ages. He is the Lord and Disposer of the whole creation, and every part of it. And in how astonishing a manner does he govern the world! How far are methods of government! Only this we know: "Thou presidest over each creature, as if it were the universe, and over the universe, as over each individual creature." Dwell a little upon this sentiment: What a glorious mystery does it contain! It is paraphrased in the words.

> FATHER, how wide Thy glories shine!
> Lord of the universe—and mine:
> Thy goodness watches o'er the whole,
> As all the world were but one soul;
> Yet keeps my every sacred hair,
> As I remain'd Thy single care!

The God Who Works

O Lord, how manifold are thy works! in wisdom hast thou made them all: the earth is full of thy riches.
Psalm 104:24

We may well cry out, "O Lord, how manifold are thy works! In wisdom hast thou made them all."

This we know, concerning the whole frame and arrangement of the visible world. But how exceeding little do we now know concerning the invisible! And we should have known still less of it, had it not pleased the Author of both worlds to give us more than natural light, to give us "his word, to be a lantern to our feet, and a light in all our paths." And holy men of old, being assisted by his Spirit, have discovered many particulars of which otherwise we should have had no conception.

And without revelation, how little certainty of invisible things did the wisest of men obtain! The small glimmerings of light which they had were merely conjectural. At best they were only a faint, dim twilight, delivered from uncertain tradition; and so obscured by heathen fables, that it was but one degree better than utter darkness.

How uncertain the best of these conjectures was, may easily be gathered from their own accounts. The most finished of all these accounts, is that of the great Roman poet. Observe how warily he begins, with that apologetic preface—*Sit mihi fas audita loqui?*: "May I be allowed to tell what I have heard?" And, in the conclusion, lest any one should imagine he believed any of these accounts, he sends the relater of them out of hades by the *ivory gate,* through which, he had just informed us, only dreams and shadows pass—a very plain intimation, that all which has gone before, is to be looked upon as a dream! . . .

So little could even the most improved reason discover concerning the invisible and eternal world! The greater cause have we to praise the Father of Lights, who has opened the eyes of our understanding, to discern those things which could not be seen by eyes of flesh and blood. . . .

These things we have believed upon the testimony of God, the Creator of all things, visible and invisible; by this testimony we already know the things that now exist, though not yet seen, as well as those that will exist in their season, until this visible world shall pass away, and the Son of Man shall come in his glory.

Man of the Book

> *I am a stranger in the earth: hide not thy*
> *commandments from me.*
> **Psalm 119:19**

To candid, reasonable men, I am not afraid to lay open what have been the inmost thoughts of my heart. I have thought, I am a creature of a day, passing through life, as an arrow through the air. I am a spirit come from God, and returning to God: just hovering over the great gulf; till a few moments hence, I am no more seen! I drop into an unchangeable eternity! I want to know one thing, the way to heaven: how to land safe on that happy shore. God himself has condescended to teach the way; for this very end he came from heaven. He has written it down in a book! Oh, give me that book! At any price, give me the book of God! I have it: here is knowledge enough for me. Let me be *homo unius libri:* "A man of one book." Here then I am far from the busy ways of men. I sit down alone: only God is here. In his presence I open, I read this book; for this end, to find the way to heaven. Is there a doubt concerning the meaning of what I read? Does anything appear dark or intricate? I lift up my heart to the Father of lights. Lord, is it not your word, "If any man lack wisdom, let him ask of God"? You "give liberally and upbraid not." You have said, "If any be willing to do my will, he shall know." I am willing to do: let me know your will. I then search after, and consider parallel passages of Scripture, "comparing spiritual things with spiritual." I meditate thereon, with all the attention and earnestness of which my mind is capable. If any doubt still remains, I consult those who are experienced in the things of God; and then, the writings whereby, being dead, they yet speak. And what I thus learn, that I teach.

4. God over All

The Law and the Gospel

Great peace have they which love thy law: and nothing shall offend them.

Psalm 119:165

The more we are alive to God, the more we shall rejoice in him; the greater measure of his strength we receive, the greater will be our consolation also. And all this, I conceive, is clearly declared in one single passage of Scripture: "The law of the Lord is perfect, converting the soul: the testimony of the Lord is sure, making wise the simple. The statutes of the Lord are right, rejoicing the heart: the commandment of the Lord is pure, enlightening the eyes. . . . More to be desired are they than gold, yea, than much fine gold: sweeter also than honey and the honeycomb" (Ps. 19:7–10). They are both food and medicine; they both refresh, strengthen, and nourish the soul.

Not that I would advise to preach the law without the gospel, any more than the gospel without the law. Undoubtedly, both should be preached in their turns; yea, both at once, or both in one: all the conditional promises are instances of this. They are law and gospel mixed together.

According to this model, I should advise every preacher continually to preach the law; the law grafted upon, tempered by, and animated with, the Spirit of the gospel. I advise him to declare, explain, and enforce every command of God; but, meantime, to declare, in every sermon (and the more explicitly the better), that the first and great command to a Christian is, "Believe in the Lord Jesus Christ"; that Christ is all in all, our "wisdom, righteousness, sanctification, and redemption"; that all life, love, strength, are from him alone, and all freely given to us through faith. And it will ever be found, that the law thus preached both enlightens and strengthens the soul; that it both nourishes and teaches; that

44

it is the guide, "food, medicine, and stay," of the believing soul.

So we preached; and so you believed. This is the scriptural way, the Methodist way, the true way. O grant we may never turn from this path to the right hand or to the left!

Stewards, Not Proprietors

My lips shall utter praise, when thou hast taught me thy statutes. My tongue shall speak of thy word: for all thy commandments are righteousness.
Psalm 119:171, 172

God has entrusted us with our bodies (those exquisitely wrought machines, so "fearfully and wonderfully made"), with all the powers and members thereof. He has entrusted us with the organs of sense; of sight, hearing, and the rest: but none of these are given us as our own, to be employed according to our own will. None of these are lent us in such a sense, as to leave us at liberty to use them as we please for a season. No: we have received them on these very terms, that, as long as they abide with us, we should employ them all, in that very manner and no other.

It is on the same terms that he imparted to us that most excellent talent of speech. "Thou hast given me a tongue," says the ancient writer, "that I may praise thee therewith." For this purpose was it given to all the children of men, to be employed in glorifying God. Nothing, therefore, is more ungrateful or more absurd, than to think or say, "Our tongues are our own." That cannot be, unless we have created ourselves, and so are independent of the Most High. Nay, but "it is he that hath made us, and not we ourselves": the manifest consequence is, that he is still Lord over us, in this as in all other respects. It follows that there is not a word of our tongue for which we are not accountable to him.

To him we are equally accountable for the use of our hands and feet, and all the members of our body. These are so many talents which are committed to our trust, until the time appointed by the Father. Until then, we have the use of all these; but as stewards, not as proprietors; to the end, we should "render them, not as instruments of unrighteousness unto sin, but as instruments of righteousness unto God."

God Is Everywhere

O Lord, thou hast searched me, and known me.
Psalm 139:1

Accordingly, I will endeavor, by the assistance of his Spirit, first, a little to explain the omnipresence of God, to show how we are to understand this glorious truth, "God is in this and every place." The psalmist, you may remember, speaks strongly and beautifully upon it, in the hundred and thirty-ninth Psalm; observing, in the most exact order. First, "God is in this place"; and then, "God is in every place." He observes, first, "Thou compassest my path and my lying down, and art acquainted with all my ways" (v. 3). "Thou hast fashioned me behind and before, and laid thine hand upon me" (v. 5). Although the manner thereof he could not explain; how it was he could not tell. "Such knowledge," says he, "is too wonderful for me; I cannot attain unto it" (v. 6). He next observes, in the most lively and affecting manner, that God is in every place. "Whither shall I go from thy Spirit? or whither shall I flee from thy presence? If I ascend up into heaven, thou art there: if I make my bed in hell, behold, thou art there" (vv. 7, 8). If I could ascend, speaking after the manner of men, to the highest part of the universe, or could I descend to the lowest point, you are alike present both in one and the other. "If I should take the wings of the morning, and remain in the uttermost parts of the sea, even there thy hand would lead me"—thy power and thy presence would be before me "and thy right hand hold me"; seeing you are equally in the length and breadth, and in the height and depth, of the universe. Indeed, your presence and knowledge not only reach the utmost bounds of creation; but

> Thine omnipresent sight,
> Even to the pathless realms extends
> Of uncreated night.

In a word, there is not a point of space, whether within or without the bounds of creation, where God is not.

The Omnipresent God

Thou knowest when I sit down and when I rise up;
thou discernest my thoughts from afar.
Psalm 139:2 (RSV)

These words sufficiently prove his omnipresence, which may be
further proved from this consideration: God acts everywhere, and,
therefore, is everywhere—for it is an utter impossibility that any
being, created or uncreated, should work where it is not. God
acts in heaven, in earth, and under the earth, throughout the whole
compass of his creation: "Thou compassest my path and my lying
down, and art acquainted with all my ways" (v. 3). He sustains
all things, without which everything would, in an instant, sink
into its primitive nothing. He governs all, every moment superintending everything he has made, strongly and sweetly influences
all, and yet without destroying the liberty of his rational creatures.
The very heathen acknowledged that the great God governs the
large and conspicuous parts of the universe; that he regulates the
motions of the heavenly bodies, of the sun, moon, and stars. . . .

But they had no conception of his having a regard to the least
things as well as the greatest; of his presiding over all that he
has made, and governing atoms as well as worlds. This we could
not have known, unless it had pleased God to reveal it unto us
himself. Had he not himself told us so, we should not have dared
to think that "one of them shall not fall on the ground without
your Father"; and much less affirm that "the very hairs of your
head are all numbered" (Matt. 10:29; Luke 12:7).

God Is Watching!

Thou compassest my path and my lying down, and art
acquainted with all my ways.
Psalm 139:3

We cannot believe the omnipotence of God unless we believe his
omnipresence. . . . To set bounds to the one is undoubtedly to
set bounds to the other also. . . .

But allowing that God is here, as in every place, that he is
"about our bed, and about our path," that he "besets us behind

and before, and lays his hand upon us," what inference should we draw from hence? What use should we make of this awful consideration? Is it not meet and right to humble ourselves before the eyes of his Majesty? Should we not labor continually to acknowledge his presence "with reverence and godly fear?"—not indeed with the fear of devils, that believe and tremble, but with the fear of angels, with something similar to that which is felt by the inhabitants of heaven, when

> Dark with excessive bright his skirts appear,
> Yet dazzle heaven, that brightest seraphim
> Approach not, but with both wings veil their eyes.

God Knows Our Thoughts

For there is not a word in my tongue, but, lo, O Lord, thou knowest it altogether.
Psalm 139:4;
see Hebrews 4:13

If there is not a word in your tongue, not a syllable you speak, but he "knoweth it altogether"; how exact should you be in "setting a watch before your mouth, and in keeping the door of your lips"! How wary does it behoove you to be in all your conversation; being forewarned by your Judge, that "by your words you shall be justified, or by your words you shall be condemned"! How cautious, lest "any corrupt communication," any uncharitable, yea, or unprofitable discourse, should "proceed out of your mouth"; instead of "that which is good to the use of edifying, and meet to minister grace to the hearers!" . . .

In order to attain [this end], spare no pains to preserve always a deep, a continual, a lively, and a joyful sense of his gracious presence. Never forget his comprehensive word to the great father of the faithful: "I am the Almighty" (rather, the All-sufficient) "God; walk before me, and be thou perfect!" Cheerfully expect that he, before whom you stand, will ever guide you with his eye, will support you by his guardian hand, will keep you from all evil, and, "when you have suffered a while, will make you perfect, will stablish, strengthen, and settle you," and then "preserve you unblamable unto the coming of our Lord Jesus Christ!"

To See God Is to Love Him

Happy is he that hath the God of Jacob for his help, whose hope is in the Lord his God: Which made heaven, and earth, the sea, and all that therein is: which keepeth truth for ever.

Psalm 146:5, 6

I want to know this great God who filleth heaven and earth; who is above, beneath, and on every side, in all places of his dominion; who just now besets me behind and before, and lays his hand upon me; and yet I am no more acquainted with him, than with one of the inhabitants of Jupiter or Saturn.

O my friend, how will you get one step farther, unless God reveal himself to your soul?

And why should this seem a thing incredible to you; that God, a Spirit, and the Father of the spirits of all flesh, should discover himself to your spirit, which is itself "the breath of God," any more than that material things should discover themselves to your material eye? Is it any more repugnant to reason, that spirit should influence spirit, than that matter should influence matter? Nay, is not the former the more intelligible of the two? For there is the utmost difficulty in conceiving how matter should influence matter at all; how that which is totally passive should act. Neither can we rationally account either for gravitation, attraction, or any natural motion whatsoever, but by supposing in all the finger of God, who alone conquers that *vis inertiae* which is essential to every particle of matter, and worketh all in all.

Now, if God should ever open the eyes of your understanding, must not the love of God be the immediate consequence? Do you imagine you can see God without loving him? Is it possible in the nature of things? That old heathen, Cicero, said: "If virtue could be made the object of sight, she would (as Plato says) excite in us a wonderful love." How much more if you see him who is the original fountain, the great archetype of all virtue, will that sight raise in you a love that is wonderful, such as the busy world knows not of!

What benevolence also, what tender love to the whole of human kind, will you drink in, together with the love of God, from the unexhausted source of love! And how easy is it to conceive that more and more of his image will be then transfused into your soul; that from disinterested love, all other divine tempers will, as it were naturally, spring: mildness, gentleness, patience, temperance, justice, sincerity, contempt of the world; yea, whatsoever things are venerable and lovely, whatsoever are justly of good report!

5. *The God of the Old and New*

God's Grace at Work

They shall not hurt nor destroy in all my holy
mountain: for the earth shall be full of the knowledge
of the Lord, as the waters cover the sea.
                            Isaiah 11:9

Is it not highly probable that God will carry on his work in the same manner as he has begun it? That he *will* carry it on, I cannot doubt; however Luther may affirm, that a revival of religion never lasts above a generation—that is, thirty years; (whereas the present revival has already continued above fifty); or however prophets of evil may say, "All will be at an end when the first instruments are removed." There will then, very probably, be a great shaking; but I cannot induce myself to think that God has wrought so glorious a work to let it sink and die away in a few years: no, I trust, this is only the beginning of a far greater work, the dawn of "the latter day glory."

And is it not probable, I say, that he will carry it on in the same manner as he has begun? At the first breaking out of this work in this or that place, there may be a shower, a torrent of grace; and so at some other particular seasons, which "the Father has reserved in his own power": but in general, it seems, the kingdom of God will not "come with observation"; but will silently increase, wherever it is set up, and spread from heart to heart, from house to house, from town to town, from one kingdom to another.

Invisible Reality

For thus saith the high and lofty One that inhabiteth
eternity, whose name is Holy; I dwell in the high and

51

holy place, with him also that is of a contrite and
humble spirit, to revive the spirit of the humble, and
to revive the heart of the contrite ones.
Isaiah 57:15

A believer, in the scriptural sense, lives in eternity, and walks in eternity. His prospect is enlarged: his view is not any longer bounded by present things, no, nor by an earthly hemisphere; though it were, as Milton speaks, "tenfold the length of this terrene." Faith places the unseen, the eternal world continually before his face. Consequently, he looks not at "the things that are seen"—

> Wealth, honour, pleasure, or what else
> This short-enduring world can give;

these are not his aim, the object of his pursuit, his desire or happiness—but at "the things that are not seen"; at the favor, the image, and the glory of God; as well knowing the "the things which are seen are temporal"—a vapor, a shadow, a dream that vanishes away; whereas "the things that are not seen are eternal"—real, solid, unchangeable.

God Fills Heaven and Earth

Do not I fill heaven and earth? saith the Lord.
Jeremiah 23:24b

How strongly and beautifully do these words express the omnipresence of God! And can there be, in the whole compass of nature, a more sublime subject? . . . What deep instruction may it convey to all the children of men; and more directly to the children of God! . . .

Indeed, this subject is far too vast to be comprehended by the narrow limits of human understanding. We can only say: The great God, the eternal, the almighty Spirit, is as unbounded in his presence as in his duration and power. In condescension, indeed, to our weak understanding, he is said to dwell in heaven; but, strictly speaking, the heaven of heavens cannot contain him; he is in every part of his dominion. The universal God dwelleth in universal space: So that we may say,

Hail, Father! whose creating call
Unnumber'd worlds attend!
Jehovah, comprehending all,
Whom none can comprehend!

If we may dare attempt illustrating this a little farther: What is the space occupied by a grain of sand, compared to that space which is occupied by the starry heavens? It is as a cipher; it is nothing; it vanishes away in the comparison. What is it, then, to the whole expanse of space, to which the whole creation is infinitely less than a grain of sand? And yet this space, to which the whole creation bears no proportion at all, is infinitely less, in comparison of the great God, than a grain of sand, yea, a millionth part of it, bears to that whole space.

God Is in This and Every Place

Can anyone hide from me? Am I not everywhere in all of heaven and earth?
Jeremiah 23:24 LB

Can there be any [subject] more worthy the consideration of every rational creature? Is there any more necessary to be considered, and to be understood, so far as our poor faculties will admit? How many excellent purposes may it answer! . . .

How is it then that so little has been written on so sublime and useful a subject? It is true that some of our most eminent writers have occasionally touched upon it; and have several strong and beautiful reflections, which were naturally suggested by it. But which of them has published a regular treatise, or so much as a sermon, upon the head? Perhaps many were conscious of their inability to do justice to so vast a subject. It is possible there may some such lie hidden in the voluminous writings of the last century. But if they are hid, even in their own country, if they are buried in oblivion, it is the same, for any use they are, as if they had never been written.

What seems to be wanting still, for general use, is a plain discourse on the omnipresence or ubiquity of God. First, in some manner explaining and proving that glorious truth, "God is in this and every place"; and then, applying it to the consciences of all thinking men, in a few practical inferences.

Cleansing

Then I will sprinkle clean water upon you, and ye shall be clean. . . . I will also save you from all your uncleannesses.
Ezekiel 36:25, 29

You have therefore good reason to believe, he is not only able, but *willing* to do this; to cleanse you from all your filthiness of flesh and spirit; to "save you from all your uncleannesses." This is the thing which you now long for; this is the faith which you now particularly need, namely, that the Great Physician, the Lover of my soul, is willing to make me clean. But is he willing to do this tomorrow or today? Let him answer for himself. "Today, if ye will hear" my "voice, harden not your hearts." If you put it off till tomorrow, you harden your hearts; you refuse to hear his voice. Believe therefore that he is willing to save you *today*. He is willing to save you *now*. "Behold, now is the accepted time." He now says, "Be thou clean!" Only believe; and you also will immediately find, "All things are possible to him that believeth."

Continue to believe in him who loved you, and gave himself for you; that bore all your sins in his own body on the tree; and he saves you from all condemnation, by his blood continually applied. Thus it is that we continue in a justified state. And when we go on "from faith to faith," when we have faith to be cleansed from indwelling sin, to be saved from all our uncleannesses, we are likewise saved from all that *guilt*, that *desert* of punishment, which we felt before. So that then we may say, not only,

"Every moment, Lord, I want
The merit of thy death;"

but, likewise, in the full assurance of faith,

"Every moment, Lord, I have
The merit of thy death!"

For, by that faith in his life, death, and intercession for us, renewed from moment to moment, we are every whit clean, and there is not only now no condemnation for us, but no such desert of punishment as was before, the Lord cleansing both our hearts and lives.

The Heavenly Teacher

And seeing the multitudes, he went up into a mountain: and when he was set, his disciples came unto him: And he opened his mouth, and taught them.
Matthew 5:1, 2

Let us observe who it is that is here speaking, that we may take heed how we hear. It is the Lord of heaven and earth, the Creator of all; who, as such has a right to dispose of all his creatures; the Lord our Governor, whose kingdom is from everlasting and rules over all; the great lawgiver, who can well enforce all his laws, being "able to save and to destroy," yea, to punish with "everlasting destruction from his presence and from the glory of his power." It is the eternal wisdom of the Father, who knows whereof we are made, and understands our inmost frame; who knows how we stand related to God, to one another, to every creature which God has made, and consequently, how to adapt every law he prescribes, to all the circumstances wherein he has placed us. It is he who is "loving unto every man, whose mercy is over all his works"; the God of love, who, having emptied himself of his eternal glory, is come forth from his Father to declare his will to the children of men, and then goes again to the Father; who is sent of God "to open the eyes of the blind, and to give light to them that sit in darkness." . . .

And what is it which he is teaching? The Son of God who came from heaven is here showing us the way to heaven; to the place which he has prepared for us; the glory he had before the world began. He is teaching us the true way to life everlasting; the royal way which leads to the kingdom; and the only true way—for there is none besides; all other paths lead to destruction. From the character of the Speaker, we are well assured that he has declared the full and perfect will of God. He has uttered not one tittle too much—nothing more than he had received of the Father; nor too little—he has not shunned to declare the whole counsel of God; much less has he uttered anything wrong, anything contrary to the will of him that sent him. All his words are true and right concerning all things, and shall stand fast forever and ever.

The Poor in Spirit

Blessed are the poor in spirit: for theirs is the kingdom of heaven.
Matthew 5:3

Poverty of spirit is a just sense of our inward and outward sins, and of our guilt and helplessness. This some have monstrously styled "the virtue of humility"; this teaching us to be proud of knowing we deserve damnation! But our Lord's expression is of quite another kind; conveying no idea to the hearer, but that of mere want, of naked sin, of helpless guilt and misery.

The great apostle, where he endeavors to bring sinners to God, speaks in a manner just answerable to this. "The wrath of God," says he, "is revealed from heaven against all ungodliness and unrighteousness of men" (Rom. 1:18)—a charge which he immediately fixes on the heathen world, and thereby proves they were under the wrath of God. He next shows that the Jews were no better than they, and were therefore under the same condemnation; and all this not in order to their attaining "the noble virtue of humility," but "that every mouth might be stopped, and all the world become guilty before God."

He proceeds to show that they were helpless as well as guilty—which is the plain purport of all those expressions: "Therefore by the deeds of the law there shall no flesh be justified" (3:20); "But now the righteousness of God [which is by faith of Jesus Christ] without the law, is manifested" (3:21); "We conclude that a man is justified by faith without the deeds of the law" (3:28)—expressions all tending to the same point, even to "hide pride from man"; to humble him to the dust, without teaching him to reflect upon his humility as a virtue; to inspire him with that full, piercing conviction of his utter sinfulness, guilt, and helplessness, which casts the sinner, stripped of all, lost and undone, on his strong helper Jesus Christ the righteous.

One cannot but observe here that Christianity begins just where heathen morality ends; poverty of spirit, conviction of sin, the renouncing of ourselves, the not having our own righteousness, (the very first point in the religion of Jesus Christ,) leaving all pagan religion behind. This was ever hid from the wise men of this world; insomuch that the whole Roman language, even with all the improvements of the Augustan age, does not afford so much as a name for *humility;* (the word from whence we borrow this, as is well known, bearing in Latin a quite different meaning); no, nor was one found in all the copious language of Greece, till it was made by the great apostle.

6. Thoughts from the Greatest Sermon of All

Blessed Are They That Mourn

Blessed are they that mourn: for they shall be comforted.
                                        Matthew 5:4

The wisdom of God is foolishness with the world. The whole affair of mourning and poverty of spirit is with them stupidity and dullness. Nay, it is well if they pass so favorable a judgment upon it; if they do not vote it to be mere moping and melancholy, if not downright lunacy and distraction. And it is no wonder at all, that this judgment should be passed by those who know not God. Suppose, as two persons were walking together, one should suddenly stop, and with the strongest signs of fear and amazement, cry out, "On what a precipice do we stand! See, we are on the point of being dashed in pieces! Another step, and we shall fall into that huge abyss! Stop! I will not go on for all the world!"— when the other, who seemed to himself at least equally sharp sighted, looked forward and saw nothing of all this; what would he think of his companion, but that he was beside himself; that his head was out of order; that much religion (if he was not guilty of much learning) had certainly made him mad?

But let not the children of God, "the mourners in Zion," be moved by any of these things. You whose eyes are enlightened, be not troubled by those who walk on still in darkness. You do not walk on in a vain shadow: God and eternity are real things. Heaven and hell are in very deed open before you; and you are on the edge of the great gulf. It has already swallowed up more than words can express, nations, and kindreds, and peoples, and tongues; and still yawns to devour, whether they see it or no, the giddy, miserable children of men. Oh cry aloud! Spare not! Lift up your voice to him who grasps both time and eternity, both for yourselves and your brethren, that you may be counted worthy to escape the destruction that comes as a whirlwind! That you may be brought safe through all the waves and storms, into the haven where you would be! Weep for yourselves, till he wipes away the tears from your eyes. And even then, weep for the miseries that come upon the earth, till the Lord of all shall put a period to misery and sin, shall wipe away the tears from all faces, and "the knowledge of the Lord shall cover the earth, as the waters cover the sea."

The Meaning of Meekness

Blessed are the meek: for they shall inherit the earth.
Matthew 5:5

"Therefore if thou bring thy gift to the altar, and there rememberest that thy brother hath ought against thee"—on account of your unkind behavior toward him, of calling him, Raca, or Thou Fool; think not that your gift will atone for your anger; or that it will find any acceptance with God, so long as your conscience is defiled with the guilt of unrepented sin. "Leave there thy gift before the altar, and go thy way; first be reconciled to thy brother," (at least do all that in you lies toward being reconciled) "and then come and offer thy gift" (Matt. 5:23, 24).

And let there be no delay in what so nearly concerns your soul. "Agree with thine adversary quickly"—now; upon the spot; "whiles thou art in the way with him"; if it be possible, before he go out of your sight; "lest at any time the adversary deliver thee to the judge"; lest he appeal to God, the judge of all; "and the judge deliver thee to the officer"; to Satan, the executioner of the wrath of God; "and thou be cast into prison"; into hell, there to be reserved to the judgment of the great day: "Verily, I say unto thee, Thou shalt by no means come out thence, till thou hast paid the uttermost farthing." But this it is impossible for you ever to do; seeing you have nothing to pay. Therefore, if you are one in that prison, the smoke of your torment must "ascend up forever and ever."

Meantime "The meek shall inherit the earth." Such is the foolishness of worldly wisdom! The wise of the world had warned them again and again, "That if they did not resent such treatment, if they would tamely suffer themselves to be thus abused, there would be no living for them upon earth; that they would never be able to procure the common necessaries of life, nor to keep even what they had; that they could expect no peace, no quiet possession, no enjoyment of anything." Most true—suppose there were no God in the world; or, suppose he did not concern himself with the children of men: but "when God ariseth to judgment, and to help all the meek upon earth," how does he laugh all this heathen wisdom to scorn, and turn the "fierceness of man to his praise!" He takes a peculiar care to provide them with all things needful for life and godliness; he secures to them the provision he has made, in spite of the force, fraud, or malice of men; and what he secures he gives them richly to enjoy. It is sweet to them, be it little or much. As in patience they possess their souls, so they truly possess whatever God has given them. They are always content, always pleased with what they have: it pleases them, because it pleases God: so that while their heart, their desire, their joy is in heaven, they may truly be said to "inherit the earth."

The Riches of Righteousness

Blessed are they which do hunger and thirst after righteousness: for they shall be filled.
Matthew 5:6

Righteousness is the image of God, the mind which was in Christ Jesus. It is every holy and heavenly temper in one; springing from, as well as terminating in, the love of God as our Father and Redeemer, and the love of all men for his sake.

"Blessed are they which do hunger and thirst after" this: To fully understand this expression, we should observe, first, that hunger and thirst are the strongest of all our bodily appetites. In like manner this hunger in the soul, this thirst after the image of God, is the strongest of all our spiritual appetites, when it is once awakened in the heart: yea, it swallows up all the rest in that one great desire—to be renewed after the likeness of him that created us. We should, secondly, observe, that from the time we begin to hunger and thirst, those appetites do not cease, but are more and more craving and importunate, till we either eat and drink, or die. And even so, from the time that we begin to hunger and thirst after the whole mind which was in Christ, these spiritual appetites do not cease, but cry after their food with more and more importunity; nor can they possibly cease, before they are satisfied, while there is any spiritual life remaining.

We may, thirdly, observe that hunger and thirst are satisfied with nothing but meat and drink. If you would give to him who is hungry all the world beside, all the elegance of apparel, all the trappings of state, all the treasure upon earth, yea, thousands of gold and silver; if you would pay him ever so much honor— he regards it not: all these things are then of no account with him. He would still say, "These are not the things I want: give me food, or else I die." The very same is the case with every soul that truly hungers and thirsts after righteousness. He can find no comfort in anything but this: he can be satisfied with nothing else. Whatever you offer besides, it is lightly esteemed: whether it be riches, or honor, or pleasure, he still says, This is not the thing which I want! Give me love, or else I die!

The Power of Purity

Blessed are the pure in heart: for they shall see God.
Matthew 5:8

How excellent things are spoken of the love of our neighbor! It is "the fulfilling of the law," "the end of the commandment." Without this, all we have, all we do, all we suffer, is of no value in the sight of God. But it is that love of our neighbor which springs from the love of God: otherwise itself is worth nothing. It behooves us, therefore, to examine well upon what foundation our love of our neighbor stands; whether it is really built upon the love of God; whether we do "love him because he first loved us"; whether we are pure in heart: for this is the foundation which shall never be moved. "Blessed are the pure in heart: for they shall see God."

"The pure in heart" are they whose hearts God has "purified even as he is pure"; who are purified through faith in the blood of Jesus, from every unholy affection; who, being "cleansed from all filthiness of flesh and spirit, perfect holiness in the [loving] fear of God." They are, through the power of his grace, purified from pride, by the deepest poverty of spirit; from anger, from every unkind or turbulent passion, by meekness and gentleness; from every desire but to please and enjoy God, to know and love him more and more, by that hunger and thirst after righteousness which now engrosses their whole soul: so that now they love the Lord their God with all their heart, and with all their soul, and mind, and strength.

Points about Peacemakers

Blessed are the peacemakers: for they shall be called the children of God.

Matthew 5:9

Let us learn in how wide a sense the term peacemakers is to be understood. In its literal meaning it implies those lovers of God and man, who utterly detest and abhor all strife and debate, all variance and contention; and accordingly labor with all their might, either to prevent this fire of hell from being kindled, or, spreading any further. They endeavor to calm the stormy spirits of men, to quiet their turbulent passions, to soften the minds of contending parties, and, if possible, reconcile them to each other. They use all innocent arts, and employ all their strength, all the talents which God has given them, as well to preserve peace where it is, as to restore it where it is not. It is the joy of their heart to promote, to confirm, to increase mutual goodwill among men, but more especially among the children of God, however distinguished by things of smaller importance; that as they have all "one Lord, one faith," as they are all "called in one hope of their calling," so they may all "walk worthy of the vocation wherewith they are called; with all lowliness and meekness, with longsuffering, forbearing one another in love; endeavoring to keep the unity of the Spirit in the bond of peace."

But, in the full extent of the word, a peacemaker is one who, as he has opportunity, "doeth good unto all men"; one who, being filled with the love of God and of all mankind, cannot confine the expressions of it to his own family, or friends, or acquaintance, or party, or to those of his own opinions—no, nor those who are partakers of like precious faith; but steps over all these narrow bounds, that he may do good to every man. . . . losing no moment wherein he may profit another. He does good, not of one particular kind, but good in general, in every possible way; employing herein all his talents of every kind, all his powers and faculties of body and soul, all his fortune, his interest, his reputation; desiring only, that when his Lord comes, he may say, "Well done, good and faithful servant!"

The Light of the World

Ye are the light of the world. A city that is set on an hill cannot be hid.
Matthew 5:14

It is impossible for any who have it to conceal the religion of Jesus Christ. This our Lord makes plain beyond all contradiction, by a twofold comparison: "Ye are the light of the world; a city set upon a hill cannot be hid." You Christians are "the light of the world," with regard both to your tempers and actions. Your holiness makes you as conspicuous as the sun in the midst of heaven. As you cannot go out of the world, so neither can you stay in it without appearing to all mankind. You may not flee from men; and while you are among them, it is impossible to hide your lowliness and meekness, and those other dispositions whereby you aspire to be perfect as your Father which is in heaven is perfect. . . . As well may men think to hide a city, as to hide a Christian; yea, as well may they conceal a city set upon a hill, as a holy, zealous, active lover of God and man.

It is true, men who love darkness rather than light, because their deeds are evil, will take all possible pains to prove that the light which is in you is darkness. They will say evil, all manner of evil, falsely, of the good which is in you; they will lay to your charge that which is farthest from your thoughts, which is the very reverse of all you are, and all you do. And your patient continuing in well-doing, your calm, humble joy in the midst of persecution, your unwearied labor to overcome evil with good, will make you still more conspicuous than you were before. . . .

Sure it is that a secret, unobserved religion cannot be the religion of Jesus Christ. Whatever religion can be concealed, is not Christianity. If a Christian could be hid, he could not be compared to a city set upon a hill; to the light of the world, the sun shining from heaven, and seen by all the world below. Never, therefore, let it enter into the heart of him whom God has renewed in the spirit of his mind, to hide that light, to keep his religion to himself; especially considering it is not only impossible to conceal true Christianity, but likewise absolutely contrary to the design of the great author of it.

The Lighted Candle

Neither do men light a candle, and put it under a bushel, but on a candlestick; and it giveth light unto all that are in the house.
Matthew 5:15

This plainly appears from the following words: "Neither do men light a candle to put it under a bushel." As if he had said: As men do not light a candle, only to cover and conceal it, so neither does God enlighten any soul with his glorious knowledge and love, to have it covered or concealed, either by prudence, falsely so-called, or shame, or voluntary humility; to have it hid either in a desert, or in the world; either by avoiding men, or in conversing with them. "But they put it on a candlestick, and it giveth light to all that are in the house." In like manner, it is the design of God that every Christian should be in an open point of view; that he may visibly express the religion of Jesus Christ.

Thus has God in all ages spoken to the world, not only by precept, but by example also. He has "not left himself without witness" in any nation where the sound of the gospel has gone forth, without a few who have testified his truth, by their lives as well as their words. These have been "as lights shining in a dark place." And from time to time they have been the means of enlightening some, of preserving a remnant, a little seed which was "counted to the Lord for a generation." They have led a few poor sheep out of the darkness of the world, and guided their feet into the way of peace.

7. Seasoning from the Sermon on the Mount

Let Your Light Shine

Let your light so shine before men, that they may see your good works, and glorify your Father which is in heaven.

Matthew 5:16

"Let your light so shine"—your lowliness of heart; your gentleness, and meekness of wisdom; your serious, weighty concern for the things of eternity, and sorrow for the sins and miseries of men; your earnest desire of universal holiness, and full happiness in God; your tender goodwill to all mankind, and fervent love to your supreme benefactor. Endeavor not to conceal this light, wherewith God has enlightened your soul; but let it shine before men, before all with whom you are, in the whole tenor of your conversation. Let it shine still more eminently in your actions, in doing all possible good to all men; and in your suffering for righteousness' sake, while you "rejoice and are exceeding glad, knowing that great is your reward in heaven."

"Let your light so shine before men, that they may see your good works"—so far let a Christian be from ever designing, or desiring to conceal his religion! On the contrary, let it be your desire not to conceal it; not to put the light under a bushel. Let it be your care to place it "on a candlestick, that it may give light to all that are in the house." Only take heed, not to seek your own praise herein, not to desire any honor to your selves. But let it be your sole aim, that all who see your good works may "glorify your Father which is in heaven."

The Law Fulfilled

Think not that I am come to destroy the law, or the prophets: I am not come to destroy, but to fulfil.

Matthew 5:17

There is, therefore, the closest connection that can be conceived, between the law and the gospel. On the one hand, the law continually makes way for, and points us to, the gospel; on the other, the gospel continually leads us to a more exact fulfilling of the law. The law, for instance, requires us to love God, to love our neighbor, to be meek, humble, or holy. We feel that we are not sufficient for these things; yea, that "with man this is impossible": but we see a promise of God, to give us that love, and to make us humble, meek, and holy: we lay hold of this gospel, of these glad tidings; it is done unto us according to our faith; and "the righteousness of the law is fulfilled in us," through faith which is in Christ Jesus. We may yet further observe, that every command in holy writ is only a covered promise. For by that solemn declaration, "This is the covenant I will make after those days, saith the Lord: I will put my laws in your minds, and write them in your hearts." God has promised to give whatsoever he commands. Does he command us then to "pray without ceasing"? To "rejoice evermore"? To be "holy as he is holy"? It is enough: he will work in us this very thing: it shall be unto us according to his word.

Righteousness

Except your righteousness shall exceed the
righteousness of the scribes and Pharisees, ye shall
in no case enter into the kingdom of heaven.
Matthew 5:20

Don't stop here! Let your righteousness "exceed the righteousness of the scribes and Pharisees." Be not content to "keep the whole law, and offend in one point." Hold fast all his commandments, and "all false ways do thou utterly abhor." Do all the things, whatsoever he has commanded, and that with all your might. You can do all things through Christ strengthening you, though without him you can do nothing.

Above all, let your righteousness exceed theirs in the purity and spirituality of it. What is the exactest form of religion to you? The most perfect outside righteousness? Go higher and deeper than all this! Let your religion be the religion of the heart. Be poor in spirit; little, and base, and mean, and vile in your own eyes; amazed and humbled to the dust at the love of God which is in Christ Jesus our Lord! Be serious: let the whole stream of your thoughts, words, and works be such as flows from the deepest conviction that you stand on the edge of the great gulf, you and all the children of men, just ready to drop in, either into everlasting glory or everlasting burnings! Be meek: let your soul be filled with mildness, gentleness, patience, longsuffering toward all men; at the same time let all that is in you be athirst for God, the living God, longing to awake up after his likeness, and to be satisfied with it. Be a lover of God, and of all mankind. In this spirit, do and suffer all things. Thus "exceed the righteousness of the scribes and Pharisees," and you shall be "called great in the kingdom of heaven."

Love for My Neighbor

Ye have heard that it hath been said, Thou shalt love thy neighbour, and hate thine enemy. But I say unto you, Love your enemies. . . . For if ye love them which love you, what reward have ye?
Matthew 5:43, 44, 46

The necessary fruit of this love of God is the love of our neighbor, of every soul which God hath made, not excepting our enemies, not excepting those who are now "despitefully using and persecuting us"—a love whereby we love every man as ourselves, as we love our own souls. Nay, our Lord has expressed it still more strongly, teaching us to "love one another even as he hath loved us." Accordingly, the commandment written in the hearts of all those that love God is no other than this: "As I have loved you, so love ye one another." Now, "herein perceive we the love of God, in that he laid down his life for us" (1 John 3:16). "We ought," then, as the apostle justly infers, "to lay down our lives for the brethren." If we feel ourselves ready to do this, then do we truly love our neighbor. Then "we know that we have passed from death unto life, because we" thus "love the brethren" (1 John 3:14). "Hereby know we" that we are born of God, that we "dwell in him, and he in us, because he hath given us of his" loving "Spirit" (4:13). For "love is of God; and every one that" thus "loveth is born of God, and knoweth God" (4:7).

Love for My Enemy

But I [Jesus] say unto you, Love your enemies, bless them that curse you, do good to them that hate you, and pray for them which despitefully use you, and persecute you.

Matthew 5:44

(1) "Love your enemies": See that you bear a tender goodwill to those who are most bitter of spirit against you, who wish you all manner of evil. (2) "Bless them that curse you": Are there any whose bitterness of spirit breaks forth in bitter words, who are continually cursing and reproaching you when you are present, and "saying all evil against you" when absent? So much the rather do you bless: In conversing with them, use all mildness and softness of language. Reprove them by repeating a better lesson before them, by showing them how they ought to have spoken. And, in speaking of them, say all the good you can, without violating the rules of truth and justice. (3) "Do good to them that hate you": Let your actions show that you are as real in love as they in hatred. Return good for evil. "Be not overcome of evil, but overcome evil with good." (4) If you can do nothing more, at least "pray for them that despitefully use you and persecute you." You can never be disabled from doing this, nor can all their malice or violence hinder you. Pour out your souls to God, not only for those who did this once, but now repent. . . . [but also for] those that do not repent, that now despitefully use thee and persecute thee. . . . Whether they repent or no, yea, though they appear farther and farther from it, yet show them this instance of kindness.

When You Pray

But thou, when thou prayest, enter into thy closet, and when thou hast shut thy door, pray to thy Father which is in secret; and thy Father which seeth in secret shall reward thee openly.

Matthew 6:6

There is a time when you are openly to glorify God, to pray to and praise him in the great congregation. But when you desire more largely and more particularly to make your requests known unto God, whether it be in the evening, or in the morning, or a noonday, "enter into thy closet, and shut thy door." Use all the privacy you can. (Only leave it not undone, whether you have any closet, any privacy, or no. Pray to God, if it be possible, when none sees but he; but, if otherwise, pray to God.) Thus "pray to thy Father which is in secret"; pour out all your heart before him; "and thy Father which seeth in secret, he shall reward thee openly."

"But when ye pray," even in secret, "use not vain repetitions as the heathen do." Do not use abundance of words without any meaning. Say not the same thing over and over again; think not the fruit of your prayers depends on the length of them, like the heathen; for "they think they shall be heard for their much speaking."

"Be not ye therefore like unto them." You who have tasted of the grace of God in Christ Jesus, are thoroughly convinced, "your Father knoweth what things ye have need of, before ye ask him." So that the end of your praying is not to inform God, as though he knew not your wants already; but rather to inform yourselves; to fix the sense of those wants more deeply in your hearts, and the sense of your continual dependence on him, who only is able to supply all your wants. It is not so much to move God, who is always more ready to give than you to ask, as to move yourselves, that you may be willing and ready to receive the good things he has prepared for you.

Our Heavenly Father

> *After this manner therefore pray ye: Our Father which art in heaven. . . .*
> **Matthew 6:9a**

"Which art in heaven"—high and lifted up; God over all, blessed forever: who, sitting on the circle of the heavens, beholds all things both in heaven and earth; whose eye pervades the whole sphere of created being; yea, and of uncreated night; unto whom "are known all his works," and all the works of every creature, not only "from the beginning of the world" (a poor, low, weak translation), but from all *eternity,* from everlasting to everlasting; who constrains the host of heaven, as well as the children of men, to cry out with wonder and amazement, "Oh, the depth! The depth of the riches, both of the wisdom and of the knowledge of God!" "Which art in heaven"—Lord and ruler of all, superintending and disposing all things; who is the King of kings, and Lord of lords, the blessed and only Potentate; who is strong and girded about with power, doing whatsoever pleases him; the Almighty; for whensoever you will, to do is present with you. "In heaven"— eminently there. Heaven is his throne, the place where his honor particularly dwells. But not there alone; for he fills heaven and earth, the whole expanse of space. "Heaven and earth are full of thy glory. Glory be to thee, O Lord most high!"

Therefore should we "serve the Lord with fear, and rejoice unto him with reverence."

8. Insights on the Lord's Prayer and Living

Hallowing God

Hallowed be thy name.

Matthew 6:9b

This is the first of the six petitions whereof the prayer itself is composed. The name of God is God himself; the nature of God, so far as it can be discovered to man. It means, therefore, together with his existence, all his attributes of perfection—his eternity, particularly signified by his great and incommunicable name, JEHOVAH, as the apostle John translates it: "The Alpha and Omega, the beginning and the end; he which is, and which was, and which is to come"; his fulness of being, denoted by his other great name, I AM THAT I AM!; his omnipresence; his omnipotence, who is indeed the only agent in the material world; all matter being essentially dull and inactive, and moving only as it is moved by the finger of God; and he is the spring of action in every creature, visible and invisible, which could neither act nor exist without the continual influx and agency of his almighty power; his wisdom, clearly deduced from the things that are seen, from the goodly order of the universe; his trinity in unity, and unity in trinity, discovered to us in the very first line of his written Word: literally, *the Gods created,* a plural noun joined with a verb of the singular number; as well as in every part of his subsequent revelations, given by the mouth of all his holy prophets and apostles; his essential purity and holiness; and above all, his love, which is the very brightness of his glory.

In praying that God, or his name, may be hallowed or glorified, we pray that he may be known, such as he is, by all who are capable thereof, by all intelligent beings, and with affections suitable to that knowledge; that he may be duly honored, and feared, and loved, by all in heaven above and in the earth beneath; by all angels and men, whom for that end he has made capable of knowing and loving him to eternity.

The Coming Kingdom

Thy kingdom come.
Matthew 6:10a

"Thy kingdom come." This has a close connection with the preceding petition. In order that the name of God may be hallowed, we pray that his kingdom, the kingdom of Christ, may come. This kingdom then comes to a particular person, when he "repents and believes the gospel"; when he is taught of God, not only to know himself, but to know Jesus Christ and him crucified. As "this is life eternal, to know the only true God, and Jesus Christ whom he hath sent"; so it is the kingdom of God begun below, set up in the believer's heart; the Lord God omnipotent then reigns, when he is known through Christ Jesus. He takes unto himself his mighty power, that he may subdue all things unto himself. He goes on in the soul conquering and to conquer, till he has put all things under his feet, till "every thought is brought into captivity to the obedience of Christ."

When therefore God shall "give his Son the heathen for his inheritance, and the uttermost parts of the earth for his possession"; when "all kingdoms shall bow before him, and all nations shall do him service"; when "the mountain of the Lord's house," the church of Christ, "shall be established in the top of the mountains"; when "the fulness of the Gentiles shall come in, and all Israel shall be saved"; then shall it be seen, that the "Lord is king, and hath put on glorious apparel," appearing to every soul of man as King of kings, and Lord of lords. And it is meet for all those who love his appearing, to pray that he would hasten the time; that this his kingdom, the kingdom of grace, may come quickly, and swallow up all the kingdoms of the earth; that all mankind, receiving him for their King, truly believing in his name, may be filled with righteousness, and peace, and joy, with holiness and happiness—till they are removed into his heavenly kingdom, there to reign with him forever and ever.

Willing to Do His Will

Thy will be done in earth, as it is in heaven.
Matthew 6:10b

"Thy will be done in earth, as it is in heaven." This is the necessary and immediate consequence wherever the kingdom of God is come—wherever God dwells in the soul by faith, and Christ reigns in the heart by love.

It is probable, many, perhaps the generality of men, at the first view of these words, are apt to imagine they are only an expression of, or petition for, resignation; for a readiness to suffer the will of God, whatsoever it be concerning us. And this is unquestionably a divine and excellent temper, a most precious gift of God. But this is not what we pray for in this petition; at least, not in the chief and primary sense of it. We pray, not so much for a passive, as for an active conformity to the will of God, in saying, "Thy will be done in earth, as it is in heaven."

How is it done by the angels of God in heaven? Those who now circle his throne rejoicing? They do it *willingly;* they love his commandments, and gladly hearken to his words. It is their meat and drink to do his will; it is their highest glory and joy. They do it *continually;* there is no interruption in their willing service. They rest not day nor night, but employ every hour (speaking after the manner of men; otherwise our measures of duration—days, and nights, and hours—have no place in eternity), in fulfilling his commands, in executing his designs, in performing the counsel of his will. And they do it *perfectly.* No sin, no defect belongs to angelic minds. It is true, "the stars are not pure in his sight," even the morning stars that sing together before him. "In his sight," that is, in comparison with him, the very angels are not pure. But this does not imply that they are not pure in *themselves.* Doubtless they are; they are without spot and blameless. They are altogether devoted to his will, and perfectly obedient in all things.

If we view them in another light, we may observe, the angels of God in heaven do *all* the will of God. And they do nothing else, nothing but what they are absolutely assured is his will. Again, they do all the will of God *as* he wills, in the manner which pleases him, and no other. Yea, and they do this, only *because* it is his will; for this end and no other reason.

When therefore we pray, that the "will of God may be done in earth, as it is in heaven," the meaning is that all the inhabitants of the earth, even the whole race of mankind, may do the will of their Father which is in heaven, as *willingly* as the holy angels; that these may do it *continually* even as they, without any interruption of their willing service; yea, and that they may do it *perfectly;* that "the God of peace, through the blood of the everlasting covenant, may make them perfect in every good work to do his will, and work in them [all] which is well pleasing in his sight."

Our Daily Bread

Give us this day our daily bread.
Matthew 6:11

In the three former petitions we have been praying for all mankind. We come now more particularly to desire a supply for our own wants. Not that we are directed, even here, to confine our prayer altogether to ourselves; but this, and each of the following petitions, may be used for the whole church of Christ upon earth.

By bread we may understand all things needful, whether for our souls or bodies—*the things pertaining to life and godliness:* we understand not barely the outward bread, what our Lord terms "the meat which perisheth"; but much more the spiritual bread, the grace of God, the food "which endureth unto everlasting life." It was the judgment of many of the ancient fathers that we are here to understand the sacramental bread also; daily received in the beginning by the whole church of Christ, and highly esteemed, till the love of many waxed cold, as the grand channel whereby the grace of this Spirit was conveyed to the souls of all the children of God.

"Our daily bread." The word we render *daily* has been differently explained by different commentators. But the most plain and natural sense of it seems to be this, which is retained in almost all translations, as well ancient as modern—what is sufficient for this day; and so for each day as it succeeds.

"Give us." For we claim nothing of right, but only of free mercy. We deserve not the air we breathe, the earth that bears us, or the sun that shines upon us. All our desert, we own, is hell: but God loves us freely; therefore we ask him to give what we can no more procure for ourselves than we can merit it at his hands. . . .

"This day." For we are to take no thought for the morrow. For this very end has our wise Creator divided life into these little portions of time, so clearly separated from each other; that we might look on every day as a fresh gift of God, another life, which we may devote to his glory; and that every evening may be as the close of life, beyond which we are to see nothing but eternity.

Forgiving Our Debtors

> *And forgive us our debts [trespasses], as we forgive our debtors [those that trespass against us].*
> **Matthew 6:12**

As nothing but sin can hinder the bounty of God from flowing forth upon every creature, so this petition naturally follows the former; that all hindrances being removed, we may the more clearly trust in the God of love for every manner of thing which is good.

"Our trespasses." The word properly signifies *our debts.* Thus our sins are frequently represented in Scripture; every sin laying us under a fresh debt to God, to whom we already owe, as it were, ten thousand talents. What then can we answer when he shall say, "Pay me that thou owest"? We are utterly insolvent; we have nothing to pay; we have wasted all our substance. Therefore if he deal with us according to the rigor of his law, if he exact what he justly may, he must command us to be "bound hand and foot, and delivered over to the tormentors.". . .

The word translated *forgive* implies either to forgive a debt, or to unloose a chain. And, if we attain the former, the latter follows of course: if our debts are forgiven, the chains fall off our hands. As soon as ever, through the free grace of God in

Christ, we "receive forgiveness of sins," we receive likewise "a lot among those which are sanctified, by faith which is in him." Sin has lost its power; it has no dominion over those who are under grace, that is, in favor with God. As "there is now no condemnation to them that are in Christ Jesus," so they are freed from sin as well as from guilt. "The righteousness of the law is fulfilled in them, and they walk not after the flesh but after the Spirit."

"As we forgive them that trespass against us." In these words our Lord clearly declares both on what condition, and in what degree or manner, we may look to be forgiven of God. All our trespasses and sins are forgiven us, *if* we forgive, and *as* we forgive others. This is a point of the utmost importance. And our blessed Lord is so jealous lest at any time we would let it slip out of our thoughts, that he not only inserts it in the body of his prayer, but presently after repeats it twice over. "If," says he, "ye forgive men their trespasses, your heavenly Father will also forgive you: But if ye forgive not men their trespasses, neither will your Father forgive your trespasses" (vv. 14, 15). Secondly, God forgives us *as* we forgive others. So that if any malice or bitterness, if any taint of unkindness or anger remain, if we do not clearly, fully, and from the heart forgive all men their trespasses, we so far cut short the forgiveness of our own; God cannot clearly and fully forgive us. He may show us some degree of mercy; but we will not suffer him to blot out all our sins, and forgive all our iniquities.

In the meantime, while we do not from our hearts forgive our neighbor his trespasses, what manner of prayer are we offering to God whenever we utter these words? We are indeed setting God at open defiance; we are daring him to do his worst. "Forgive us our trespasses, as we forgive them that trespass against us!" That is, in plain terms, "Do not thou forgive us at all: we desire no favor at your hands. We pray that you will keep our sins in remembrance, and that your wrath may abide upon us." But can you seriously offer such a prayer to God? And has he not yet cast you quick into hell? O tempt him no longer! Now, even now, by his grace, forgive as you would be forgiven! Now have compassion on your fellow servant, as God has had, and will have, pity on you!

Handling Temptation

And lead us not into temptation, but deliver us from evil.

Matthew 6:13a

"And lead us not into temptation." The word translated *temptation,* means trial of any kind. And so the English word *temptation* was formerly taken in an indifferent sense; although now it is usually understood of solicitation to sin. St. James uses the word in both these senses; first, in its general, then in its restrained, acceptation. He takes it in the former sense when he says, "Blessed is the man that endureth temptation: for when he is tried, [or approved of God,] he shall receive the crown of life" (1:12). He immediately adds, taking the word in the latter sense, "Let no man say when he is tempted, I am tempted of God: for God cannot be tempted with evil, neither tempteth he any man: but every man is tempted when he is *drawn away* of his own lust," or *desire*—drawn out of God, in whom alone he is safe—"*and enticed"*; caught as a fish with a bait. Then it is, when he is thus *drawn away and enticed,* that he properly enters into temptation. Then temptation covers him as a cloud; it overspreads his whole soul. Then how hardly shall he escape out of the snare!

Therefore, we beseech God "not to lead us into temptation," that is, (seeing God tempteth no man,) not to suffer us to be led into it. "But deliver us from evil," rather—*"from the evil one."* He is unquestionably *the wicked one,* emphatically so called, the prince and god of this world, who works with mighty power in the children of disobedience. But all those who are the children of God, by faith, are delivered out of his hands. He may fight against them; and so he will. But he cannot conquer, unless they betray their own souls. He may torment for a time, but he cannot destroy; for God is on their side, who will not fail, in the end, to "avenge his own elect, that cry unto him day and night."

Lord, when we are tempted, suffer us not to enter into temptation! Make a way for us to escape, that the wicked one touch us, not!

The Doxology

For thine is the kingdom, and the power, and the glory, for ever. Amen.
Matthew 6:13b*

The conclusion of this divine prayer, commonly called the doxology, is a solemn thanksgiving, a compendious acknowledgment of the attributes and works of God. "For thine is the kingdom"—the sovereign right of all things that are or ever were created; yea, thy kingdom is an everlasting kingdom, and thy dominion endureth throughout all ages. "The power"—the executive power whereby you govern all things in your everlasting kingdom, whereby you do whatsoever pleases you, in all places of your dominion. "And the glory"—the praise due from every creature, for your power, and the mightiness of your kingdom, and for all your wondrous works which you work from everlasting, and shall do, world without end, "forever and ever! Amen!" So be it!

---

* Editor's note: We are fully aware that later printings of the King James Bible omitted these words, but felt Wesley's comments so pertinent that they should be retained.

9. Life in Perspective

Philosophy for Living

Lay not up for yourselves treasures upon earth, where moth and rust doth corrupt, and where thieves break through and steal: But lay up for yourselves treasures in heaven, where neither moth nor rust doth corrupt, and where thieves do not break through nor steal: For where your treasure is, there will your heart be also.
Matthew 6:19–21

You may gain all you can, without hurting either your soul or body; you may save all you can, by carefully avoiding every needless expense; and yet never lay up treasures on earth, nor either desire or endeavor so to do. . . .

Forty-two years ago, having a desire to furnish poor people with cheaper, shorter, and plainer books than any I had seen, I wrote many small tracts, generally a penny a-piece; and afterward several larger. Some of these had such a sale as I never thought of; and, by this means, I unawares became rich. But I never desired or endeavored after it. And now that it is come upon me unawares, I lay up no treasures upon earth: I lay up nothing at all. I cannot help leaving my book [assets] behind me whenever God calls me hence; but, in every other respect, my own hands will be my executors.

Where Is Your Treasure?

For where your treasure is, there will your heart be also.
Matthew 6:21

As it comes, daily or yearly, so let it go: otherwise you "lay up treasures upon earth." And this our Lord as flatly forbids as murder and adultery. By doing it, therefore, you would "treasure up to yourselves wrath against the day of wrath and revelation of the righteous judgment of God."

But suppose it were not forbidden, how can you, on principles of reason, spend your money in a way which God may *possibly forgive,* instead of spending it in a manner which he will *certainly reward?* You will have no reward in heaven for what you *lay up;* you will, for what you *lay out.* Every pound you put into the earthly bank is sunk: It brings no interest above. But every pound you give to the poor is put into the bank of heaven. And it will bring glorious interest; yea, and as such, will be accumulating to all eternity.

Who then is a wise man, and endued with knowledge among you? Let him resolve this day, this hour, this moment, the Lord assisting him, to choose in all the preceding particulars the "more excellent way": And let him steadily keep it, both with regard to sleep, prayer, work, food, conversation, and diversions; and particularly with regard to the employment of that important talent, money. Let *your* heart answer to the call of God, "From this moment, God being my helper, I will lay up no more treasure upon earth: This one thing I will do, I will lay up treasure in heaven; I will render unto God the things that are God's: I will give him all my goods, and all my heart!"

The Single Eye

The light of the body is the eye: if therefore thine eye be single, thy whole body shall be full of light.
Matthew 6:22

"If thine eye be [thus] single," thus fixed on God, "thy whole body shall be full of light." "Thy whole body"—all that is guided by the intention, as the body is by the eye: all you are; all you do; your desires, tempers, affections; your thoughts, words, and actions. The whole of these "shall be full of light"; full of true divine knowledge. This is the first thing we may here understand by light. "In his light thou shalt see light." "He who of old com-

manded light to shine out of darkness, shall shine in thy heart":
he shall enlighten the eyes of your understanding with the knowledge of the glory of God. His Spirit shall reveal unto you the
deep things of God. The inspiration of the Holy One shall give
you understanding, and cause you to know wisdom secretly. Yea,
the anointing which you receive of him "shall abide in thee, and
teach thee of all things."

How does experience confirm this! Even after God has opened
the eyes of our understanding, if we seek or desire anything else
than God, how soon is our foolish heart darkened! Then clouds
again rest upon our souls. Doubts and fears again overwhelm us.
We are tossed to and fro, and know not what to do, or which is
the path wherein we should go. But when we desire and seek
nothing but God, clouds and doubts vanish away. We "who were
sometimes darkness, are now light in the Lord." The night now
shines as the day; and we find "the path of the upright is light."
God shows us the path wherein we should go, and makes plain
the way before our face.

The Lighted Life

> *The light of the body is the eye: if therefore thine eye
> be single, thy whole body shall be full of light. But if
> thine eye be evil, thy whole body shall be full of
> darkness. If therefore the light that is in thee be
> darkness, how great is that darkness!*
> **Matthew 6:22, 23**

First, "If thine eye be single, thy whole body shall be full of light."
If your eye be single; if God be in all your thoughts; if you are
constantly aiming at him who is invisible; if it be your intention
in all things, small and great, in all your conversation, to please
God, to do, not your own will, but the will of him who sent
you into the world; if you can say, not to any creature, but to
him who made you for himself, "I view thee, Lord and End of
my desires"—then the promise will certainly take place: "Thy
whole body shall be full of light"; your whole soul shall be filled
with the light of heaven—with the glory of the Lord resting upon
you. In all your actions and conversation, you shall have not only
the testimony of a good conscience toward God, but likewise of

his Spirit, bearing witness with your spirit, that all your ways are acceptable to him.

When your whole soul is full of this light, you will be able (according to St. Paul's direction to the Thessalonians) to "rejoice evermore," to "pray without ceasing," and "in everything to give thanks." For who can be constantly sensible of the loving presence of God without "rejoicing evermore"? Who can have the loving eye of his soul perpetually fixed upon God, but he will "pray without ceasing"? For his "heart is unto God without a voice, and his silence speaketh unto him." Who can be sensible that this loving Father is well-pleased with all he does and suffers, but he will be constrained "in everything to give thanks," knowing that all things "work together for good"?

The Surrendered Life

> *Therefore I say unto you, Take no thought for your life, what ye shall eat, or what ye shall drink; nor yet for your body, what ye shall put on. Is not the life more than meat, and the body than raiment?*
> **Matthew 6:25**

This is a deep and weighty commandment, which we would do well to consider, and thoroughly to understand. Our Lord does not here require that we should be utterly without thought, even touching the concerns of this life. A giddy, careless temper is farthest from the whole religion of Jesus Christ. Neither does he require us to be "slothful in business," to be slack and dilatory therein. This, likewise, is contrary to the whole spirit and genius of his religion. A Christian abhors sloth as much as drunkenness; and flees from idleness as he does from adultery. He well knows that there is one kind of thought and care, with which God is pleased; which is absolutely needful for the due performance of those outward works, unto which the providence of God has called him.

It is the will of God, that every man should labor to eat his own bread; yea, and that every man should provide for his own, for them of his own household. It is likewise his will that we should "owe no man any thing, but provide things honest in the sight of all men." But this cannot be done without taking some thought, without having some care upon our minds; yea often, not without long and serious thought, not without much and earnest care. Consequently this care, to provide for ourselves and our household, this thought how to render to all their dues, our blessed Lord does not condemn. Yea, it is good and acceptable in the sight of God our Savior.

It is good and acceptable to God that we should so take thought concerning whatever we have in hand, as to have a clear comprehension of what we are about to do, and to plan our business before we enter upon it. And it is right that we should carefully consider, from time to time, what steps we are to take therein; as well as that we should prepare all things beforehand, for the carrying it on in the most effectual manner. This care, termed by some, "the care of the head," was by no means our Lord's design to condemn.

What he here condemns is the care of the heart; the anxious, uneasy care. . . . This care is not only a sore disease, a grievous sickness of soul, but also a heinous offense against God, a sin of the deepest dye. . . . It plainly implies that he is wanting; either in wisdom, if he does not know what things we stand in need of; or in goodness, if he does not provide those things for all who put their trust in him. Beware, therefore, that you take no thought in this sense: be anxiously careful for nothing. Take no uneasy thought: this is a plain, sure rule—uneasy care is unlawful care. With a single eye to God, do all that in you lies, to provide things honest in the sight of all men: and then give up all into better hands; leave the whole event to God.

Live for Today

Take therefore no thought for the morrow: for the morrow shall take thought for . . . itself. Sufficient unto the day is the evil thereof.
Matthew 6:34

"Let the morrow," therefore, "take thought for the things of itself"; that is, when the morrow comes, then think of it. Live today. Be it your earnest care to improve the present hour. This is your own; and it is your all. The past is as nothing, as though it had never been. The future is nothing to you: it is not yours; perhaps it never will be. There is no depending on what is yet to come; for you "know not what a day may bring forth." Therefore, live today: lose not an hour; use this moment, for it is your portion. "Who knoweth the things which have been before him, or which shall be after him under the sun?" The generations that were from the beginning of the world, where are they now? Fled away: forgotten. They were; they lived their day; they were shook off the earth, as leaves off their trees: they moldered away into common dust! Another and another race succeeded; then they "followed the generation of their fathers, and shall never more see the light." Now is your turn upon the earth. "Rejoice, O young man, in the days of thy youth!" Enjoy the very, very now, by enjoying him, "whose years fail not." Now let your eye be singly fixed on him, "with whom is no variableness, neither shadow of turning!" Now give him your heart; now stay yourself on him: now be holy, as he is holy! Now lay hold on the blessed opportunity of doing his acceptable and perfect will! Now "rejoice to suffer the loss of all things, so thou mayest win Christ!"

Gladly suffer today, for his name's sake, whatsoever he permits this day to come upon you. But look not at the sufferings of tomorrow. "Sufficient unto the day is the evil thereof." Evil it is, speaking after the manner of men; whether it be reproach or want, pain or sickness; but in the language of God, all is a blessing: it is a precious balm, prepared by the wisdom of God, and variously dispensed among his children, according to the various sicknesses of their souls. And he gives in one day, sufficient for the day; proportioned to the want and strength of the patient. If, therefore, you snatch today what belongs to you tomorrow; if you add this to what is given you already, it will be more than you can bear: this is the way not to heal, but to destroy your own soul. Take, therefore, just as much as he gives you today: today, do and suffer his will!

The Fruit of Faith

Even so every good tree bringeth forth good fruit; but a corrupt tree bringeth forth evil fruit. A good tree cannot bring forth evil fruit, neither can a corrupt tree bring forth good fruit.
Matthew 7:17, 18

Faith in general is a divine, supernatural *evidence* or *conviction* "of things not seen," not discoverable by our bodily senses, as being either past, future, or spiritual. Justifying faith implies not only a divine evidence or conviction that "God was in Christ reconciling the world unto himself," but a sure trust and confidence that Christ died for *my* sins, and gave himself for *me*. And at whatsoever time a sinner thus believes, be it in early childhood, in the strength of his years, or when he is old and hoary headed, God justifies that ungodly one: God for the sake of his Son pardons and absolves him, who had in him till that time no good thing. Repentance, indeed, God had given him before; but that repentance was neither more nor less than a deep sense of the want of all good, and the presence of all evil. And whatever good he had or does from that hour, when he first believes in God through Christ, faith does not *find,* but *bring.* This is the fruit of faith. First the tree is good, and then the fruit also.

10. Faith at Work

Of Faith and Fruit

Even so every good tree bringeth forth good fruit; but a corrupt tree bringeth forth evil fruit. . . . Wherefore by their fruits ye shall know them.
Matthew 7:17, 20

The tree is known by its fruits. For as the Christian loves God, so he keeps his commandments; not only some, or most of them, but all, from the least to the greatest. He is not content to "keep the whole law, and offend in one point," but has in all points, "a conscience void of offense toward God and toward man." Whatever God has forbidden, he avoids; whatever God has ordered, he does; and that whether it be little or great, hard or easy, joyous or grievous to the flesh. He "runs the way to God's commandments," now he has set his heart at liberty. It is his glory so to do; it is his daily crown of rejoicing, "to do the will of God on earth, as it is done in heaven"; knowing it is the highest privilege of "the angels of God, of those that excel in strength, to fulfill his commandments, and hearken to the voice of his word."

All the commandments of God he accordingly keeps, and that with all his might. For his obedience is in proportion to his love, the source from whence it flows. And therefore, loving God with all his heart, he serves him with all his strength. He continually presents his soul and body a living sacrifice, holy, acceptable to God; entirely and without reserve devoting himself, all he has, and all he is, to his glory. All the talents he has received, he constantly employs according to his Master's will; every power and faculty of his soul, every member of his body. Once he "yielded" them "unto sin" and the devil, "as instruments of unrighteousness"; but now, "being alive from the dead," he yields them all "as instruments of righteousness unto God."

Building on a Rock

Therefore whosoever heareth these sayings of mine,
and doeth them, I will liken him unto a wise man,
which built his house upon a rock.
Matthew 7:24

He is a wise man, even in God's account; for "he buildeth his house upon a rock"; upon the rock of ages, the everlasting rock, the Lord Jesus Christ. Fitly is he so called; for he changes not: he is "the same yesterday, and today, and forever." To him both the man of God of old, and the apostle citing his words, bear witness, "Thou, Lord, in the beginning hast laid the foundation of the earth; and the heavens are the works of thine hands: they shall perish; but thou remainest: and they all shall wax old as doth a garment; and as a vesture shalt thou fold them up, and they shall be changed: but thou art the same, and thy years shall not fail" (Heb. 1:10–12). Wise, therefore, is the man who builds on him; who lays him for his only foundation; who builds only upon his blood and righteousness, upon what he has done and suffered for us. On this cornerstone he fixes his faith, and rests the whole weight of his soul upon it. He is taught of God to say, "Lord, I have sinned; I deserve the nethermost hell; but I am justified freely by thy grace, through the redemption that is in Jesus Christ; and the life I now live, I live by faith in him, who loved me and gave himself for me: the life I now live; namely, a divine, heavenly life; of pure love both to God and man; a life of holiness and happiness; praising God, and doing all things to his glory."

Yet, let not such a one think that he shall not see war anymore; that he is now out of the reach of temptation. It still remains for God to prove the grace he has given: he shall be tried as gold in the fire. He shall be tempted not less than they who know not God—perhaps abundantly more, for Satan will not fail to try to the uttermost those whom he is not able to destroy. Accordingly, "the rain" will impetuously descend; only at such times and in such a manner as seems good, not to the prince of the power of the air, but to him "whose kingdom ruleth over all.". . . "The winds will blow, and beat upon that house," as though they would tear it up from the foundation. But they cannot prevail; it falls not, for it is founded upon a rock. He builded on Christ by faith and love; therefore he shall not be cast down. He "shall not fear though the earth be moved, and though the hills be carried into the midst of the sea." "Though the waters thereof rage and swell, and the mountains shake at the tempest of the same" still he "dwelleth under the defense of the Most High, and is safe under the shadow of the Almighty."

Finding the Infinite

Are not two sparrows sold for a farthing? and one of them shall not fall on the ground without your Father [knowing it].
Matthew 10:29

He is concerned every moment for what befalls every creature upon earth; and more especially for everything that befalls any of the children of men. It is hard, indeed, to comprehend this; nay, it is hard to believe it, considering the complicated wickedness, and the complicated misery, which we see on every side. But believe it we must, unless we will make God a liar; although it is sure, no man can comprehend it. It behooves us, then, to humble ourselves before God, and to acknowledge our ignorance. Indeed how can we expect that a man should be able to comprehend the ways of God? Can a worm comprehend a man? How much less can it be supposed, that a man can comprehend God! For how can finite measure infinite?

He is infinite in wisdom as well as in power: And all his wisdom is continually employed in managing all the affairs of his creation for the good of all his creatures. For his wisdom and goodness go hand in hand: They are inseparably united, and continually act in concert with Almighty power, for the real good of all his creatures. His power being equal to his wisdom and goodness, continually cooperates with them. And to him all things are possible: he does whatsoever pleases him, in heaven and earth, and in the sea, and all deep places. And we cannot doubt of his exerting all his power, as in sustaining, so in governing, all that he has made.

The Nature of True Religion

*For what is a man profited, if he shall gain the whole
world, and lose his own soul? or what shall a man
give in exchange for his soul?*
Matthew 16:26

Such a man supposes, first, that "a life of religion is a life of
misery." *That religion is misery!* How is it possible that anyone should entertain so strange a thought? Do any of *you* imagine this? If you do, the reason is plain; you know not what
religion is. "No! but I do, as well as you." What is it then?
"Why, the doing no harm." Not so; many birds and beasts do
no harm; yet they are not capable of religion. "Then it is going
to church and sacrament." Indeed it is not. This may be an excellent help to religion; and everyone who desires to save his soul
should attend them at all opportunities; yet it is possible, you may
attend them all your days, and still have no religion at all. Religion
is a higher and deeper thing than any outward ordinance whatever.

What is religion then? It is easy to answer, if we consult the
oracles of God. According to these, it lies in one single point; it
is neither more nor less than love; it is love which "is the fulfilling
of the law, the end of the commandment." Religion is the love
of God and our neighbor; that is, every man under heaven. This
love ruling the whole life, animating all our tempers and passions,
directing all our thoughts, words, and actions, is "pure religion
and undefiled."

Speaking the Truth in Love

*Moreover if thy brother shall trespass against thee,
go and tell him his fault between thee and him alone:
if he shall hear thee, thou hast gained thy brother.*
Matthew 18:15

First, "If thy brother shall sin against thee, go and tell him of
his fault between thee and him alone." The most literal way of
following this first rule, where it is practicable, is the best: therefore
if you see with your own eyes a brother, a fellow Christian, commit

undeniable sin, or hear it with your own ears, so that it is impossible for you to doubt the fact, then your part is plain: take the very first opportunity of going to him; and, if you can, "tell him of his fault between thee and him alone." Indeed great care is to be taken that this is done in a right spirit, and in a right manner.

The success of a reproof greatly depends on the spirit wherein it is given. . . . See that you speak in a meek as well as a lowly spirit; for the "wrath of man worketh not the righteousness of God." If he be "overtaken in a fault," he cannot otherwise be restored, than "in the spirit of meekness." If he opposes the truth, yet he cannot be brought to the knowledge thereof, but by gentleness. Still speak in a spirit of tender love, "which many waters cannot quench." If love is not conquered, it conquers all things. Who can tell the force of love?

> Love can bow down the stubborn neck
>   The stone to flesh convert;
> Soften, and melt, and pierce, and break
>   An adamantine heart.

Confirm then your love toward him, and you will thereby "heap coals of fire upon his head."

But see that the manner also wherein you speak, be according to the gospel of Christ. Avoid everything in look, gesture, word, and tone of voice, that savors of pride or self-sufficiency. Studiously avoid everything magisterial or dogmatical, everything that looks like arrogance or assuming. Beware of the most distant approach to disdain, overbearing, or contempt. With equal care avoid all appearance of anger; and though you use great plainness of speech, yet let there be no reproach, no railing accusation, no token of any warmth, but that of love. Above all, let there be no shadow of hate or ill will, no bitterness or sourness of expression; but use the air and language of sweetness as well as gentleness, that all may appear to flow from love in the heart. And yet this sweetness need not hinder your speaking in the most serious and solemn manner; as far as may be, in the very words of the oracles of God (for there are none like them), and as under the eye of him who is coming to judge the quick and dead.

The Wedding Garment

And he saith unto him, Friend, how camest thou in hither not having a wedding garment? And he was speechless.

Matthew 22:12

Does not that expression, "the righteousness of the saints," describe the "wedding garment" in the parable? It is the "holiness without which no man shall see the Lord." The righteousness of Christ is doubtless necessary for any soul who enters into glory: But so is personal holiness, too, for every child of man. But it is highly needful to be observed, that they are necessary in different respects. The former is necessary to entitle us to heaven; the latter to qualify us for it. Without the righteousness of Christ we would have no claim to glory; without holiness we could have no fitness for it. By the former we become members of Christ, children of God, and heirs of the kingdom of heaven. By the latter "we are made meet to be partakers of the inheritance of the saints in light."

Choose Life

And he saith unto him, Friend, how camest thou in hither not having a wedding garment? . . . Then said the king to the servants . . . take him away, and cast him into outer darkness; there shall be weeping and gnashing of teeth. For many are called, but few are chosen.

Matthew 22:12–14

The sum of all is this: The God of love is willing to save all the souls he has made. This he has proclaimed to them in his Word, together with the terms of salvation, revealed by the Son of his love, who gave his own life that they who believe in him might have everlasting life. And for these he has prepared a kingdom, from the foundation of the world. But he will not force them to accept it; he leaves them in the hands of their own counsel; he says, "Behold, I set before you life and death, blessing and cursing: Choose life, that ye may live." Choose holiness, by my grace; which is the way, the only way, to everlasting life. He cries aloud,

"Be holy, and be happy; happy in this world, and happy in the world to come." "Holiness becometh his house forever!" This is the wedding garment of all who are called to "the marriage of the Lamb." Clothed in this, they will not be found naked: "They have washed their robes and made them white in the blood of the Lamb." But as to all those who appear in the last day without the wedding garment, the Judge will say, "Cast them into outer darkness; there shall be weeping and gnashing of teeth."

11. *Faith with Feet on It*

Loving God and Neighbor

Jesus said unto him, Thou shalt love the Lord thy God with all thy heart, and with all thy soul, and with all thy mind. This is the first and great commandment. And the second is like unto it, Thou shalt love thy neighbour as thyself.

Matthew 22:37–39

Is it not reasonable to love God? Has he not given you life, and breath, and all things? Does he not continue his love to you, filling your heart with food and gladness? What have you which you have not received of him? And does not love demand a return of love? Whether, therefore, you do love God or not, you cannot but own it is reasonable so to do; nay, seeing he is the Parent of all good, to love him with all your heart.

Is it not reasonable also to love our neighbor, every man whom God has made? Are we not brethren, the children of one Father? Ought we not, then, to love one another? And should we only love those who love us? Is that acting like our Father which is in heaven? He causes his sun to shine on the evil and on the good, and sends rain on the just and on the unjust. And can there be a more equitable rule than this: "Thou shalt love thy neighbor as thyself"? You will plead for the reasonableness of this; as also for the golden rule (the only adequate measure of brotherly love, in all our words and actions), "Whatsoever ye would that men should do unto you, even so do unto them."

Is it not reasonable then, that, as we have opportunity, we should do good unto all men; not only friends, but enemies; not only to the deserving, but likewise to the evil and unthankful? Is it not right that all our life should be one continued labor of love?

The Rewards of Righteousness

*When the Son of man shall come in his glory, and all
the holy angels with him, then shall he sit upon the
throne of his glory.*
Matthew 25:31

Reason alone will convince every fair inquirer, that God "is a
rewarder of them that diligently seek him." This alone teaches
him to say, "Doubtless there is a reward for the righteous"; "there
is a God that judgeth the earth." But how little information do
we receive from unassisted reason touching the particulars contained in this general truth! As eye has not seen, nor ear heard,
so neither could it naturally enter into our hearts to conceive
the circumstances of that awful day wherein God will judge the
world. No information of this kind could be given but from the
great Judge himself. And what an amazing instance of condescension it is, that the Creator, the Governor, the Lord, the Judge
of all, should deign to give us so clear and particular an account
of that solemn transaction! If the learned heathen acknowledged
the sublimity of that account which Moses gives of the creation,
what would he have said, if he had heard this account of the
Son of Man coming in his glory? Here, indeed, is no labored pomp
of words, no ornaments of language. This would not have suited
either the Speaker or the occasion. But what inexpressible dignity
of thought! See him "coming in the clouds of heaven; and all the
angels with him"! See him "sitting on the throne of his glory, and
all the nations gathered before him"! And shall he separate them,
placing the good on his right hand, and the wicked on his left?
"Then shall the King say"—with what admirable propriety is the
expression varied! "The Son of man" comes down to judge the
children of men. "The King" distributes rewards and punishments
to his obedient or rebellious subjects—"Then shall the King say to
them on his right hand, Come, ye blessed of my Father, inherit
the kingdom prepared for you from the foundation of the world."

Inheriting the Kingdom

*Come, ye blessed of my Father, inherit the kingdom
prepared for you from the foundation of the world.*
Matthew 25:34

"Prepared for you from the foundation of the world"—does this agree with the common supposition, that God created man merely to supply the vacant thrones of the rebel angels? Does it not rather seem to imply that he would have created man, though the angels had never fallen? inasmuch as he then prepared the kingdom for his human children, when he laid the foundation of the earth.

"Inherit the kingdom"—as being "heirs of God, and joint heirs" with his beloved Son. It is your right; seeing I have purchased eternal redemption for all them who obey me; and you did obey me in the days of your flesh. You "believed in the Father, and also in me." You loved the Lord your God; and that love constrained you to love all mankind. You continued in the faith that was wrought by love. You showed your faith by your works. "For I was hungry, and ye gave me meat: I was thirsty, and ye gave me drink: I was a stranger, and ye took me in: naked, and ye clothed me: I was sick, and in prison, and ye came unto me."

Good Works

Then shall he answer them, saying, Verily I say unto you, Inasmuch as ye did it not to one of the least of these, ye did it not to me.
Matthew 25:45

To you who believe the Christian revelation, I may speak in a still stronger manner. You believe your blessed Master "left you an example, that you might tread in his steps." Now, you know his whole life was one long labor of love. You know "how he went about doing good," and that without intermission; declaring to all, "My Father worketh hitherto, and I work." Is not that, then, the language of your heart?

> Thy mind throughout my life be shown,
>   White, list'ning to the wretches' cry,
> The widows' and the orphans' groan,
>   On mercy's wings I swiftly fly,
> The poor and helpless to relieve,
> My life, my all, for them to give!

Occasions of doing this can never be wanting; for "the poor ye have always with you." But what a peculiar opportunity does the solemnity of this day furnish you with, of "treading in his steps," after a manner which you did not before conceive? Did he say to the poor afflicted parent (doubtless to the surprise of many), "Weep not"? And did he surprise them still more, when he stopped her flowing tears, by restoring life to her dead son, and "delivering him to his mother"? Did he (notwithstanding all that "laughed him to scorn") restore to life the daughter of Jairus? How many things of a nearly resembling sort, "if human we may liken to divine," have been done, and continue to be done daily, by these lovers of mankind! Let everyone then be ambitious of having a share in this glorious work! Let everyone (in a stronger sense than Mr. Herbert meant) join hands with God, to make a poor man live! By your generous assistance, be partakers of their work, and partakers of their joy.

To you I need add but one word more. Remember (what was spoken at first) the solemn declaration of him, whose you are, and whom you serve, coming in the clouds of heaven! While you are promoting this comprehensive charity, which contains feeding the hungry, clothing the naked, lodging the stranger; indeed all good works in one; let those animating words be written on your hearts, and sounding in your ears: "Inasmuch as ye have done it unto one of the least of these, ye have done it unto *me.*"

On Repentance and Faith

The time is fulfilled, and the kingdom of God is at hand: repent ye, and believe the gospel.
Mark 1:15

By the same faith we feel the power of Christ every moment resting upon us, whereby alone we are what we are; whereby we are enabled to continue in spiritual life, and without which, notwithstanding all our present holiness, we should be devils the next moment. But as long as we retain our faith in him, we "draw water out of the wells of salvation." Leaning on our beloved, even Christ in us the hope of glory, who dwells in our hearts by faith, who likewise is ever interceding for us at the right hand of God, we receive help from him to think, and speak, and act what is acceptable in his sight. Thus does he "prevent" them that believe, in all their "doings, and further them with his continual help," so that all their designs, conversations, and actions are "begun, continued, and ended in him." Thus does he "cleanse the thoughts of their hearts, by the inspiration of his Holy Spirit, that they may perfectly love him, and worthily magnify his holy name."

Thus it is, that in the children of God, repentance and faith exactly answer each other. By repentance, we feel the sin remaining in our hearts, and cleaving to our words and actions: by faith we receive the power of God in Christ, purifying our hearts, and cleansing our hands. By repentance we are still sensible that we deserve punishment for all our tempers, and words, and actions: by faith we are conscious, that our Advocate with the Father is continually pleading for us, and thereby continually turning aside all condemnation and punishment from us. By repentance we have an abiding conviction, that there is no help in us: by faith we receive not only mercy, "but grace to help in" *every* "time of need." Repentance disclaims the very possibility of any other help: faith accepts all the help we stand in need of, from him who has all power in heaven and earth. Repentance says, "Without him I can do nothing"; faith says, "I can do all things through Christ strengthening me." Through him I can not only overcome, but expel, all the enemies of my soul. Through him I can "love the Lord my God with all my heart, mind, soul, and strength"; yea, and "walk in holiness and righteousness before him all the days of my life."

Beginning with Repentance and Faith

Repent and believe the good news!
Mark 1:15 (NIV)

It is generally supposed that repentance and faith are only the gate of religion; that they are necessary only at the beginning of our Christian course, when we are setting out in the way to the kingdom. And this may seem to be confirmed by the great apostle, where, exhorting the Hebrew Christians to "go on to perfection," he teaches them to *leave* these "first principles of the doctrine of Christ"; "not laying again the foundation of repentance from dead works, and of faith towards God"; which must at least mean that they should comparatively leave these, that at first took up all their thoughts, in order to "press forward towards the prize of the high calling of God in Christ Jesus."

And this is undoubtedly true, that there is a repentance and a faith, which are, more especially, necessary at the beginning: a repentance, which is a conviction of our utter sinfulness, and guiltiness, and helplessness; and which precedes our receiving that kingdom of God, which our Lord observes, is "within us"; and a faith, whereby we receive that kingdom, even "righteousness, and peace, and joy in the Holy Ghost."

But, notwithstanding this, there is also a repentance and a faith (taking the words in another sense, a sense not quite the same, nor yet entirely different), which are requisite after we have "believed the gospel"; yea, and in every subsequent stage of our Christian course, or we cannot "run the race which is set before us." And this repentance and faith are full as necessary, in order to our *continuance* and *growth* in grace, as the former faith and repentance were, in order to our *entering* into the kingdom of God.

The Everlasting God

The Lord our God is one Lord.
Mark 12:29b

As there is one God, so there is one religion and one happiness for all men. God never intended there should be any more; and it is not possible there should. Indeed, in another sense, as the apostle observes, "There are gods many, and lords many." All the heathen nations had their gods, whole shoals of them. And generally, the more polished they were, the more gods they heaped up to themselves. But to us, to all who are favored with the Christian Revelation, "there is but one God"; who declares of himself, "Is there any God beside me? There is none; I know not any."

But who can search out this God to perfection? None of the creatures that he has made. Only some of his attributes he has been pleased to reveal to us in his Word. Hence we learn that God is an eternal Being. "His goings forth are from everlasting," and will continue to everlasting. As he ever was, so he ever will be; as there was no beginning of his existence, so there will be no end. This is universally allowed to be contained in his very name, Jehovah, which the apostle John accordingly renders: "He that was, and that is, and that is to come." Perhaps it would be as proper to say, "He is from everlasting to everlasting."

12. Life at Its Utmost

Believe, Love . . . and Obey

And thou shalt love the Lord thy God with all thy heart, and with all thy soul, and with all thy mind, and with all thy strength: this is the first commandment.

Mark 12:30

To *believe* is the first thing we are to understand by serving God. The second is, to *love* him.

Now to love God, in the manner the Scripture describes, in the manner God himself requires of us . . . is to love him as the *one* GOD; that is, "with all our heart, and with all our soul, and with all our mind, and with all our strength"; it is to desire God alone for his own sake; and nothing else, but with reference to him; to rejoice in God; to delight in the Lord; not only to seek but find happiness in him; to enjoy God as the chiefest among ten thousand; to rest in him, as our God and our all—in a word, to have such a possession of God, as makes us always happy.

A third thing we are to understand by serving God, is, to *resemble,* or *imitate* him.

So the ancient father said: *Optimus Dei cultus, imitari quem colis:* "It is the best worship or service of God, to imitate him you worship."

We here speak of imitating or resembling him in the spirit of our minds: for here the true Christian imitation of God begins. God is a Spirit; and they that imitate or resemble him, must do it in spirit and in truth.

Now God is love: therefore they who resemble him in the spirit of their minds, are transformed into the same image. They are merciful, even as he is merciful. Their soul is all love. They are kind, benevolent, compassionate, tenderhearted; and that not only to the good and gentle, but also to the froward. Yea, they are, like him, loving unto every man, and their mercy extends to all his works.

One thing more we are to understand by serving God, and that is, *obeying* him; glorifying him with our bodies, as well as with our spirits; keeping his outward commandments; zealously doing whatever he has enjoined; carefully avoiding whatever he has forbidden; performing all the ordinary actions of life with a single eye and a pure heart, offering them all in holy, fervent love, as sacrifices to God, through Jesus Christ.

Omnipresent—Not Uncaring

For with God nothing shall be impossible.
Luke 1:37

The omnipresent God sees and knows all the properties of the beings whom he has made. He knows all the connections, dependencies, and relations, and all the ways wherein one of them can affect another. In particular, he sees all the inanimate parts of the creation, whether in heaven above, or in the earth beneath. He knows how the stars, comets, or planets above influence the inhabitants of the earth beneath; what influence the lower heavens, with their magazines of fire, hail, snow, and vapors, winds, and storms, have on our planet; and what effects may be produced in the bowels of the earth by fire, air, or water; what exhalations may be raised therefrom, and what changes wrought thereby; what effects every mineral or vegetable may have upon the children of men: all these lie naked and open to the eye of the Creator and Preserver of the universe.

He knows all the animals of the lower world, whether beasts, birds, fishes, reptiles, or insects. He knows all the qualities and powers he has given them, from the highest to the lowest. He knows every good angel and every evil angel in every part of his dominions; and looks from heaven upon the children of men over the whole face of the earth. He knows all the hearts of the sons of men, and understands all their thoughts. He sees what any angel, any devil, any man, either thinks, or speaks, or does; yea, and all they feel. He sees all their sufferings, with every circumstance of them.

And is the Creator and Preserver of the world unconcerned for what he sees therein? Does he look upon these things either with a malignant or heedless eye? Is he an Epicurean god? Does he sit at ease in the heaven, without regarding the poor inhabitants of earth? It cannot be. He has made us, not we ourselves, and he cannot despise the work of his own hands. We are his children: and can a mother forget the children of her womb? Yea, she may forget; yet will God not forget us! On the contrary, he has expressly declared, that his "eyes are over all the earth," so he "is loving to every man, and his mercy is over all his works."

Faith . . . and Peace

And he [Jesus] said to the woman, Thy faith hath saved thee; go in peace.
Luke 7:50

Now, faith (supposing the Scripture to be of God) is "the demonstrative evidence of things unseen," the supernatural evidence of things invisible, not perceivable by eyes of flesh, or by any of our natural senses or faculties. Faith is that divine evidence whereby the spiritual man discerns God, and the things of God. It is, with regard to the spiritual world, what sense is with regard to the natural. It is the spiritual sensation of every soul that is born of God.

Perhaps you have not considered it in this view. I will, then, explain it a little further.

Faith, according to the scriptural account, is the eye of the newborn soul. Hereby every true believer in God "seeth him who is invisible." Hereby (in a more particular manner, since life and immortality have been brought to light by the gospel) he "seeth the light of the glory of God in the face of Jesus Christ"; and "beholdeth what manner of love it is which the Father hath bestowed upon us, that we," who are born of the Spirit, "should be called the sons of God."

It is the ear of the soul, whereby a sinner "hears the voice of the Son of God, and lives"; even that voice which alone wakes the dead, "Son, thy sins are forgiven thee."

It is (if I may be allowed the expression) the palate of the soul;

for hereby a believer "tastes the good word, and the powers of the world to come"; and "hereby he both tastes and sees that God is gracious," yea, "and merciful to him a sinner."

It is the feeling of the soul, whereby a believer perceives, through the "power of the Highest overshadowing him" both the existence and the presence of him in whom "he lives, moves, and has his being"; and indeed the whole invisible world, the entire system of things eternal. And hereby, in particular, he feels "the love of God shed abroad in his heart."

Self-Denial

> *And he said to them all, If any man will come after me, let him deny himself, and take up his cross daily, and follow me.*
>
> **Luke 9:23**

What is self-denial? Wherein are we to deny ourselves? And whence does the necessity of this arise? I answer, the will of God is the supreme, unalterable rule for every intelligent creature; equally binding every angel in heaven, and every man upon earth. Nor can it be otherwise: this is the natural, necessary result of the relation between creatures and their Creator. But if the will of God be our one rule of action in everything, great and small, it follows, by undeniable consequence, that we are not to do our own will in anything. Here, therefore, we see at once the nature, with the ground and reason, of self-denial. We see the nature of self-denial: it is the denying or refusing to follow our own will, from a conviction that the will of God is the only rule of action to us. And we see the reason thereof, because we are creatures; because "it is he that hath made us, and not we ourselves."

This reason for self-denial must hold, even with regard to the angels of God in heaven; and with regard to man innocent and holy, as he came out of the hands of his Creator. But a further reason for it arises from the condition wherein all men are since the fall. We are all now "shapen in wickedness, and in sin did our mother conceive us." Our nature is altogether corrupt, in every power and faculty. And our will, depraved equally with the rest, is wholly bent to indulge our natural corruption. On the other hand, it is the will of God, that we resist and counteract that corruption, not at some times, or in some things only, but at all times, and in all things. Here, therefore, is further ground for constant and universal self-denial.

Prayer Is Asking

If ye then, being evil, know how to give good gifts unto your children: how much more shall your heavenly Father give the Holy Spirit to them that ask him?
Luke 11:13

All who desire the grace of God are to wait for it in the way of prayer. This is the express direction of our Lord himself. In his Sermon upon the Mount, after explaining at large wherein religion consists, and describing the main branches of it, he adds, "Ask, and it shall be given you; seek, and ye shall find; knock, and it shall be opened unto you: For every one that asketh receiveth; and he that seeketh findeth; and to him that knocketh it shall be opened" (Matt. 7:7, 8). Here we are in the plainest manner directed to ask, in order to, or as a means of, receiving; to seek, in order to find, the grace of God, the pearl of great price; and to knock, to continue asking and seeking, if we would enter into his kingdom.

That no doubt might remain, our Lord labors this point in a more peculiar manner. He appeals to every man's own heart. "What man is there of you, whom if his son ask bread, will he give him a stone? Or if he ask a fish, will he give him a serpent? If ye then, being evil, know how to give good gifts unto your children, how much more shall your Father which is in heaven," the Father of angels and men, the Father of the spirits of all flesh, "give good things to them that ask him?" (9–11). Or, as he expresses himself on another occasion, including all good things in one, "How much more shall your heavenly Father give the Holy Spirit to them that ask him?" (Luke 11:13). It should be particularly observed here, that the persons directed to ask had not then received the Holy Spirit: nevertheless our Lord directs them to use this means, and promises that it should be effectual; that upon asking they should receive the Holy Spirit, from him whose mercy is over all his works.

The absolute necessity of using this means, if we would receive any gift from God, yet further appears from that remarkable passage which immediately precedes these words: "And he said unto them," whom he had just been teaching how to pray, "Which of you shall have a friend, and shall go unto him at midnight, and say unto him, Friend, lend me three loaves; And he from within shall answer and say, Trouble me not: . . . I cannot rise and give thee. I say unto you, Though he will not rise and give him, because he is his friend, yet because of his importunity he will rise and give him as many as he needeth. And I say unto you, Ask, and it shall be given you" (Luke 11:5, 7–9).

Of Hair and Sparrows

But even the very hairs of your head are all numbered.
Fear not therefore: ye are of more value than many
sparrows.
                                        Luke 12:7

In the verses preceding the text, our Lord has been arming his disciples against the fear of man: "Be not afraid," says he, (v. 4) "of them that kill the body, and after that have no more that they can do." He guards them against this fear, first, by reminding them of what was infinitely more terrible than anything which man could inflict: "Fear him, which after he hath killed hath power to cast into hell." He guards them further against it, by the consideration of an overruling providence: "Are not five sparrows sold for two farthings, and not one of them is forgotten before God?" Or, as the words are repeated by Matthew, with a very inconsiderable variation, (10:29, 30): "Not one of them shall fall on the ground without your Father. But the very hairs of your head are all numbered."

We must indeed observe that this strong expression, though repeated by both the evangelists, need not imply (though if any one thinks it does, he may think so very innocently), that God does literally number all the hairs that are on the heads of all his creatures. But it is a proverbial expression, implying that nothing is so small or insignificant in the sight of men as not to be an object of the care and providence of God, before whom nothing is small that concerns the happiness of any of his creatures.

And as this all-wise, all-gracious Being created all things, so he sustains all things. He is the Preserver as well as the Creator of everything that exists. "He upholdeth all things by the word of his power"; that is, by his powerful word. Now it must be that he knows everything he has made, and everything he preserves, from moment to moment; otherwise, he could not preserve it, he could not continue giving to it the being which he has given it. And it is nothing strange that he who is omnipresent, who "filleth heaven and earth," who is in every place, should see what is in every place, where he is intimately present. If the eye of man discerns things at a small distance; the eye of an eagle, what is at a greater; the eye of an angel, what is at a thousand times greater distance (perhaps taking in the surface of the earth at one view); how shall not the eye of God see everything, through the whole extent of creation? especially considering that nothing is distant from him in whom we all "live, and move, and have our being."

The Care and Feeding of the Soul

But God said unto him, Thou fool, this night thy soul shall be required of thee: then whose shall those things be, which thou hast provided?
Luke 12:20

Let us consider this man's words a little more attentively. He said within himself, "What shall I do?" And is not the answer ready? Do good. Do all the good you can. Let your plenty supply your neighbor's wants; and you will never want something to do. Can you find none who need the necessaries of life, who are wasted with pining sickness; none who are languishing in prison? If you duly considered our Lord's words, "The poor have you always with you," you would no more ask, "What shall I do?"

How different was the purpose of this poor madman! "I will pull down my barns, and build greater; and there will I bestow all my goods." You may just as well bury them in the earth, or cast them into the sea. This will just as well answer the end for which God entrusted you with them.

But let us examine a little further the remaining part of his resolution. "I will say to my soul, Soul, thou hast much goods laid up for many years; take thy ease, eat, drink and be merry." What, are these the goods of a never-dying spirit? As well may your body feed on the fleeting breeze, as your soul on earthly fruits. Excellent counsel then to such a spirit, to eat and drink! To a spirit made equal to angels, made an incorruptible picture of the God of glory, to feed not on corruptible things, but on the fruit of the tree of life, which grows in the midst of the paradise of God.

It is no marvel, then, that God should say unto him, "Thou fool!" For this terrible reason, were there no other: "This night shall thy soul be required of thee!"

> And art thou born to die,
> To lay this body down?
> And must thy trembling spirit fly
> Into a land unknown?
>
> A land of deepest shade,
> Unpierced by human thought;
> The dreary regions of the dead,
> Where all things are forgot?

13. How to Live As a Christian

Give All to God

Sell that ye have, and give alms; provide yourselves bags which wax not old, a treasure in the heavens that faileth not, where no thief approacheth, neither moth corrupteth.

Luke 12:33

[Here we] see the nature and extent of truly Christian prudence, so far as it relates to the use of that great talent, money. Gain all you can without hurting either yourself or your neighbor, in soul or body, by applying hereto with unintermitted diligence, and with all the understanding which God has given you; save all you can, by cutting off every expense which serves only to indulge foolish desire; to gratify either the desire of the flesh, the desire of the eye, or the pride of life; waste nothing, living or dying, on sin or folly, whether for yourself or your children; and then, give all you can, or, in other words, give all you have to God. . . . Render unto God, not a tenth, not a third, not half, but all that is God's, be it more or less; by employing all, on yourself, your household, the household of faith, and all mankind, in such a manner that you may give a good account of your stewardship, when you can be no longer stewards; in such a manner as the oracles of God direct, both by general and particular precepts; in such a manner, that whatever you do may be "a sacrifice of a sweet-smelling savor to God," and that every act may be rewarded in that day, when the Lord cometh with all his saints.

The Habit of Doing Good

Let your loins be girded about, and your lights burning;
And ye yourselves like unto men that wait for their
lord, when he will return from the wedding; that when

he cometh and knocketh, they may open unto him immediately. Blessed are those servants, whom the lord when he cometh shall find watching.

Luke 12:35–37a

We "charge" you, therefore, "who are rich in this world," as having authority from our great Lord and Master—to be *habitually doing good,* to live in a course of good works. "Be ye merciful, as your Father who is in heaven is merciful" who does good and ceases not. "Be ye merciful"—how far? After your power; with all the ability which God gives. Make this your only measure of doing good, not any beggarly maxims or customs of the world. We "charge you to be rich in good works"; as you have much, to give plenteously. "Freely ye have received; freely give"; so as to lay up no treasure but in heaven. Be ye "ready to distribute" to everyone according to his necessity. Disperse abroad; give to the poor; deal your bread to the hungry. Cover the naked with a garment; entertain the stranger; carry or send relief to them who are in prison. Heal the sick; not by miracle, but through the blessing of God upon your seasonable support. Let the blessing of him that was ready to perish, through pining want, come upon you. Defend the oppressed, plead the cause of the fatherless, and make the widow's heart sing for joy.

The Faithful and Wise Steward

And the Lord said, Who then is that faithful and wise steward, whom his lord shall make ruler over his household . . . ?

Luke 12:42

If you desire to be "a faithful and a wise steward," out of that portion of your Lord's goods which he has for the present lodged in your hands, but with the right of resumption whenever it pleases him: (1) provide things needful for yourself; food to eat, raiment to put on; whatever nature moderately requires, for preserving you both in health and strength; (2) provide these for your wife, your children, your servants, or any others who pertain to your household. If, when this is done, there is a surplus left, then do good to "them that are of the household of faith." If there be a surplus still, "as you have opportunity, do good unto all men."

In so doing, you *give all you can;* nay, in a sound sense, all you have. For all that is laid out in this manner is really given to God. You render unto God the things that are God's, not only by what you give to the poor, but also by that which you expend in providing things needful for yourself and your household.

The Proper Use of Money

And I say unto you, Make to yourselves friends of the mammon of unrighteousness; that, when ye fail, they may receive you into everlasting habitations.
Luke 16:9*

An excellent branch of Christian wisdom is here inculcated by our Lord on all his followers, namely, the right use of money— a subject largely spoken of, after their manner, by men of the world; but not sufficiently considered by those whom God has chosen out of the world. These, generally, do not consider, as the importance of the subject requires, the use of this excellent talent. Neither do they understand how to employ it to the greatest advantage; the introduction of which into the world, is one admirable instance of the wise and gracious providence of God. It has, indeed, been the manner of poets, orators, and philosophers, in almost all ages and nations, to rail at this as the grand corrupter of the world, the bane of virtue, the pest of human society. Hence, nothing so commonly heard, as,

Gold, more mischievous than keenest steel.

Hence the lamentable complaint,

Wealth is dug up, incentive to all ill.

Nay, one celebrated writer gravely exhorts his countrymen, in order to banish all vice at once, to "throw all their money into the sea."

---

* Editor's note: This verse has always been difficult of interpretation, and Wesley's explanation is particularly helpful. A more modern translation of the verse bears this out: "I tell you, use worldly wealth to gain friends for yourselves, so that when it is gone, you will be welcomed into eternal dwellings" (NIV).

But is not all this mere empty rant? Is there any solid reason therein? By no means. For, let the world be as corrupt as it will, is gold or silver to blame? "The love of money," we know, "is the root of all evil"; but not the thing itself. The fault does not lie in the money, but in them that use it. It may be used ill: and what may not? But it may likewise be used well: it is full as applicable to the best, as to the worst uses. It is of unspeakable service to all civilized nations, in all the common affairs of life: it is a most compendious instrument of transacting all manner of business, and (if we use it according to Christian wisdom) of doing all manner of good. It is true, were man in a state of innocence, or were all men "filled with the Holy Ghost," so that, like the infant church at Jerusalem, "no man counted anything he had his own," but "distribution was made to every one as he had need," the use of it would be superseded; as we cannot conceive there is anything of the kind among the inhabitants of heaven. But, in the present state of mankind, it is an excellent gift of God, answering the noblest ends. In the hands of his children, it is food for the hungry, drink for the thirsty, raiment for the naked: it gives to the traveller and the stranger where to lay his head. By it we may supply the place of a husband to the widow, and of a father to the fatherless. We may be a defense for the oppressed, a means of health to the sick, of ease to them that are in pain; it may be as eyes to the blind, as feet to the lame; yea, a lifter up from the gates of death!

Of Religion and Riches

There was a certain rich man, which was clothed in purple and fine linen, and fared sumptuously every day.

Luke 16:19

"There was a certain rich man." It is no more sinful to be rich than to be poor. But it is dangerous beyond expression. Therefore, I remind all of you who are of this number, who have the conveniences of life, and something over, that you walk upon slippery ground. You continually tread on snares and deaths. You are every moment on the verge of hell! "It is easier for a camel to go through the eye of a needle," than for you to enter into the kingdom of heaven.

"Who was clothed in purple and fine linen." And some may have a plea for this. Our Lord mentions those who "dwell in kings' houses," as wearing gorgeous, that is, splendid apparel, and does not blame them for it. But certainly this is no plea for any who do not dwell in kings' houses. Let all of them, therefore, beware how they follow his example who is "lifting up his eyes in hell"! Let us follow the advice of the apostle, being "adorned with good works, and with the ornament of a meek and quiet spirit."

"He fared sumptuously every day." Reconcile this with religion who can. I know how plausibly the prophets of smooth things can talk in favor of hospitality; of making our friends welcome; of keeping a handsome table, to do honor to religion; of promoting trade, and the like. But God is not mocked: He will not be put off with such pretenses as these. Whoever you are who shares in the sin of this rich man, were it no other than "faring sumptuously every day," you shall as surely be a sharer in his punishment, except you repent, as if you were already crying for a drop of water to cool your tongue!

Comfort for the Poor

And there was a certain beggar named Lazarus, which was laid at his gate, full of sores, And desiring to be fed with the crumbs which fell from the rich man's table.
Luke 16:20, 21

It seems both the rich man and his guests were too *religious* to relieve *common beggars!*—a sin of which pious Mr. H. earnestly warns his readers; and an admonition of the same kind I have read on the gate of the good city of Winchester! I wish the gentlemen who placed it there had seen a little circumstance which occurred some years since. At Epworth, In Lincolnshire, the town where I was born, a beggar came to a house in the marketplace, and begged a morsel of bread, saying she was very hungry. The master bid her *be gone,* for *a lazy jade.* She called at a second, and begged a little drink, saying she was very thirsty. She had

112

much the same answer. At a third door she begged a little water, saying she was very faint. But this man also was too conscientious to encourage common beggars. The boys, seeing a ragged creature turned from door to door, began to pelt her with snowballs. She looked up, lay down, and died!

Would you wish to be the man who refused that poor wretch a morsel of bread, or a cup of water? "Moreover the dogs came and licked his sores," being more compassionate than their master. "And it came to pass, that the beggar died, and was carried by angels into Abraham's bosom."

Hear this, all you who are poor in this world. You who, many times, have not food to eat, or raiment to put on; you who have not a place where to lay your head, unless it be a cold garret, or a foul and damp cellar! You are now reduced to "solicit the cold hand of charity." Yet lift up your load; it shall not always be thus. I love you, I pity you, I admire you, when "in patience ye possess your souls." Yet I cannot help you. But there is One who can—the Father of the fatherless, and the Husband of the widow. "The poor crieth unto the Lord; and he heareth him, and delivereth him out of all his troubles." Yet a little while, if you truly turn to him, his angels shall carry you into Abraham's bosom. There you shall "hunger no more, and thirst no more"; you shall feel no more sorrow or pain; but "the Lamb shall wipe away all tears from your eyes, and lead you forth beside fountains of living waters."

Lessons from Lazarus

And it came to pass, that the beggar died, and was carried by the angels into Abraham's bosom: the rich man also died, and was buried. . . . And he (Abraham) said unto him, If they hear not Moses and the prophets, neither will they be persuaded, though one rose from the dead.

Luke 16:22, 31

Before, or about the same time that Lazarus was carried into Abraham's bosom, another Lazarus, the brother of Martha and Mary, was actually raised from the dead. But were even those who believed the fact persuaded to repent? So far from it, that "they took counsel to kill Lazarus," as well as his Master! Away then with the fond imagination, that those who "hear not Moses and the prophets, would be persuaded, though one rose from the dead!"

From the whole we may draw this general conclusion. That standing revelation is the best means of rational conviction; far preferable to any of those extraordinary means which some imagine would be more effectual. It is therefore our wisdom to avail ourselves of this; to make full use of it; so that it may be a lantern to our feet, and a light in all our paths. Let us take care that our whole heart and life be conformable thereto; that it be the constant rule of all our tempers, all our words, and all our actions. So shall we preserve in all things the testimony of a good conscience toward God; and when our course is finished, we too shall be "carried by angels into Abraham's bosom."

14. Christ and the New Birth

Constant Communion

And he took bread, and gave thanks, and brake it, and gave unto them, saying, This is my body which is given for you: this do in remembrance of me.
Luke 22:19

Consider the Lord's Supper as a mercy from God to man. As God, whose mercy is over all his works, and particularly over the children of men, knew there was but one way for man to be happy like himself; namely, by being like him in holiness; as he knew we could do nothing toward this of ourselves, he has given us certain means of obtaining his help. One of these is the Lord's Supper, which, of his infinite mercy, he has given for this very end; that through this means we may be assisted to attain those blessings which he has prepared for us, that we may obtain holiness on earth, and everlasting glory in heaven.

I ask, then, why do you not accept of his mercy as often as ever you can? God now offers you his blessing—why do you refuse it? You have now an opportunity of receiving his mercy—why do you not receive it? You are weak—why do not you seize every opportunity of increasing your strength? In a word: Considering this as a command of God, he who does not communicate as often as he can has no piety; considering it as a mercy, he who does not communicate as often as he can has no wisdom.

These two considerations will yield a full answer to all the common objections which have been made against constant communion; indeed to all that ever were or can be made. In truth, nothing can be objected it, but upon supposition that, this particular time, either the communion would be no mercy, or I am not commanded to receive it. Nay, should we grant it would be no mercy, that is not enough; for still the other reason would hold: whether it does you any good or none, you are to obey the command of God.

Communion and Communication

And he took bread, and gave thanks, and brake it, and gave unto them, saying, This is my body which is given for you: this do in remembrance of me.
Luke 22:19;
see 1 Corinthians 11:23b, 24

All who desire an increase of the grace of God are to wait for it in partaking of the Lord's Supper: for this also is a direction he himself has given. "The same night in which he was betrayed [he] took bread: And when he had given thanks, he brake it, and said, Take, eat: this is my body," that is, the sacred sign of my body, "this do in remembrance of me." Likewise, he took the cup, saying, "This cup is the new testament," or covenant, "in my blood," the sacred sign of that covenant; "this do ye . . . in remembrance of me. For as often as ye eat this bread, and drink this cup, ye do shew the Lord's death till he come" (1 Cor. 11:23–26): you openly exhibit the same, by these visible signs, before God, and angels, and men; you manifest your solemn remembrance of his death, till he comes in the clouds of heaven.

Only let a man first examine himself, whether he understand the nature and design of this holy institution, and whether he really desire to be himself made comformable to the death of Christ; and so, nothing doubting, "let him eat of that bread, and drink of that cup."

Here, then, the direction first given by our Lord is expressly repeated by the apostle. Let him eat; let him drink (the imperative mood; words not implying a bare permission only, but a clear, explicit command; a command to all those who either already are filled with peace and joy in believing, or can truly say, "The remembrance of our sins is grievous unto us, the burden of them is intolerable").

And that this is also an ordinary, stated means of receiving the grace of God, is evident from those words of the apostle which occur in the preceding chapter. "The cup of blessing which we bless, is it not the communion [or *communication*] of the blood of Christ? The bread which we break, is it not the communion of the body of Christ?" (1 Cor. 10:16). Is not the eating of that bread, and the drinking of that cup, the outward, visible means,

116

whereby God conveys into our souls all that spiritual grace, that righteousness, and peace, and joy in the Holy Ghost, which were purchased by the body of Christ once broken, and the blood of Christ once shed for us? Let all, therefore, who truly desire the grace of God, eat of that bread, and drink of that cup.

Christ—Prophet, King, and Priest

. . . Jesus of Nazareth, which was a prophet mighty in deed and word before God and all the people.
Luke 24:19b

The holiest of men still need Christ as their Prophet, as the "light of the world." For he does not give them light but from moment to moment; the instant He withdraws, all is darkness. They still need Christ as their King, for God does not give them a stock of holiness. But unless they receive a supply every moment, nothing but unholiness would remain. They still need Christ as their Priest, to make atonement for their holy things. Even perfect holiness is acceptable to God only through Jesus Christ.

The Word Made Flesh

In the beginning was the Word, and the Word was with God, and the Word was God. The same was in the beginning with God. All things were made by him; and without him was not any thing made that was made.
John 1:1-3

In the beginning, the heavenly Word—being a Spirit that issued from the Father, and the Word of his power—made man an image of immortality, according to the likeness of the Father; but he who had been made in the image of God, afterward became mortal, when the more powerful Spirit was separated from him. To remedy this, the Word became Man, that man by receiving the adoption might become a son of God once more; that the light of the Father might rest upon the flesh of our Lord, and come bright from thence unto us; and so man, being encompassed with the light of the Godhead, might be carried into immortality. When he was

incarnate and became man, he recapitulated in himself all generations of mankind, making himself the center of our salvation, that
what we lost in Adam, even the image and likeness of God, we
might receive in Christ Jesus. By the Holy Ghost coming upon
Mary, and the power of the highest overshadowing her, the incar-
nation of Christ was wrought, and a new birth, whereby man
should be born of God, was shown; that as by our first birth we
did inherit death, so by this birth we might inherit life.

This is no other than what St. Paul teaches us: "The first man,
Adam, was made a living soul, but the Second Adam was made
a quickening spirit." All that the first man possessed of himself,
all that he has transmitted to us, is "a living soul"; a nature endued
with an animal life, and receptive of a spiritual. But the Second
Adam is, and was made to us, "a quickening spirit"; by a strength
from him as our Creator, we were at first raised above ourselves;
by a strength from him as our Redeemer, we shall again live
unto God.

Happiness in the Heart

Jesus saw Nathanael coming to him, and saith of him,
Behold an Israelite indeed, in whom is no guile!
John 1:47

What does it mean to be "without guile"? Nathanael is our example
of one whose heart was true to God, for that is the meaning in
a nutshell.

We may, first, observe what is implied in having our hearts
true to God. Does this imply any less than is included in that
gracious command, "My son, give me thy heart"? Then only is
our heart *true to God,* when we give it to him. We give him our
heart, in the lowest degree, when we seek our happiness in him;
when we do not seek it in gratifying "the desire of the flesh"—
in any of the pleasures of sense; nor in gratifying "the desire of
the eye"—in any of the pleasures of the imagination, arising from
grand, or new, or beautiful objects, whether of nature or art; neither
in "the pride of life"—in "the honour that cometh of men," in
being beloved, esteemed, and applauded by them; no, nor yet in
what some term, with equal impudence and ignorance, *the main*

118

chance, the "laying up treasures on earth." When we seek happiness in none of these, but in God alone, then we, in some sense, give him our heart.

But in a more proper sense, we give God our heart when we not only seek but find happiness in him. This happiness undoubtedly begins when we begin to know him by the teaching of his own Spirit; when it pleases the Father to reveal his Son in our hearts, so that we can humbly say, "My Lord and my God"; and when the Son is pleased to reveal his Father in us, by "the Spirit of adoption, crying in our hearts, Abba, Father," and bearing his "testimony of our spirits that we are the children of God." Then it is that "the love of God also is shed abroad in our hearts." And according to the degree of our love, is the degree of our happiness.

The Nature of the New Birth

Jesus answered and said unto him, Verily, verily, I say unto thee, Except a man be born again, he cannot see the kingdom of God. Nicodemus saith unto him, How can a man be born when he is old? can he enter a second time into his mother's womb, and be born?
John 3:3, 4

It suffices for every rational and Christian purpose, that without descending into curious, critical inquiries, we can give a plain scriptural account of the nature of the new birth. This will satisfy every reasonable man, who desires only the salvation of his soul. The expression, being born again, was not first used by our Lord in his conversation with Nicodemus: it was well known before that time, and was in common use among the Jews when our Savior appeared among them. When an adult heathen was convinced that the Jewish religion was of God, and desired to join therein, it was the custom to baptize him first, before he was admitted to circumcision. And when he was baptized, he was said to be born again; by which they meant, that he who was before a child of the devil, was now adopted into the family of God, and accounted one of his children. This expression, therefore, which Nicodemus, being "a teacher in Israel," ought to have understood well, our Lord uses in conversing with him; only in a stronger sense than he was accustomed to. And this might be the reason of his asking, "How can these things be?" They cannot be, literally: a man cannot "enter a second time into his mother's womb, and be born"—but they may, spiritually: a man may be born from above, born of God, born of the spirit, in a manner which bears a very near analogy to the natural birth.

From hence it manifestly appears what is the nature of the new birth. It is the great change which God works in the soul, when he brings it into life; when he raises it from the death of sin to the life of righteousness. It is the change wrought in the whole soul by the almighty Spirit of God, when it is "created anew in Christ Jesus," when it is "renewed after the image of God, in righteousness and true holiness"; when the love of the world is changed into the love of God; pride into humility; passion into meekness; hatred, envy, malice, into a sincere, tender, disinterested love for all mankind. In a word, it is that change whereby the earthly, sensual, devilish mind is turned into the "mind which was in Christ Jesus." This is the nature of the new birth: "So is every one that is born of the Spirit."

Why We Must Be Born Again

Jesus answered, Verily, verily, I say unto thee, Except a man be born of water and of the Spirit, he cannot enter into the kingdom of God.
John 3:5

Although man was made in the image of God, yet he was not made immutable. This would have been inconsistent with that state of trial in which God was pleased to place him. He was therefore created able to stand, and yet liable to fall. And this God himself apprised him of, and gave him a solemn warning against it. Nevertheless, man did not abide in honor: he fell from his high estate. He lost the life of God: he was separated from him, in union with whom his spiritual life consisted. The body dies when it is separated from the soul; the soul, when it is separated from God. But this separation from God, Adam sustained in the day, the hour, he ate of the forbidden fruit. And of this he gave immediate proof; presently showing by his behavior, that the love of God was extinguished in his soul, which was now "alienated from the life of God." Instead of this he was now under the power of servile fear, so that he fled from the presence of the Lord.

In Adam all died, all humankind, all the children of men who were then in Adam's loins. The natural consequence of this is, that everyone descended from him comes into the world spiritually dead, dead to God, wholly dead in sin; entirely void of the life of God; void of the image of God, of all that righteousness and holiness wherein Adam was created. Instead of this, every man born into the world now bears the image of the devil, in pride and self-will; the image of the beast, in sensual appetites and desires. This then is the foundation of the new birth, the entire corruption of our nature. Hence it is, that being born in sin, we must be "born again." Hence everyone that is born of a woman, must be born of the Spirit of God.

15. Gems from the Apostle John

No Neutral Ground

Marvel not that I said unto thee, Ye must be born again.

John 3:7

Why must we be born again? What is the foundation of this doctrine? The foundation of it lies near as deep as the creation of the world; in the scriptural account whereof we read, "And God," the three-one God, "said, Let us make man in our image, after our likeness: . . . So God created man in his own image, in the image of God created he him" (Gen. 1:26, 27)—not barely in his *natural image,* a picture of his own immortality; a spiritual being, endued with understanding, freedom of will, and various affections; nor merely in his *political image,* the governor of this lower world, having "dominion over the fishes of the sea, and over all the earth"; but chiefly in his *moral image,* which, according to the apostle, is "righteousness and true holiness" (Eph. 4:24). In this image of God was man made. "God is love": accordingly man at his creation was full of love; which was the sole principle of all his tempers, thoughts, words, and actions. God is full of justice, mercy, and truth; so was man as he came from the hands of his Creator. God is spotless purity; and so man was in the beginning pure from every sinful blot; otherwise God could not have pronounced him, as well as all the other works of his hands, "very good" (Gen. 1:31). This he could not have been, had he not been pure from sin, and filled with righteousness and true holiness. For there is no medium: if we suppose an intelligent creature not to love God, not to be righteous and holy, we necessarily suppose him not to be good at all: much less to be "very good."

A Living Faith

So is everyone that is born of the Spirit.
John 3:8b

What is the new birth? Perhaps it is not necessary to give a definition of this, seeing the Scripture gives none. But as the question is of the deepest concern to every child of man; since, "except a man be born again," born of the Spirit, "he cannot see the kingdom of God," I propose to lay down the marks of it in the plainest manner, just as I find them laid down in Scripture.

The first of these, and the foundation of all the rest, is faith. So St. Paul, "Ye are all the children of God by faith in Christ Jesus" (Gal. 3:26). So St. John, "To them gave he power [*right* or *privilege,* it may rather be translated] to become the sons of God, even to them that believe on his name; which were born," when they believed, "not of blood, nor of the will of the flesh," not by natural generation, "nor of the will of man," like those children adopted by men, in whom no inward change is thereby wrought, "but of God" (1:12, 13). And again in his general epistle, "Whosoever believeth that Jesus is the Christ is born of God" (1 John 5:1).

But it is not a barely notional or speculative faith that is here spoken of by the apostles. It is not a bare assent to this proposition, Jesus is the Christ; nor indeed to all the propositions contained in our creed, or in the Old and New Testaments.

For all this is no more than a dead faith. The true, living, Christian faith, which whosoever is born of God has, is not only assent, an act of the understanding; but a disposition, which God has wrought in his heart; "a sure trust and confidence in God, that through the merits of Christ his sins are forgiven, and he reconciled to the favour of God." This implies that a man . . . comes to God as a lost, miserable, self-destroyed, self-condemned, undone, helpless sinner; as one whose mouth is utterly stopped, and who is altogether "guilty before God." Such a sense of sin (commonly called despair, by those who speak evil of the things they know not) together with a full conviction, such as no words can express, that of Christ only comes our salvation, and an earnest desire of that salvation must precede a living faith, a trust in him, who for us paid our ransom by his death, and for us fulfilled the law in his life.

Possessions in Perspective

[John the Baptist said:] He who comes from above is above all; he who is of earth belongs to the earth, and of the earth he speaks; he who comes from heaven is above all.

John 3:31 (RSV)

What can be a fitter employment for a wise man than to meditate upon these things, frequently to expand his thoughts "beyond the bounds of this diurnal sphere," and to expatiate above even the starry heavens, in the fields of eternity? What a means might it be to confirm his contempt of the poor little things of earth!

When a man of huge possessions was boasting to his friend of the largeness of his estate, Socrates desired him to bring a map of the earth, and to point out Attica therein. When this was done (although not very easily, as it was a small country), he next desired Alcibiades to point out his own estate therein. When he could not do this, it was easy to observe how trifling the possessions were in which he so prided himself, in comparison to the whole earth.

How applicable is this to the present case! Does anyone value himself on his earthly possessions? Alas, what is the whole globe of earth to the infinity of space? A mere speck of creation. And what is the life of man, yea, the duration of the earth itself, but a speck of time, if it be compared to the length of eternity? Think of this: Let it sink into your thought, till you have some conception, however imperfect, of that

> Boundless, fathomless abyss,
> Without a bottom or a shore.

True Worship

But the hour cometh, and now is, when the true worshippers shall worship the Father in spirit and in truth: for the Father seeketh such to worship him.

John 4:23

How shall we secure the favor of this great God? How, but by worshiping him in spirit and in truth; by uniformly imitating him we worship, in all his imitable perfections, without which the most accurate systems of opinions, all external modes of religion, are idle cobwebs of the brain, dull farce and empty show? Now, God is love: Love God, then, and you are a true worshiper. Love mankind, and God is your God, your Father, and your Friend. But see that you deceive not your own soul; for this is not a point of small importance. And by this you may know: If you love God, then you are happy in God; if you love God, riches, honors, and the pleasures of sense are no more to you than bubbles on the water: You look on dress and equipage, as the tassels of a fool's cap; diversions, as the bells on a fool's coat. If you love God, God is in all your thoughts, and your whole life is a sacrifice to him. And if you love mankind, it is your one design, desire, and endeavor, to spread virtue and happiness all around you, to lessen the present sorrows, and increase the joys, of every child of man; and, if it be possible, to bring them with you to the rivers of pleasure that are at God's right hand forever more.

Worshiping in Spirit and in Truth

God is a Spirit: and they that worship him must worship him in spirit and in truth.
John 4:24

God is a Spirit; and they that worship him must worship him in spirit and in truth. Yea, and this is enough: we ought to employ the whole strength of our mind therein. But then I would ask, what is it to worship God, a Spirit, in spirit and in truth? Why, it is to worship him with our spirit; to worship him in that manner which none but spirits are capable of. It is to believe in him, as a wise, just, holy being, of purer eyes than to behold iniquity; and yet merciful, gracious, and longsuffering; forgiving iniquity, and transgression, and sin; casting all our sins behind his back, and accepting us in the Beloved. It is: to love him; to delight in him; to desire him with all our heart, and mind, and soul, and strength; to imitate him we love, by purifying ourselves even as he is pure; and to obey him whom we love, and in whom we believe, both in thought, and word, and work. Consequently, one branch of worshiping God in spirit and in truth is in keeping his outward commandments. To glorify him therefore with our bodies, as well as with our spirits; to go through outward work with hearts lifted up to him; to make our daily employment a sacrifice to God; to buy and sell, to eat and drink, to his glory— this is worshiping God in spirit and in truth, as much as the praying to him in a wilderness.

Search the Scriptures

Search the scriptures; for in them ye think ye have eternal life: and they are they which testify of me.
John 5:39

All who desire the grace of God are to wait for it in searching the Scriptures.

Our Lord's direction, with regard to the use of this means, is likewise plain and clear. "Search the Scriptures," says he to the unbelieving Jews, "for they testify of me" (John 5:39). And for this very end did he direct them to search the Scriptures, that they might believe in him.

And what a blessing from God attends the use of this means appears from what is recorded concerning the Bereans; who, after hearing St. Paul, "searched the Scriptures daily, whether those things were so. Therefore many of them believed"—found the grace of God, in the way which he had ordained (Acts 17:11, 12).

And that this is a means whereby God not only gives, but also confirms and increases, true wisdom, we learn from the words of St. Paul to Timothy: "From a child thou hast known the holy scriptures, which are able to make thee wise unto salvation through faith which is in Christ Jesus" (2 Tim. 3:15). The same truth (namely, that this is the great means God has ordained for conveying his manifold grace to man) is delivered, in the fullest manner that can be conceived, in the words which immediately follow: "All scripture is given by inspiration of God"; consequently, all Scripture is infallibly true; "and is profitable for doctrine, for reproof, for correction, for instruction in righteousness"; to the end "that the man of God may be perfect, throughly furnished unto all good works" (vv. 16, 17).

First Things First

Labour not for the meat which perisheth, but for that meat which endureth unto everlasting life, which the Son of man shall give unto you: for him hath God the Father sealed.

John 6:27

Now hunger and thirst, not for "the meat which perisheth, but for that which endureth unto everlasting life." Trample underfoot the world, and the things of the world; all these riches, honors, pleasures. What is the world to you? Let the dead bury their dead; but follow after the image of God. And beware of quenching that blessed thirst, if it is already excited in your soul, by what is vulgarly called religion; a poor, dull farce, a religion of form, of outside show, which leaves the heart still cleaving to the dust, as earthly and sensual as ever. Let nothing satisfy you but the power of godliness, but a religion that is spirit and life; the dwelling in God and God in you; the being an inhabitant of eternity; the entering in by the blood of sprinkling "within the veil," and "sitting in heavenly places with Christ Jesus!"

Now, seeing you can do all things through Christ strengthening you, be merciful as your Father in heaven is merciful! Love your neighbor as yourself! Love friends and enemies as your own soul! And let your love be longsuffering and patient to all men. Let it be kind, soft, benign; inspiring you with the most amiable sweetness, and the most fervent and tender affection. Let it rejoice in the truth, wheresoever it is found; the truth that is after godliness. Enjoy whatsoever brings glory to God, and promotes peace and goodwill among men. In love, cover all things—of the dead and the absent speaking nothing but good; believe all things which may any way tend to clear your neighbor's character; hope all things, in his favor; and endure all things triumphing over all opposition: for true love never faileth, in time or in eternity.

Now be pure in heart; purified through faith from every unholy affection; "cleansing thyself from all filthiness of flesh and spirit, and perfecting holiness in the fear of God." Being, through the power of his grace, purified from pride, by deep poverty of spirit; from anger, from every unkind or turbulent passion, by meekness and mercifulness; from every desire but to please and enjoy God, by hunger and thirst after righteousness; now love the Lord your God with all your heart, and with all your strength!

16. Obedient Faith

Mirror Image

> [*Jesus said:*] *And whosoever liveth and believeth in me shall never die. Believest thou this?*
> ### John 11:26

Do you now believe? Then the love of God is now shed abroad in your heart. We love him, because he first loved us. And, because you love God, you love your brother also. And, being filled with "love, joy, peace," you are also filled with "longsuffering, gentleness, goodness, faith, meekness, temperance," and all the other fruits of the same Spirit; in a word, with whatever dispositions are holy, are heavenly, or divine. For while you behold with open, uncovered face, (the veil being now taken away,) "the glory of the Lord," his glorious love, and the glorious image wherein you were created, you are "changed into the same image, from glory to glory, by the Spirit of the Lord."

Faith for Children of Light

> *While ye have light, believe in the light, that ye may be the children of light. These things spake Jesus. . . . Jesus cried and said, He that believeth on me, believeth not on me, but on him that sent me. I am come a light into the world, that whosoever believeth on me should not abide in darkness.*
> ### John 12:36, 44, 46

The best guide of the blind, the surest light of them that are in darkness, the most perfect instructer of the foolish, is faith. But it must be such a faith as is "mighty through God, to the pulling down of strongholds," to the overturning of all the prejudices of corrupt reason, all the false maxims revered among men, all evil customs and habits, all that "wisdom of the world which is foolishness with God"; as "casteth down imaginations [reasonings], and every high thing that exalteth itself against the knowledge of God, and bringeth into captivity every thought to the obedience of Christ."

"All things are possible to him that [thus] believeth." "The eyes of his understanding being enlightened," he sees what is his calling; even to glorify God, who hath bought him with so high a price, in his body and in his spirit, which now are God's by redemption, as well as by creation. He feels what is "the exceeding greatness of his power," who, as he raised up Christ from the dead, so is able to quicken us, dead in sin, "by his Spirit which dwelleth in us." "This is the victory which overcometh the world, even our faith"; that faith, which is not only an unshaken assent to all that God has revealed in Scripture—and in particular to those important truths, "Jesus Christ came into the world to save sinners"; "He bare our sins in his own body on the tree"; "He is the propitiation for our sins, and not for ours only, but also for the sins of the whole world"—but likewise the revelation of Christ in our hearts; a divine evidence or conviction of his love, his free, unmerited love to me, a sinner; a sure confidence in his pardoning mercy, wrought in us by the Holy Ghost; a confidence, whereby every true believer is enabled to bear witness, "I know that my Redeemer liveth," that I have an "Advocate with the Father," and that "Jesus Christ the righteous" is my Lord, and "the propitiation for my sins,"—I know he hath "loved me, and given himself for me"—he hath reconciled me, even me, to God; and I "have redemption through his blood, even the forgiveness of sins."

Such a faith as this cannot fail to show evidently the power of Him that inspires it, by delivering his children from the yoke of sin, and "purging their consciences from dead works"; by strengthening them so that they are no longer constrained to obey sin in the desires thereof; but instead of "yielding their members unto it, as instruments of unrighteousness" they now "yield themselves" entirely "unto God, as those that are alive from the dead."

130

Love One Another

A new commandment I give unto you, That ye love one another; as I have loved you, that ye also love one another. By this shall all men know that ye are my disciples, if ye have love one to another.

John 13:34, 35

There is a peculiar love which we owe to those who love God. So says David: "All my delight is upon the saints that are in the earth, and upon such as excel in virtue." And so says a greater than he: "A new commandment I give unto you, That ye love one another; as I have loved you, that ye also love one another. By this shall all men know that ye are my disciples, if ye have love one to another" (John 13:34, 35). This is that love on which the apostle John so frequently and strongly insists: "This," says he, "is the message that ye heard from the beginning, that we should love one another" (1 John 3:11). "Hereby perceive we the love of God, because he laid down his life for us: and we ought [if love should call us thereto] to lay down our lives for the brethren" (v. 16). And again: "Beloved, let us love one another: for love is of God. . . . He that loveth not knoweth not God; for God is love" (1 John 4:7, 8). "Not that we loved God, but that he loved us, and sent his Son to be the propitiation for our sins. Beloved, if God so loved us, we ought also to love one another" (vv. 10, 11).

All men approve of this. But do all men practice it? Daily experience shows the contrary. Where are even the Christians who "love one another, as he hath given us commandment"? How many hindrances lie in the way! The two grand, general hindrances are, first, that they cannot all think alike; and, in consequence of this, secondly, they cannot all walk alike; but in several smaller points their practice must differ, in proportion to the difference of their sentiments.

But although a difference in opinions or modes of worship may prevent an entire external union; yet need it prevent our union in affection? Though we cannot think alike, may we not love alike? May we not be of one heart, though we are not of one opinion? Without all doubt we may. Herein all the children of God may unite, notwithstanding these smaller differences. These remaining

131

as they are, they may forward one another in love and in good works.

The Meaning of Obedience

He that hath my commandments, and keepeth them, he it is that loveth me: and he that loveth me shall be loved of my Father, and I will love him, and will manifest myself to him.
John 14:21

A Christian can be described in those words: "He that feareth God, and keepeth his commandments." Even one who has gone thus far in religion, who obeys God out of fear, is not in anywise to be despised, seeing "the fear of the Lord is the beginning of wisdom." Nevertheless, he should be exhorted not to stop there; not to rest till he attains the adoption of sons; till he obeys his master out of love, which is the privilege of all the children of God.

Exhort him to press on, by all possible means, till he passes "from faith to faith;" from the faith of a *servant* to the faith of a *son;* from the spirit of bondage unto fear, to the spirit of childlike love. He will then have "Christ revealed in his heart," enabling him to testify, "The life that I now live in the flesh, I live by faith in the Son of God, who loved *me,* and gave himself for *me*"—the proper voice of a child of God. He will then be "born of God"; inwardly changed by the mighty power of God, from "an earthly, sensual, devilish" mind, to the "mind which was in Christ Jesus." He will experience what St. Paul means by those remarkable words to the Galatians, "Ye are the sons of God by faith; and because ye are sons, God hath sent forth the Spirit of his Son into your hearts, crying, Abba, Father." "He that believeth," as a son (as St. John observes), "hath the witness in himself." "The Spirit itself witnesses with his spirit, that he is a child of God." "The love of God is shed abroad in his heart by the Holy Ghost which is given unto him."

We Are His Friends

Ye are my friends, if ye do whatsoever I command you.
John 15:14

132

In all his providences relating to themselves, to their souls or bodies, the pure in heart do more particularly see God. They see his hand ever over them for good; giving them all things in weight and measure, numbering the hairs of their head, making a hedge round about them, and all that they have, and disposing all the circumstances of their life, according to the depth both of his wisdom and mercy.

But in a more especial manner they see God in his ordinances. Whether they appear in the great congregation, to "pay him the honor due unto his name," "and worship him in the beauty of holiness"; or "enter into their closets," and there pour out their souls before their "Father which is in secret"; whether they search the oracles of God, or hear the ambassadors of Christ proclaiming glad tidings of salvation; or by eating of that bread, and drinking of that cup, "show forth his death till he come" in the clouds of heaven—in all these his appointed ways, they find such a near approach as cannot be expressed. They see him, as it were, face to face, and "talk with him, as a man talketh with his friend"— a fit preparation for those mansions above, wherein they shall see him as he is.

Filled and Led by the Spirit

And when they had prayed, the place was shaken where they were assembled together; and they were all filled with the Holy Ghost, and they spake the word of God with boldness.

Acts 4:31

Do some of you ask, What does it mean to be "filled by the Spirit"? "But dost thou acknowledge the inward principle?" I do, my friends: And I would to God every one of you acknowledged it as much. I say, all religion is either empty show, or perfection by inspiration; in other words, the obedient love of God, by the supernatural knowledge of God. Yea, all that which "is not of faith is sin"—all which does not spring from this loving knowledge of God, which knowledge cannot begin or subsist one moment without immediate inspiration; not only all public worship, and all private prayer, but every thought in common life, and word, and work. What think you of this? Do you not stagger? Dare you carry the inward principle so far? Do you acknowledge it? Do you experience this principle in yourself? What says your heart? Does God dwell therein? And does it now echo to the voice of God? Have you the continual inspiration of his Spirit, filling your heart with his love, as with a well of water, springing up into everlasting life?

Are you acquainted with the "leading of his Spirit," not by notion only but by living experience? I fear very many of you talk of this, who do not so much as know what it means. How does the Spirit of God lead his children to this or that particular action? Do you imagine it is by blind impulse only? By moving you to do it, you know not why? Not so. He leads us by our eye, at least, as much as by the hand; and by light as well as by heat. He shows us the way wherein we should go, as well as incites us to walk therein. For example: Here is a man ready to perish with hunger. How am I "led by the Spirit" to relieve him? First, by his convincing me it is the will of God I should; and second, by his filling my heart with love toward him. Both this light and this heat are the gift of God; are wrought in me by the same Spirit, who leads me, by this conviction as well as love, to go and feed that man. This is the plain, rational account of the ordinary leading of the Spirit.

Living Witnesses

And we are his witnesses of these things; and so is also the Holy Ghost, whom God hath given to them that obey him.

Acts 5:32

You may all be living witnesses of these things; of remission of sins, and the gift of the Holy Ghost. "If thou canst believe, all things are possible to him that believeth." "Who among you is there, that feareth the Lord, and yet walketh in darkness, and hath no light?" I ask you, in the name of Jesus, do you believe that his arm is not shortened at all? That he is still mighty to save? That he is the same yesterday, today, and forever? That he has power on earth to forgive sins? "Son, be of good cheer; thy sins are forgiven." God, for Christ's sake, has forgiven you.

Receive this, "not as the word of man; but as it is, indeed, the word of God" and you are justified freely through faith. You shall be sanctified also through faith which is in Jesus, and it shall be set to your seal, that "God hath given unto us eternal life, and this life is in his Son."

Men and brethren, let me freely speak unto you; and suffer this word of exhortation, even from one the least esteemed in the church. . . . "This is eternal life, to know the only true God, and Jesus Christ whom he hath sent." This experimental knowledge, and this alone, is true Christianity. He is a Christian who has received the Spirit of Christ. He is not a Christian who has not received him. Neither is it possible to have received him, and not know it. "For, at that day," (when he comes, says our Lord,) "ye shall know that I am in my Father, and you in me, and I in you." "[This is that] Spirit of Truth; whom the world cannot receive, because it seeth him not, neither knoweth him: but ye know him; for he dwelleth with you, and shall be in you" (John 14:17).

17. From Love to Justification

Unmerited Love

And they said, Believe on the Lord Jesus Christ, and thou shalt be saved, and thy house.
Acts 16:31

What does the covenant of forgiveness say of unmerited love, of pardoning mercy? "Believe in the Lord Jesus Christ, and thou shalt be saved." In the day you believe, you shall surely live. You shall be restored to the favor of God; and in his pleasure is life. You shall be saved from the curse, and from the wrath of God. You shall be quickened, from the death of sin, into the life of righteousness. And if you endure to the end, believing in Jesus, you shall never taste the second death; but, having suffered with your Lord, shall also live, and reign with him forever and ever.

Now "this word is nigh thee." This condition of life is plain, easy, always at hand. "It is in thy mouth, and in thy heart," through the operation of the Spirit of God. The moment "thou believest in thine heart" in him whom God "hath raised from the dead," and "confessest with thy mouth the Lord Jesus," as your Lord and your God, you shall be saved from condemnation, from the guilt and punishment of your former sins, and shall have power to serve God in true holiness all the remaining days of your life.

The Properties of Love

[Paul said:] I am verily a man which am a Jew, born in Tarsus, a city in Cilicia, yet brought up in this city at the feet of Gamaliel, and taught according to the perfect manner of the law of the fathers, and was zealous toward God, as ye all are this day.
Acts 22:3

The properties of love are the properties of zeal also. Now, one of the chief properties of love is humility: "Love is not puffed up." Accordingly, this is a property of true zeal: Humility is inseparable from it. As is the degree of zeal, such is the degree of humility: They must rise and fall together. The same love which fills a man with zeal for God, makes him little, and poor, and vile in his own eyes.

Another of the properties of love is meekness; consequently, it is one of the properties of zeal. It teaches us to be meek, as well as lowly; to be equally superior to anger or pride. Like as the wax melts at the fire, so before this sacred flame all turbulent passions melt away, and leave the soul unruffled and serene.

Yet another property of love, and consequently of zeal, is unwearied patience: For "love endureth all things." It arms the soul with entire resignation to all the disposals of Divine Providence, and teaches us to say, in every occurrence, "It is the Lord; let him do what seemeth him good." It enables us, in whatever station, therewith to be content; to repine at nothing, to murmur at nothing, "but in everything to give thanks." This is the way in which the Christian is to walk.

Glory in Another World

> *But this I confess unto thee, that after the way which they call heresy, so worship I the God of my fathers, believing all things which are written in the law and in the prophets: And have hope toward God, which they themselves also allow, that there shall be a resurrection of the dead, both of the just and unjust.*
> **Acts 24:14, 15**

When we are washed from the guilt of our sins, and cleansed from all filthiness of flesh and spirit, by faith in the Lord Jesus Christ, then we shall long to be dissolved, and to be with our exalted Savior; we shall be always ready to take wing for the other world, where we shall at last have a body suited to our spiritual appetites.

From hence we may see how to account for the different degrees of glory in the heavenly world. For although all the children of God shall have glorious bodies, yet the glory of them all shall not be equal. "As one star differeth from another star in glory, so also is the resurrection of the dead." They shall all shine as stars; but those who, by a constant diligence in well-doing, have attained to a higher measure of purity than others, shall shine more brightly than others. They shall appear as more glorious stars. It is certain that the most heavenly bodies will be given to the most heavenly souls; so that this is no little encouragement to us to make the greatest progress we possibly can in the knowledge and love of God, since the more we are weaned from the things of the earth now, the more glorious will our bodies be at the resurrection.

The Christian's Conscience

And herein do I exercise myself, to have always a conscience void of offence toward God, and toward men.

Acts 24:16

This is properly the account of a good conscience; which may be in other terms expressed thus: A divine consciousness of walking in all things according to the written Word of God. It seems, indeed, that there can be no conscience which has not a regard to God. If you say, "Yes, there certainly may be a consciousness of having done right or wrong, without any reference to him"; I answer, This I cannot grant: I doubt whether the very words, right and wrong, according to the Christian system, do not imply, in the very idea of them, agreement and disagreement to the will and Word of God. If so, there is no such thing as conscience in a Christian, if we leave God out of the question.

In order to the very existence of a good conscience, as well as to the continuance of it, the continued influence of the Spirit of God is absolutely needful. Accordingly, the apostle John declares to the believers of all ages, "Ye have an unction from the Holy One, and ye know all things." All things that are needful to your having a "conscience void of offense toward God and toward man." So he adds, "Ye have no need that anyone should teach you," otherwise "than as that anointing teacheth you." That anointing clearly teaches us those three things—first, the true meaning of God's Word; second, our own tempers and lives; bringing all our thoughts, words, and actions, to remembrance; and, third, the agreement of all with the commandments of God.

Two Loves

Then Agrippa said unto Paul, Almost thou persuadest me to be a Christian.

Acts 26:28

If it be inquired, what is implied in the being altogether a Christian? I answer,

(1) First, the love of God. For thus saith his Word, "Thou shalt love the Lord thy God, with all thy heart, and with all thy soul, and with all thy mind, and with all thy strength." Such a love of God is this, as engrosses the whole heart, as takes up all the affections, as fills the entire capacity of the soul, and employs the utmost extent of all its faculties. He that thus loves the Lord his God, his spirit, continually "rejoiceth in God his Saviour." His delight is in the Lord, his Lord and his All, to whom "in everything he giveth thanks." "All his desire is unto God, and to the remembrance of his name." His heart is ever crying out, "Whom have I in heaven but thee, and there is none upon earth that I desire beside thee." Indeed, what can he desire beside God? Not the world, or the things of the world. For he is "crucified to the world, and the world crucified to him." . . .

(2) The second thing implied in the being altogether a Christian, is the love of our neighbor. For thus said our Lord, in the following words, "Thou shalt love thy neighbor as thyself." If any man ask, Who is my neighbor? we reply, every man in the world; every child of his, who is the Father of the spirits of all flesh. Nor may we in any wise except our enemies, or the enemies of God and their own souls. But every Christian loves these also as himself, yea, "as Christ loved us." He who would more fully understand what manner of love this is, may consider St. Paul's description of it. It is "longsuffering and kind." It "envieth not." It is not rash or hasty in judging. It "is not puffed up," but makes him that loves, the least, the servant of all. Love "doth not behave itself unseemly," but becomes "all things to all men." She "seeketh not her own," but only the good of others, that they may be

139

saved. "Love is not provoked." It casts out wrath, which he who has, is not "made perfect in love." "It thinketh no evil. It rejoiceth not in iniquity, but rejoiceth in the truth. It covereth all things, believeth all things, hopeth all things, endureth all things." "Every one," says the beloved disciple, "that believeth, is born of God." "To as many as received him, gave he power to become the sons of God, even to them that believe in his name." And "this is the victory that overcometh the world, even our faith."

Faith and Law

Do we then make void the law through faith? God forbid: yea, we establish the law.
Romans 3:31

The most important way we establish the law is by establishing it in our own hearts and lives. Indeed without this, what would all the rest avail? We might establish it by our doctrine; we might preach it in its whole extent; might explain and enforce every part of it; we might open it in its most spiritual meaning, and declare the mysteries of the kingdom; we might preach Christ in all his offices, and faith in Christ as opening all the treasures of his love; and yet all this time, if the law we preached were not established in our hearts, we should be of no more account before God, than "sounding brass, or tinkling cymbals": all our preaching would be so far from profiting ourselves, that it would only increase our damnation.

This is, therefore, the main point to be considered, how may we establish the law in our own hearts, so that it may have its full influence on our lives? And this can only be done by faith.

Faith alone it is which effectually answers this end, as we learn from daily experience. For so long as we walk by faith, not by sight, we go swiftly on in the way of holiness. While we steadily look, not at the things which are seen, but at those which are not seen, we are more and more crucified to the world, and the world crucified to us. Let but the eye of the soul be constantly fixed, not on the things which are temporal, but on those which are eternal, and our affections are more and more loosened from earth, and fixed on things above. So that faith, in general, is the

140

most direct and effectual means of promoting all righteousness and true holiness; of establishing the holy and spiritual law, in the hearts of them that believe.

Justification

For what saith the scripture? Abraham believed God, and it was counted unto him for righteousness.
Romans 4:3

Justification is being cleared from accusation, particularly that of Satan, easily provable from any clear text of Holy Writ. In the whole scriptural account of this matter, as above laid down, neither that accuser, nor his accusation, appears to be at all taken in. It cannot indeed be denied, that he is the "accuser" of men, emphatically so called. But it does in no wise appear, that the great apostle has any reference to this, more or less, in all that he has written touching justification, either to the Romans or the Galatians.

It is also far easier to take for granted, than to prove from any clear Scripture testimony, that justification is our clearance from the accusation brought against us by the law: at least, if this forced, unnatural way of speaking mean either more or less than this, that whereas we have transgressed the law of God, and thereby deserved the damnation of hell, God does not inflict on those who are justified the punishment which they had deserved.

Least of all does justification imply that God is deceived in those whom he justifies; that he thinks them to be what in fact they are not; that he accounts them to be otherwise than they are. It does by no means imply that God judges concerning us contrary to the real nature of things; that he esteems us better than we really are, or believes us righteous when we are unrighteous. Surely not. The judgment of the all-wise God is always according to truth. Neither can it ever consist with his unerring wisdom to think that I am innocent, to judge that I am righteous or holy, because another is so. He can no more in this manner confound me with Christ, than with David or Abraham. Let any man to whom God has given understanding weigh this without prejudice; and he cannot but perceive that such a notion of justification is neither reconcilable to reason nor Scripture.

The plain scriptural notion of justification is pardon, the forgiveness of sins. It is that act of God the Father, whereby, for the sake of the propitiation made by the blood of his Son, he "showeth forth his righteousness [or mercy] by the remission of the sins that are past."

18. The Fruit of a Living Faith

Justified by Faith

Therefore being justified by faith, we have peace with God through our Lord Jesus Christ.
Romans 5:1

Faith, therefore, is the necessary condition of justification; yea, and the *only necessary* condition thereof. . . . The very moment God giveth faith (for *it is the gift of God*) to the "ungodly," . . . that "faith is counted to him for righteousness." He hath no righteousness at all, antecedent to this, not so much as negative righteousness, or innocence. But "faith is imputed to him for righteousness," the very moment that he believeth. Not that God (as was observed before) thinketh him to be what he is not. But as "he made Christ to be sin for us," he counteth us righteous, from the time we believe in him. That is, he doth not punish us for our sins; yea, treats us as though we were guiltless and righteous.

Surely the difficulty of assenting to this proposition, that "faith is the *only condition* of justification," must arise from not understanding it. We mean thereby this much, that it is the only thing without which none is justified, the only thing that is immediately, indispensably, absolutely requisite in order to pardon. As, on the one hand, though a man should have everything else without faith, yet he cannot be justified; so, on the other, though he be supposed to want everything else, yet if he hath faith, he cannot but be justified. For suppose a sinner of any kind or degree, in a full sense of his total ungodliness, of his utter inability to think, speak, or do good, and his absolute meetness for hellfire; suppose, I say, this sinner, helpless and hopeless, casts himself wholly on the mercy of God in Christ (which indeed he cannot do but by the grace of God), who can doubt but he is forgiven in that moment? Who will affirm that any more is *indispensably required* before that sinner can be justified?

Now, if there ever was one such instance from the beginning of the world (and have there not been, and are there not, ten thousand times ten thousand?), it plainly follows that faith is, in the above sense, the sole condition of justification.

Of Joy and Faith

By whom also we have access by faith into this grace wherein we stand, and rejoice in hope of the glory of God. And not only so, but we glory in tribulations also: knowing that tribulation worketh patience.
Romans 5:2, 3

The joy of the Christian does not arise from any dullness or callousness of conscience. A kind of joy, it is true, may arise from this, in those whose "foolish hearts are darkened"; whose heart is callous, unfeeling, dull of sense, and, consequently, without spiritual understanding. Because of their senseless, unfeeling hearts, they may rejoice even in committing sin; and this they may probably call *liberty!*—which is indeed mere drunkenness of soul . . . such as he could not have conceived before. He never had such a tenderness of conscience as he has had since the love of God has reigned in his heart. And this also is his glory and joy, that God has heard his daily prayer:

> Oh that my tender soul might fly
>   The first abhorr'd approach of ill;
> Quick, as the apple of an eye,
>   The slightest touch of sin to feel.

Christian joy is joy in obedience; joy in loving God and keeping his commandments, and yet not in keeping them as if we were thereby to fulfill the terms of the covenant of works; as if by any works or righteousness of ours, we were to procure pardon and acceptance with God. Not so: we are already pardoned and accepted, through the mercy of God in Christ Jesus. . . . We rejoice in knowing that, "being justified through his grace," we have "not received that grace of God in vain"; that God having freely (not for the sake of our willing or running, but through the blood of the Lamb) reconciled us to himself, we run, in the strength which he has given us, the way of his commandments. He has "girded us with strength unto the war," and we gladly "fight the good fight of faith." We rejoice, through him who lives in our hearts by faith, to "lay hold of eternal life." This is our rejoicing, that as our "Father worketh hitherto," so (not by our own might or wisdom, but through the power of his Spirit, freely given in Christ Jesus) we also work the works of God. And may he work in us whatsoever is well pleasing in his sight! To whom be the praise forever and ever!

Faith . . . and Love

> *And hope does not disappoint us, because God's love has been poured into our hearts through the Holy Spirit which has been given to us.*
> **Romans 5:5 (RSV)**

> *So faith, hope, love abide, these three; but the greatest of these is love.*
> **1 Corinthians 13:13 (RSV)**

Now is not this love "the fulfilling of the law"? The sum of all Christian righteousness?—of all inward righteousness, for it necessarily implies "bowels of mercy, humbleness of mind" (seeing "love is not puffed up"), "gentleness, meekness, longsuffering" (for love "is not provoked," but "believeth, hopeth, endureth all things"); and of all outward righteousness, for "love worketh no evil to his neighbor," either by word or deed. It cannot willingly either hurt or grieve anyone. And it is zealous of good works. Every lover of mankind, as he has opportunity, "doeth good unto all men," being (without partiality, and without hypocrisy) "full of mercy, and good fruits."

But true religion, or a heart right toward God and man, implies happiness, as well as holiness. For it is not only righteousness, but also "peace and joy in the Holy Ghost." What peace? *The peace of God,* which God only can give, and the world cannot take away; the peace which passeth all understanding," all (barely) rational conception; being a supernatural sensation, a divine taste of "the powers of the world to come"; such as the natural man knows not, however wise in the things of this world, nor, indeed, can he know it, in his present state, "because it is spiritually discerned." It is a peace that banishes all doubt, all painful uncertainty; the Spirit of God bearing witness with the spirit of a Christian, that he is *a child of God.* And it banishes fear, all such fear as has torment; the fear of the wrath of God; the fear of hell; the fear of the devil; and, in particular, the fear of death: he who has the peace of God, desiring, if it were the will of God, "to depart, and to be with Christ."

Peace—Fruit of a Living Faith

And not only so, but we also joy in God through our Lord Jesus Christ, by whom we have now received the atonement.

Romans 5:11

Another fruit of living faith is peace. For, "being justified by faith," having all our sins blotted out, "we have peace with God, through our Lord Jesus Christ" (Rom. 5:1). This indeed our Lord himself, the night before his death, solemnly bequeathed to all his followers: "Peace," said he, "I leave with you"; (you who "believe in God," and "believe also in me") "my peace I give unto you: not as the world giveth, give I unto you. Let not your heart be troubled, neither let it be afraid" (John 14:27). And again, "These things have I spoken unto you, that in me ye might have peace" (John 16:33). This is that "peace of God which passeth all understanding," that serenity of soul which it has not entered into the heart of a natural man to conceive, and which it is not possible for even the spiritual man to utter. And it is a peace which all the powers of earth and hell are unable to take from him. Waves and storms beat upon it, but they shake it not; for it is founded upon a rock. It keeps the hearts and minds of the children of God, at all times and in all places. Whether they are in ease or in pain, in sickness or health, in abundance or want, they are happy in God. In every state they have learned to be content, yea, to give thanks unto God through Christ Jesus; being well assured that "whatsoever is, is best," because it is his will concerning them: so that in all the vicissitudes of life their "heart standeth fast, believing in the Lord."

146

Death by Sin

As by one man sin entered into the world, and death
by sin; and so death passed upon all men.
Romans 5:12a

Thus "by one man sin entered into the world, and death by sin. And so death passed upon all men," as being contained in him who was the common father and representative of us all. Thus, "through the offense of one," all are dead, dead to God, dead in sin, dwelling in a corruptible, mortal body, shortly to be dissolved, and under the sentence of death eternal. For as, "by one man's disobedience," all "were made sinners"; so, by that offense of one, "judgment came upon all men to condemnation" (Rom. 5:19).

In this state we were, even all mankind, when "God so loved the world, that he gave his only begotten Son, to the end we might not perish, but have everlasting life." In the fulness of time he was made man, another common head of mankind, a second general parent and representative of the whole human race. And as such it was that "he bore our griefs," "the Lord laying upon him the iniquities of us all." Then was he "wounded for our transgressions, and bruised for our iniquities." . . .

In consideration of this, that the Son of God has "tasted death for every man," God has now "reconciled the world to himself, not imputing to them their former trespasses." And thus, "as, by the offense of one, judgment came upon all men to condemnation, even so by the righteousness of one, the free gift came upon all men unto justification." So that for the sake of his well beloved Son of what he has done and suffered for us, God now vouchsafes, on only one condition (which himself also enables us to perform), both to remit the punishment due to our sins, to reinstate us in his favor, and to restore our dead souls to spiritual life, as the earnest of life eternal.

Love in the Light of Sin

And so death spread to all men because all men sinned.
. . . Death reigned from Adam to Moses, even over
those whose sins were not like the transgression of
Adam.
Romans 5:12b, 14a (RSV)

Was it not to remedy this very thing that "the Word was made flesh," that "as in Adam all died," so in Christ all might "be made alive"? Unless, then, many had been made sinners by the disobedience of one, by the obedience of one many would not have been made righteous (v. 19). So there would have been no room for that amazing display of the Son of God's love to mankind: there would have been no occasion for his being "obedient unto death, even the death of the cross." It could not then have been said, to the astonishment of all the hosts of heaven, "God so loved the world," yea, the ungodly world, which had no thought or desire of returning to him, "that he gave his Son" out of his bosom, his only begotten Son, "to the end that whosoever believeth on him should not perish, but have everlasting life." Neither could we then have said, "God was in Christ reconciling the world to himself"; or, that he "made him to be sin," that is, a *sin offering*, "for us, who knew no sin, that we might be made the righteousness of God through him." There would have been no such occasion for such "an Advocate with the Father," as "Jesus Christ the righteous"; neither for his appearing "at the right hand of God, to make intercession for us."

What is the necessary consequence of this? It is this: There could then have been no such thing as faith in God thus loving the world, giving his only Son for us men, and for our salvation. There could have been no such thing as faith in the Son of God, as "loving us and giving himself for us." There could have been no faith in the Spirit of God, as renewing the image of God in our hearts, as raising us from the death of sin into the life of righteousness. Indeed, the whole privilege of justification by faith could have had no existence; there could have been no redemption in the blood of Christ; neither could Christ have been "made of God unto us," either "wisdom, righteousness, sanctification," or "redemption."

The Gift of Grace

But not as the offence, so also is the free gift. For if through the offence of one many be dead, much more the grace of God, and the gift of grace, which is by one man, Jesus Christ, hath abounded unto many.
Romans 5:15

148

It is then we shall be enabled fully to comprehend, not only the advantages which accrue at the present time to the sons of men by the fall of their first parent, but the infinitely greater advantages which they may reap from it in eternity. To form some conception of this, we may remember the observation of the apostle: As "one star differeth from another star in glory, so also is the resurrection of the dead." The most glorious stars will undoubtedly be those who are the most holy, who bear most of that image of God wherein they were created; the next in glory to these will be those who have been most abundant in good works; and next to them, those who have suffered most according to the will of God. But what advantages, in every one of these respects, will the children of God receive in heaven, by God's permitting the introduction of pain upon earth in consequence of sin! By occasion of this they attained many holy tempers, which otherwise could have had no being—resignation to God; confidence in him in times of trouble and danger; patience, meekness, gentleness, longsuffering, and the whole train of passive virtues. And on account of this superior holiness, they will then enjoy superior happiness.

19. Of Law and Grace

Grace—Gift of God

> *But the free gift is not like the trespass. For if many died through one man's trespass, much more have the grace of God and the free gift in the grace of that one man Jesus Christ abounded for many.*
>
> **Romans 5:15 (RSV)**

May not your own experience teach you this? Can you give yourself this faith? Is it now in your power to see, or hear, or taste, or feel God? Have you already, or can you raise in yourself, any perception of God, or of an invisible world? I suppose you do not deny that there is an invisible world; you will not charge it in poor old Hesiod to Christian prejudice of education when he says, in those well-known words,

> Millions of spiritual creatures walk the earth
> Unseen, whether we wake, or if we sleep.

Now, is there any power in your soul whereby you discern either these, or him that created them? Or, can all your wisdom and strength open an avenue between yourself and the world of spirits? Is it in your power to burst the veil that is on your heart, and let in the light of eternity? You know it is not. You not only do not, but cannot, by your own strength, thus believe. The more you labor so to do, the more you will be convinced "it is the gift of God."

Abundance of Grace

> *If, because of one man's trespass, death reigned through that one man, much more will those who receive the abundance of grace and the free gift of*

righteousness reign in life through the one man Jesus
Christ. Then as one man's trespass led to
condemnation for all men, so one man's act of
righteousness leads to acquittal and life for all men.
Romans 5:17, 18 (RSV)

By faith in this fact we are saved from all uneasiness of mind, from the anguish of a wounded spirit, from discontent, from fear and sorrow of heart, and from that inexpressible listlessness and weariness, both of the world and of ourselves, which we had so helplessly labored under for many years; especially when we were out of the hurry of the world, and sunk into calm reflection. In this we find that love of God, and of all mankind, which we had elsewhere sought in vain. This we know and feel, and therefore cannot but declare, saves every one that partakes of it, both from sin and misery, from every unhappy and every unholy temper.

> Soft peace she brings, wherever she arrives;
> She builds our quiet, as she forms our lives;
> Lays the rough paths of peevish nature even,
> And opens in each breast a little heaven.

If you ask, "Why then have not all men this faith? All, at least, who conceive it to be so happy a thing? Why do they not believe immediately?"

We answer, (on the Scripture hypothesis,) "It is the gift of God." No man is able to work it in himself. It is a work of omnipotence. It requires no less power thus to quicken a dead soul, than to raise a body that lies in the grave. It is a new creation; and none can create a soul anew, but he who at first created the heavens and the earth.

Abundant Forgiveness

For the wages of sin is death; but the gift of God is
eternal life through Jesus Christ our Lord.
Romans 6:23

There is one advantage more that we reap from Adam's fall, which is not unworthy of our attention. Unless in Adam all had died,

151

being in the loins of their first parent, every descendant of Adam, every child of man, must have personally answered for himself to God. It seems to be a necessary consequence of this, that if he had once fallen, once violated any command of God, there would have been no possibility of his rising again; there was no help, but he must have perished without remedy. For that covenant knew not to show mercy: The word was, "The soul that sinneth, it shall die." Now who would not rather be on the footing he is now—under a covenant of mercy? Who would wish to hazard a whole eternity upon one stake? Is it not infinitely more desirable to be in a state wherein, though encompassed with infirmities, yet we do not run such a desperate risk, but if we fall, we may rise again?—wherein we may say,

> My trespass is grown up to heaven;
> But far above the skies,
> In Christ abundantly forgiven
> I see thy mercies rise!

The Fruit of the Spirit

Wherefore, my brethren, ye also are become dead to the law by the body of Christ; that ye should be married to another, even to him who is raised from the dead, that we should bring forth fruit unto God.
Romans 7:4

Two inferences may be drawn from the whole. The first: Let none ever presume to rest in any supposed testimony of the Spirit, which is separate from the fruit of it. If the Spirit of God does really testify that we are children of God, the immediate consequence will be the fruit of the Spirit, even "love, joy, peace, longsuffering, gentleness, goodness, fidelity, meekness, temperance." And however this fruit may be clouded for a while, during the time of strong temptation, so that it does not appear to the tempted person, while Satan is sifting him as wheat; yet the substantial part of it remains, even under the thickest cloud. It is true, joy in the Holy Ghost may be withdrawn during the hour of trial; yea, the soul may be "exceeding sorrowful," while "the hour and power of darkness" continue; but even this is generally restored with increase, till we rejoice "with joy unspeakable and full of glory."

The second inference is: Let none rest in any supposed fruit of the Spirit without the witness. There may be foretastes of joy, of peace, of love, and those not delusive, but really from God, long before we have the witness in ourselves; before the Spirit of God witnesses with our spirits that we have "redemption in the blood of Jesus, even the forgiveness of sins." Yea, there may be a degree of longsuffering, of gentleness, of fidelity, meekness, temperance (not a shadow thereof, but a real degree, by the preventing grace of God), before we "are accepted in the Beloved," and consequently, before we have a testimony of our acceptance: but it is by no means advisable to rest here; it is at the peril of our souls if we do. If we are wise, we shall be continually crying to God, until his Spirit cry in our heart, *Abba, Father!* This is the privilege of all the children of God, and without this we can never be assured that we are his children.

Law and Grace

O wretched man that I am! who shall deliver me from the body of this death?
Romans 7:24

How lively a portrait is this of one *under the law!* One who feels the burden he cannot shake off; who longs for liberty, power, and love, but is in fear and bondage still; until the time that God answers the wretched man—crying out, "Who shall deliver me" from this bondage of sin, from this body of death? "The grace of God, through Jesus Christ thy Lord."

Then it is that this miserable bondage ends, and he is no more "under the law, but under grace." This state we are to consider; the state of one who has found *grace* or favor in the sight of God, even the Father; and who has the *grace* or power of the Holy Ghost, reigning in his heart: who has received, in the language of the apostle, the "Spirit of adoption, whereby" he now cries, "Abba, Father!"

No Condemnation

There is therefore now no condemnation to them which are in Christ Jesus, who walk not after the flesh, but after the Spirit.

Romans 8:1

We are saved from the guilt of all past sin: for, whereas all the world is guilty before God, insomuch, that should he "be extreme to mark what is done amiss, there is none that could abide it"; and whereas, "by the law is" only "the knowledge of sin," but no deliverance from it, so that, "by fulfilling the deeds of the law, no flesh can be justified in his sight"; now, "the righteousness of God, which is by faith of Jesus Christ, is manifested unto all that believe." Now, "they are justified freely by his grace, through the redemption that is in Jesus Christ." "Him God hath set forth to be a propitiation, through faith in his blood; to declare his righteousness for [or by] the remission of the sins that are past." Now has Christ taken away "the curse of the law, being made a curse for us." He has "blotted out the handwriting that was against us, taking it out of the way, nailing it to his cross." "There is, therefore, no condemnation now, to them which" believe in Christ Jesus.

And being saved from guilt, they are saved from fear. Not indeed from a filial fear of offending; but, from all servile fear; from that fear which hath torment; from fear of punishment; from fear of the wrath of God, whom they now no longer regard as a severe Master, but as an indulgent Father. "They have not received again the spirit of bondage, but the spirit of adoption, whereby they cry, Abba, Father; the Spirit itself also bearing witness with their spirits, that they are the children of God."

The Flesh . . . and the Spirit

For what the law could not do, in that it was weak through the flesh, God sending his own Son in the likeness of sinful flesh, and for sin, condemned sin in the flesh: That the righteousness of the law might be fulfilled in us, who walk not after the flesh, but after the Spirit.

Romans 8:3, 4

154

The sum of all is this: There are in every person, even after he is justified, two contrary principles, nature and grace, termed by St. Paul, the *flesh* and the *Spirit.* Hence, although even babes in Christ are *sanctified,* yet it is only in part. In a degree, according to the measure of their faith, they are spiritual; yet, in a degree they are carnal. Accordingly, believers are continually exhorted to watch against the flesh, as well as the world and the devil. And to this agrees the constant experience of the children of God. While they feel this witness in themselves, they feel a will not wholly resigned to the will of God. They know they are in him; and yet find a heart ready to depart from him, a proneness to evil in many instances, and a backwardness to that which is good. The contrary doctrine is wholly new; never heard of in the church of Christ, from the time of his coming into the world, till the time of Count Zinzendorf; and it is attended with the most fatal consequences. It cuts off all watching against our evil nature, against the Delilah which we are told is gone, though she is still lying in our bosom. It tears away the shield of weak believers, deprives them of their faith, and so leaves them exposed to all the assaults of the world, the flesh, and the devil.

20. A Vital Dimension of Faith

Holiness

The Spirit itself beareth witness with our spirit, that we are the children of God.

Romans 8:16

Now this is properly the testimony of our own spirit; even the testimony of our own conscience, that God has given us to be holy of heart, and holy in outward conversation. It is a consciousness of our having received, in and by the spirit of adoption, the tempers mentioned in the Word of God, as belonging to his adopted children; even a loving heart toward God, and toward all mankind; hanging with childlike confidence on God our Father, desiring nothing but him, casting all our care upon him, and embracing every child of man with earnest, tender affection; so as to be ready to lay down our life for our brother, as Christ laid down his life for us: a consciousness that we are inwardly conformed, by the Spirit of God, to the image of his Son, and that we walk before him in justice, mercy, and truth, doing the things which are pleasing in his sight.

But what is that testimony of God's Spirit, which is superadded to and associated with this? How does he "bear witness with our spirit that we are the children of God"? It is hard to find words in the language of men to explain "the deep things of God." Indeed, there are none that will adequately express what the children of God experience. But perhaps one might say (desiring any who are taught of God, to correct, to soften, or strengthen the expression), the testimony of the Spirit is an inward impression on the soul, whereby the Spirit of God directly witnesses to my spirit, that I am a child of God; that Jesus Christ has loved me, and given himself for me; and that all my sins are blotted out, and I, even I, am reconciled to God. He who now loves God, who delights and rejoices in him with a humble joy, holy delight, and an obedient love, is a child of God.

Called Creatures

For the earnest expectation of the creature waiteth for the manifestation of the sons of God. For the creature was made subject to vanity, not willingly, but by reason of him who hath subjected the same in hope, Because the creature itself also shall be delivered from the bondage of corruption into the glorious liberty of the children of God. For we know that the whole creation groaneth and travaileth in pain together until now.

Romans 8:19–22

But will "the creature," will even the brute creation, always remain in this deplorable condition? God forbid that we should affirm this; yea, or even entertain such a thought! While "the whole creation groaneth together" (whether men attend or not), their groans are not dispersed in idle air, but enter in to the ears of him who made them. While his creatures "travail together in pain," he knows all their pain, and is bringing them nearer and nearer to the birth which shall be accomplished in its season. He sees "the earnest expectation" wherewith the whole animated creation "waiteth for" that final "manifestation of the sons of God"; in which "they themselves also shall be delivered" (not by annihilation; annihilation is not deliverance) from the present "bondage of corruption, into" a measure of "the glorious liberty of the children of God."

Nothing can be more express: Away with vulgar prejudices, and let the plain Word of God take place. They "shall be delivered from the bondage of corruption, into glorious liberty"—even a measure, according as they are capable, of "the liberty of the children of God."

Liberty to Love

Because the creature itself also shall be delivered from the bondage of corruption into the glorious liberty of the children of God.

Romans 8:21

"Where the Spirit of the Lord is, there is liberty" (2 Cor. 3:7). Liberty, not only from guilt and fear, but from sin, from that

157

heaviest of all yokes, that basest of all bondage. His labor is not now in vain. The snare is broken, and he is delivered. He not only strives, but likewise prevails; he not only fights, but conquers also. "Henceforth we should not serve sin" (Rom. 6:6ff). "He is dead unto sin, and alive unto God"; "sin doth not now reign," even "in his mortal body," nor doth he "obey it in the desires thereof." He does not "yield his members as instruments of unrighteousness unto sin, but as instruments of righteousness unto God." For "being now made free from sin, he is become the servant of righteousness."

Thus, "having peace with God, through our Lord Jesus Christ," "rejoicing in hope of the glory of God," and having power over all sin, over every evil desire, and temper, and word, and work, he is a living witness of the "glorious liberty of the sons of God"; all of whom, being partakers of like precious faith, bear record with one voice, "We have received the spirit of adoption, whereby we cry, Abba, Father!"

It is this Spirit which continually "worketh in them, both to will and to do of his good pleasure." It is he who sheds the love of God abroad in their hearts, and the love of all mankind; thereby purifying their hearts from the love of the world, from the lust of the flesh, and lust of the eye, and the pride of life. It is by him they are delivered from anger and pride, from all vile and inordinate affections. In consequence they are delivered from evil words and works, from all unholiness of conversation; doing no evil to any child of man, and being zealous of all good works.

The Nature of Predestination

For whom he did foreknow, he also did predestinate to be conformed to the image of his Son, that he might be the firstborn among many brethren.
Romans 8:29

Indeed, if man were not free, he could not be accountable either for his thoughts, words, or actions. If he were not free, he would not be capable either of reward or punishment; he would be incapable either of virtue or vice, of being either morally good or bad. If he had no more freedom than the sun, the moon, or the stars, he would be no more accountable than they. On supposition that he had no more freedom than they, the stones of the earth would be as capable of reward, and as liable to punishment, as man: one would be as accountable as the other. Yea, and it would be as absurd to ascribe it to the stock of a tree.

But to proceed: "Whom he did foreknow, them he did predestinate to be conformed to the image of his Son." In other words, God decrees, from everlasting to everlasting, that all who believe in the Son of his love, shall be conformed to his image; shall be saved from all inward and outward sin, into all inward and outward holiness. Accordingly, it is a plain undeniable fact all who truly believe in the name of the Son of God do now "receive the end of their faith, the salvation of their souls"; and this by virtue of the unchangeable, irreversible, irresistible decree of God—"He that believeth shall be saved"; "he that believeth not, shall be damned."

Called . . . and Justified

Moreover whom he did predestinate, them he also called: and whom he called, them he also justified: and whom he justified, them he also glorified.
Romans 8:30

"Whom he did predestinate, them he also called." This is the next step (still remembering that we speak after the manner of men). To express it a little more largely: According to his fixed decree that believers shall be saved, those whom he foreknows as such, he calls both outwardly and inwardly—*outwardly* by the Word of his grace, and *inwardly* by his Spirit. This inward application of his Word to the heart, seems to be what some term "effectual calling." And it implies the calling them children of God; the accepting them "in the Beloved"; the justifying them "freely by his grace, through the redemption that is in Jesus Christ."

"Whom he called, them he also justified." This is the next step. It is generally allowed that the word "justified" here is taken in a peculiar sense; that it means he made them just or righteous. He executed his decree, "conforming them to the image of his Son"; or, as we usually speak, sanctified them.

It remains, "whom he justified, them he also glorified." This is the final step. Having made them "meet to be partakers of the inheritance of the saints in light," he gives them "the kingdom which was prepared for them before the world began." This is the order wherein, "according to the counsel of his will," the plan he has laid down from eternity, he saves those whom he foreknew; the true believers in every place and generation.

A Vital Dimension of Faith

> *He that spared not his own Son, but delivered him up for us all, how shall he not with him also freely give us all things?*
>
> **Romans 8:32**

Without the truth of this verse, a vital dimension of our faith would be missing.

We might have loved the Author of our being, the Father of angels and men, as our Creator and Preserver. We might have said, "O Lord our Governor, how excellent is thy name in all the earth!" But we could not have loved him under the nearest and dearest relation—as delivering up his Son for us all. We might have loved the Son of God, as being "the brightness of his Father's glory, the express image of his person" (although this ground seems to belong rather to the inhabitants of heaven than earth); but we could not have loved him as "bearing our sins in his own body on the tree," and "by that one oblation of himself once offered, making a full sacrifice, oblation, and satisfaction for the sins of the whole world." We would not have been "made conformable to his death," nor have known "the power of his resurrection." We could not have loved the Holy Ghost, as revealing to us the Father and the Son; as opening the eyes of our understanding; bringing us out of darkness into his marvelous light; renewing the image of God in our soul, and sealing us unto the day of redemption. So that, in truth, what is now "in the sight of God, even the Father," not of fallible men, "pure religion and undefiled," would then have had no being; inasmuch as it wholly depends on those grand principles, "By grace ye are saved through faith" and, "Jesus Christ is of God made unto us wisdom, and righteousness, and sanctification, and redemption."

160

Of Works . . . and Grace

What shall we say then? That the Gentiles, which followed not after righteousness, have attained to righteousness, even the righteousness which is of faith. But Israel, which followed after the law of righteousness, hath not attained to the law of righteousness.

Romans 9:30, 31

What is the difference then between the "righteousness which is of the law," and the "righteousness which is of faith"? Between the first covenant, or the covenant of works, and the second, the covenant of grace? The essential, unchangeable difference is this: The one supposes him to whom it is given to be already holy and happy, created in the image and enjoying the favor of God; and prescribes the condition whereon he may continue therein, in love and joy, life and immortality. The other supposes him to whom it is given to be now unholy and unhappy; fallen short of the glorious image of God, having the wrath of God abiding on him, and hastening through sin, whereby his soul is dead, to bodily death, and death everlasting. And to man in this state it prescribes the condition, whereon he may regain the pearl he has lost; may recover the favor and image of God; may retrieve the life of God in his soul, and be restored to the knowledge and the love of God, which is the beginning of life eternal.

Again, the covenant of works, in order to effect man's *continuance* in the favor of God, in his knowledge and love, in holiness and happiness, required, of perfect man, a *perfect* and uninterrupted *obedience* to every point of the law of God. Whereas, the covenant of grace, in order to bring about man's *recovery* of the favor and the life of God, requires only *faith*—living faith in him, who, through God, justifies him that obeyed not.

Yet, again: the covenant of works required of Adam, and all his children, to pay the price themselves, in consideration of which they were to receive all the future blessings of God. But, in the covenant of grace, seeing we have nothing to pay, God "frankly forgives us all": provided only that we believe in him, who has paid the price for us; who has given himself a "propitiation for our sins, for the sins of the whole world."

21. Holiness—A Fruit of Faith

Faith Shown by Fruit

So then faith cometh by hearing, and hearing by the word of God.

Romans 10:17

Faith works by love; faith overcomes the world, faith purifies the heart; faith, in the smallest measure, removes mountains. If you can believe, all things are possible to you. If you are justified by faith, you have peace with God, and rejoice in hope of his glorious appearing.

He who believes has the witness in himself; he has the earnest of heaven in his heart; he has love stronger than death. Death to a believer has lost its sting; "therefore will he not fear, though the earth be removed, and though the mountains be carried into the midst of the sea" (Psalm 46:2). For he knows in whom he has believed; and that "neither life nor death shall be able to separate him from the love of God which is in Christ Jesus his Lord."

Do you so believe? Prove your own self by the infallible Word of God. If you do not have the fruits, effects, or inseparable properties of faith, you do not have faith. Come, then, to the Author and Finisher of faith, confessing your sins, and the root of all your unbelief, till he forgive you your sins, and cleanse of all your unbelief and unrighteousness. Come to the Friend of sinners, weary and heavy laden, and he will give you pardon! Cast your poor desperate soul on his undying love! Enter into the rock, the ark, the city of refuge! Ask, and you shall receive faith and forgiveness together. He waited to be gracious. He has spared you for this very thing; that your eyes might see his salvation. Whatever judgments come in these latter days, yet whosoever shall call on the name of the Lord Jesus shall be delivered.

Choose Holiness

I beseech you therefore, brethren, by the mercies of
God, that ye present your bodies a living sacrifice, holy,
acceptable unto God, which is your reasonable service.
Romans 12:1

Holiness is having "the mind that was in Christ," and "walking as Christ walked." Such has been my judgment for these threescore years without any material alteration. Only about fifty years ago I had a clearer view than before of justification by faith; and in this, from that very hour, I never varied, no, not a hair's breadth. Nevertheless, an ingenious man has publicly accused me of a thousand variations. I pray God not to lay this to his charge! I am now on the borders of the grave; but, by the grace of God, I still witness the same confession. Indeed, some have supposed, that when I began to declare, "By grace ye are saved through faith," I retracted what I had before maintained: "Without holiness no man shall see the Lord." But . . . these scriptures will consist with each other; the meaning of the former being plainly this: By faith we are saved from sin, and made holy. The imagination—that faith supersedes holiness—is the marrow of Antinomianism.

The sum of it all is this: The God of love is willing to save all the souls that he has made. This he has proclaimed to them in his Word, together with the terms of salvation, revealed by the Son of his love, who gave his own life that they who believe in him might have everlasting life. And for these he has prepared a kingdom, from the foundation of the world. But he will not force them to accept of it; he leaves them in the hands of their own counsel; he says, "Behold, I set before you life and death, blessing and cursing: choose life that ye may live." Choose holiness, by my grace which is the way, the only way, to everlasting life. . . . This is the wedding garment of all who are called to "the marriage of the Lamb." Clothed in this, they will not be found naked: "They have washed their robes and made them white in the blood of the Lamb." But as to all those who appear in the last day without the wedding garment, the Judge will say, "Cast them into outer darkness; there shall be weeping and gnashing of teeth."

Reason and Holiness

I appeal to you therefore, brethren, by the mercies of God, to present your bodies as a living sacrifice, holy and acceptable to God, which is your spiritual worship.
Romans 12:1 (RSV)

You see how many admirable ends it answers, were it only in the things of this life. Of what unspeakable use is even a moderate share of reason in all our worldly employments, from the lowest and meanest offices of life, through all the intermediate branches of business; till we ascend to those that are of the highest importance and the greatest difficulty? When therefore you despise or depreciate reason, you must not imagine you are doing God service. Least of all, are you promoting the cause of God when you are endeavoring to exclude reason out of religion? Unless you willfully shut your eyes, you cannot but see of what service it is both in laying the foundation of true religion, under the guidance of the Spirit of God, and in raising the superstructure. You see it directs us in every point both of faith and practice. It guides us with regard to every branch both of inward and outward holiness. Do we not glory in this, that the whole of our religion is a "reasonable service"? Yea, and that every part of it, when it is duly performed, is the highest exercise of our understanding?

Permit me to add a few words to you, likewise, who overvalue reason. Why should you run from one extreme to the other? Is not the middle way best? Let reason do all that reason can: Employ it as far as it will go. But, at the same time, acknowledge it is utterly incapable of giving either faith, or hope, or love; and, consequently, of producing either real virtue, or substantial happiness. Expect these from a higher source, even from the Father of the spirits of all flesh. Seek and receive them, not as your own acquisition, but as the gift of God. Lift up your hearts to him who "giveth to all men liberally, and upbraideth not." He alone can give that faith, which is "the evidence" and conviction "of things not seen." He alone can "beget you unto a lively hope" of an inheritance eternal in the heavens; and he alone can "shed his love abroad in your heart by the Holy Ghost given unto you." Ask, therefore, and it shall be given you! Cry unto him, and you shall not cry in vain!

Glorifying God by Your Love

Let love be without dissimulation. Abhor that which is evil; cleave to that which is good.
Romans 12:9

Let this be our one ultimate end in all things. With this view, be plain, open, undisguised. Let your love be without dissimulation: why should you hide fair, disinterested love? Let there be no guile found in your mouth; let your words be the genuine picture of your heart. Let there be no darkness or reservedness in your conversation, no disguise in your behavior. Leave this to those who have other designs in view; designs which will not bear the light. Be artless and simple to all mankind; that all may see the grace of God which is in you. And although some will harden their hearts, yet others will take knowledge that you have been with Jesus, and, by returning themselves to the great Bishop of their souls, "glorify your Father which is in heaven" (Matt. 5:16).

With this one design, that men may glorify God in you, go on in his name, and in the power of his might. Be not ashamed even to stand alone, so it be in the ways of God. Let the light, which is in your heart, shine in all good works, both works of piety and works of mercy. And to enlarge your ability of doing good, renounce all superfluities. Cut off all unnecessary expense in food, in furniture, in apparel. Be a good steward of every gift of God, even of these his lowest gifts. Cut off all unnecessary expense of time, all needless or useless employments; and "whatsoever thy hand findeth to do, do it with thy might." In a word, be full of faith and love; do good; suffer evil. And herein be "steadfast, unmoveable; [yea,] always abounding in the work of the Lord; forasmuch as thou knowest that thy labour is not in vain in the Lord."

Men of Upright Hearts

Let love be without dissimulation. Abhor that which is evil; cleave to that which is good. Be kindly affectioned one to another with brotherly love; in honour preferring one another.
Romans 12:9, 10

Even among men of an upright heart, men who desire to "have a conscience void of offense," it must needs be, that, as long as there are various opinions, there will be various ways of worshiping God; seeing a variety of opinions necessarily implies a variety of practice. And as, in all ages, men have differed in nothing more than in their opinions concerning the Supreme Being, so in nothing have they more differed from each other, than in the manner of worshiping him. Had this been only in the heathen world, it would not have been at all surprising: for we know, these "by [their] wisdom knew not God"; nor, therefore, could they know how to worship him. But is it not strange, that even in the Christian world, although they all agree in the general, "God is a Spirit, and they that worship him must worship him in spirit and in truth," yet the particular modes of worshiping God are almost as various as among the heathen?

And how shall we choose among so much variety? No man can choose for, or prescribe to, another. But everyone must follow the dictates of his own conscience, in simplicity and godly sincerity. He must be fully persuaded in his own mind, and then act according to the best light he has. Nor has any creature power to constrain another to walk by his own rule. God has given no right to any of the children of men, thus to lord it over the conscience of his brethren; but every man must judge for himself, as every man must give an account of himself to God.

Brotherly Love

Let love be genuine . . . love one another with brotherly affection; outdo one another in showing honor.
Romans 12:9, 10 (RSV)

Let *love* not visit you as a transient guest, but be the constant temper of your soul. See that your heart be filled at all times, and on all occasions, with real, undissembled benevolence; not to those only that love *you,* but to every soul of man. Let it pant in your heart; let it sparkle in your eyes; let it shine on all your actions. Whenever you open your lips, let it be with love; and let there be in your tongue the law of kindness. Your word will then distill as the rain, and as the dew upon the tender herb. Be not straitened or limited in your affection, but let it embrace every child of man. Everyone born of a woman has a claim to your goodwill. You owe this, not to some, but to all. And let all men know that you desire both their temporal and eternal happiness, as sincerely as you do your own.

Prayer—the Voice of a Thankful Heart

Rejoicing in hope; patient in tribulation; continuing instant in prayer.
Romans 12:12

[When, you pray,] consider both your outward and inward state, and vary your prayers accordingly. For instance, suppose your outward state is prosperous; suppose you are in a state of health, ease, and plenty, having your lot cast among kind relations, good neighbors, and agreeable friends who love you, and you them; then your outward state manifestly calls for praise and thanksgiving to God. On the other hand, if you are in a state of adversity; if God has lain trouble upon you; if you are in poverty, in want, in outward distress; if you are in imminent danger; if you are in pain and sickness; then you are clearly called to pour out your soul before God in such prayer as is suited to your circumstances. In like manner you may suit your devotions to your inward state, the present state of your mind.

22. The Marks of a Christian

Weep with the Weeping

Rejoice with them that do rejoice, and weep with them that weep.

Romans 12:15

Weep with them who weep. If you can do no more, at least mix your tears with theirs; and give them healing words, such as may calm their minds, and mitigate their sorrows. But if you can, if you are able to give them actual assistance, let it not be wanting. Be as eyes to the blind, as feet to the lame, a husband to the widow, and a father to the fatherless. This will greatly tend to conciliate the affection, and to give a profitable pleasure, not only to those who are immediate objects of your compassion, but to others likewise who "see your good works, and glorify your Father which is in heaven."

Love Is God's Highest Call

Love worketh no ill to his neighbour: therefore love is the fulfilling of the law.

Romans 13:10

This cannot be denied, our Lord himself has said, "Ye shall know them by their fruits." By their works you know them that believe, and them that believe not. But yet it may be doubted, whether there is not a surer proof of the sincerity of our faith than even our works, that is our willingly suffering for righteousness' sake—especially if, after suffering reproach, and pain, and loss of friends and substance, a man gives up life itself; yea, by a shameful and painful death, by giving his body to be burned, rather than he would give up faith and a good conscience by neglecting his known duty.

It is proper to observe here, first, what a beautiful gradation there is, each step rising above the other, in the enumeration of those several things which some or other of those who are called Christians, and are usually accounted so, really believe will supply the absence of love. In Romans 13, St. Paul begins at the lowest point, *talking well,* and advances step by step; everyone rising higher than the preceding, till he comes to the highest of all. A step above eloquence is knowledge. Faith is a step above this. Good works are a step above that faith; and even above this, is suffering for righteousness' sake. Nothing is higher than this, but Christian love—the love of our neighbor, flowing from the love of God.

The Mark of Meekness

Let every one of us please his neighbour for his good to edification.
Romans 15:2

If you would please your neighbor for his good, study to be *lowly* in heart. Be little and vile in your own eyes, in honor preferring others before yourself. Be deeply sensible of your own weaknesses, follies, and imperfections; as well as of the sin remaining in your heart, and cleaving to all your words and actions. And let this spirit appear in all you speak or do. "Be clothed with humility." Reject with horror that favorite maxim of the old heathen, sprung from the bottomless pit: "The more you value yourself, the more others will value you." Not so; on the contrary, both God and man "resist the proud." And, as "God giveth grace to the humble," so humility, not pride, recommends us to the esteem and favor of men, especially those who fear God.

If you desire to please your neighbor for his good to edification, you should also labor and pray that you may be *meek* as well as lowly in heart. Labor to be of a calm, dispassionate temper; gentle toward all men; and let the gentleness of your disposition

169

appear in the whole tenor of your conversation. Let all your words and all your actions be regulated thereby. Remember, likewise, that advice of St. Peter: As an addition to your gentleness, be merciful; "be courteous." Be pitiful; be tenderly compassionate to all who are in distress; to all who are under any affliction of mind, body, or estate. Let

> The various scenes of human woe
> Excite our softest sympathy.

God's Faithfulness

God is faithful, by whom ye were called into the fellowship of his Son Jesus Christ our Lord.
1 Corinthians 1:9

"How then is God faithful?" I answer: In fulfilling every promise which he hath made, to all to whom it is made, all who fulfill the condition of that promise. More particularly, (1) "God is faithful" in that "[he] will not suffer you to be tempted above that you are able [to bear]" (1 Cor. 10:13). (2) "The Lord is faithful, who shall stablish you, and keep you from evil" (if you put your trust in him); from all the evil which you might otherwise suffer, through "unreasonable and wicked men" (2 Thess. 3:2, 3). (3) "Quench not the Spirit; hold fast that which is good; Abstain from all appearance of evil; [and] your whole spirit and soul and body be preserved blameless unto the coming of our Lord Jesus Christ. Faithful is he that calleth you, who also will do it" (1 Thess. 5:19, 21–23). (4) Be not disobedient unto the heavenly calling; and "God is faithful, by whom ye were called . . . [to] confirm you unto the end, that ye may be blameless in the day of our Lord Jesus Christ" (1 Cor. 1:8, 9). Yet, notwithstanding all this, unless you fulfill the condition, you cannot attain the promise.

"Nay, but are not 'all the promises, yea and amen?' " They are firm as the pillars of heaven. Perform the condition, and the promise is sure. Believe, and thou shalt be saved.

170

The Trinity

But God hath revealed them unto us by his Spirit: for the Spirit searcheth all things, yea, the deep things of God.

1 Corinthians 2:10

This is a point much to be observed. There are many things "which eye hath not seen, nor ear heard, neither hath it entered into the heart of man to conceive." Part of these God has "revealed to us by his Spirit"— *"revealed,"* that is, unveiled, uncovered. That part he requires us to believe. Part of them he has not revealed; that we need not, and indeed cannot, believe. It is far above, out of our sight.

Now, where is the wisdom of rejecting what is revealed, because we do not understand what is not revealed? Of denying the *fact* which God had unveiled, because we cannot see the *manner,* which is veiled still?

Especially when we consider that what God has been pleased to reveal upon this head is far from being a point of indifference, is a truth of the last importance. It enters into the very heart of Christianity; it lies at the root of all vital religion.

Unless these Three are One, how can "all men honor the Son, even as they honor the Father"? "I know not what to do," says Socinus in a letter to his friend, "with my untoward followers: they will not worship Jesus Christ. I tell them it is written, 'Let all the angels of God worship him.' They answer: However that be, if he is not God, we dare not worship him. For 'it is written, Thou shalt worship the Lord thy God, and him only shalt thou serve.' "

But the thing which I here particularly mean is this: The knowledge of the three-one God is interwoven with all true Christian faith, with all vital religion.

I do not say that every real Christian can say with the Marquis de Renty, "I bear about with me continually an experimental verity, and a plenitude of the presence of the ever-blessed Trinity." I apprehend this is not the experience of "babies," but rather "fathers in Christ."

But I know not how anyone can be a Christian believer till he "hath," as St. John speaks, "the witness in himself"; till "the

171

Spirit of God witnesses with his spirit, that he is a child of God"; that is, in effect, till God the Holy Ghost witnesses that God the Father has accepted him through the merits of God the Son: and, having this witness, he honors the Son, and the blessed Spirit, "even as he honors the Father."

Reward for Suffering

Now he that planteth and he that watereth are one: and every man shall receive his own reward according to his own labour.
1 Corinthians 3:8

Everyone will then "receive his own reward according to his own labor." Every individual will be "rewarded according to his work." But the Fall gave rise to innumerable good works, which could otherwise never have existed: such as ministering to the necessities of saints; yea, relieving the distressed in every kind. And hereby innumerable stars will be added to their eternal crown. Yet again: there will be an abundant reward in heaven for *suffering* as well as for *doing* the will of God: "These light afflictions, which are but for a moment, work out for us a far more exceeding and eternal weight of glory." Therefore that event which occasioned the entrance of suffering into the world, has thereby occasioned to all the children of God an increase of glory to all eternity. For although the sufferings themselves will be at an end; although

> The pain of life shall then be o'er,
>   The anguish and distracting care;
> There sighing grief shall weep no more;
>   And sin shall never enter there;

yet the joys occasioned thereby shall never end, but flow at God's right hand for evermore.

Christians in Business

Whether therefore ye eat, or drink, or whatsoever ye do, do all to the glory of God.
1 Corinthians 10:31

172

How do you transact your worldly business? I trust, with diligence, whatever your hand finds to do, doing it with your might; with justice, rendering to all their due, in every circumstance of life; yea, and with mercy, doing unto every man what you would he should do unto you. This is well: But a Christian is called to go still farther—to add piety to justice; to intermix prayer especially the prayer of the heart, with all the labor of his hands. Without this, all his diligence and justice only show him to be an honest heathen; and many there are who profess the Christian religion, who go no farther than honest Heathenism.

In what *spirit* do you go through your business? In the spirit of the world, or in the Spirit of Christ? I am afraid thousands of those who are called good Christians do not understand the question. If you act in the Spirit of Christ, you carry the end you at first proposed through all your work from first to last. You do everything in the spirit of sacrifice, giving up your will to the will of God; and continually aiming, not at ease, pleasure, or riches, not at anything "this short-enduring world can give," but merely at the glory of God. Now, can anyone deny that this is the most excellent way of pursuing worldly business?

23. The More Excellent Way

The Lord's Supper

*For as often as ye eat this bread, and drink this cup,
ye do shew the Lord's death till he come.*
1 Corinthians 11:26

In this world we are never free from temptations. Whatever way
of life we are in, whatever our condition be, whether we are sick
or well, in trouble or at ease, the enemies of our souls are watching
to lead us into sin. And too often they prevail over us. Now,
when we are convinced of having sinned against God, what surer
way have we of procuring pardon from him, than the "showing
forth the Lord's death"; and beseeching him, for the sake of his
Son's sufferings, to blot out all our sins?

The grace of God given herein confirms to us the pardon
of our sins, and enables us to leave them. As our bodies are
strengthened by bread and wine, so are our souls by these
tokens of the body and the blood of Christ. This is the food of
our souls; this gives strength to perform our duty, and leads us
on to perfection. If, therefore, we have any regard for the plain
command of Christ, if we desire the pardon of our sins, if we
wish for strength to believe, to love and obey our Savior, if
we wish for strength to believe, to love and obey God, then
we should neglect no opportunity of receiving the Lord's Supper; then we must never turn our backs on the feast which our
Lord has prepared for us. . . . Whoever, therefore, does not receive, but goes from the holy table, when all things are prepared,
either does not understand his duty, or does not care for the
dying command of his Savior, the forgiveness of his sins, the
strengthening of his soul, and the refreshing it with the hope of
glory.

Love—the More Excellent Way

Covet earnestly the best gifts: and yet shew I unto you a more excellent way.
1 Corinthians 12:31

In the preceding verses, St. Paul has been speaking of the extraordinary gifts of the Holy Spirit such as healing the sick; prophesying, in the proper sense of the word, that is, foretelling things to come; speaking with strange tongues, such as the speaker had never learned; and the miraculous interpretation of tongues. And these gifts the apostle allows to be desirable; yea, he exhorts the Corinthians, at least the teachers among them (to whom chiefly, if not solely, they were wont to be given in the first ages of the church), to *covet* them *earnestly,* that thereby they might be qualified to be more useful either to Christians or heathens. "And yet," says he, "I show unto you a more excellent way"; far more desirable than all these put together. Inasmuch as it will infallibly lead you to happiness, both in this world and in the world to come; whereas you might have all those gifts, yea, in the highest degree, and yet be miserable both in time and eternity. That "more excellent way" was the way of love. That is the gift to be sought above all others!

Come Up Higher

But eagerly desire the greater gifts. And now I will show you the most excellent way.
1 Corinthians 12:31 (NIV)

From long experience and observation I am inclined to think that whoever finds redemption in the blood of Jesus, whoever is justified, has the choice of walking in a higher or lower path. I believe the Holy Spirit at that time sets before him the "more excellent way," and incites him to walk therein; to choose the narrowest path in the narrow way; to aspire after the heights and depths of holiness—after the entire image of God. But if he does not accept this offer, he insensibly declines into the lower order of Christians. He still goes on in what may be called a good way, serving God in his degree, and finds mercy in the close of life, through the blood of the covenant.

I would be far from quenching the smoking flax—from discouraging those that serve God in a low degree. But I could not wish them to stop here: I would encourage them to come up higher. Without thundering hell and damnation in their ears, without condemning the way wherein they were, telling them it is the way that leads to destruction, I will endeavor to point out to them what is, in every respect, "a more excellent way."

Prayer and the Inner Man

But earnestly desire the higher gifts. And I will show you a still more excellent way.
1 Corinthians 12:31 (RSV)

Most Christians, as soon as they rise, are accustomed to use some kind of *prayer;* and probably to use the same form still, which they learned when they were eight or ten years old. Now, I do not condemn those who proceed thus, (though many do) as mocking God; though they have used the same form, without any variation, for twenty or thirty years together. But surely there is "a more excellent way" of ordering our private devotions. . . . Is your soul in heaviness, either from a sense of sin, or through manifold temptations? Then let your prayer consist of such confessions, petitions, and supplications as are agreeable to your distressed situation of mind. On the contrary, is your soul in peace? Are you rejoicing in God? Are his consolations not small with you? Then say, with the psalmist, "Thou art my God, and I will love thee: Thou art my God, and I will praise thee." You may, likewise, when you have time, add to your other devotions a little reading and meditation, and perhaps a psalm of praise—the natural effusion of a thankful heart. You must certainly see that this is "a more excellent way" than the poor dry form which you used before.

The Constraining Love of God

Though I speak with the tongues of men and of angels, and have not charity [love], I am become as sounding brass, or a tinkling cymbal.
1 Corinthians 13:1

Of what kind of love is the apostle speaking throughout the chapter? Many persons of eminent learning and piety think it is the love of God. But from reading the whole chapter numberless times, and considering it in every light, I am thoroughly persuaded that what St. Paul is here directly speaking of is the love of our neighbor. I believe whoever carefully weighs the whole tenor of his discourse, will be fully convinced of this. But it must be allowed to be such a love of our neighbor, as can only spring from a love of God. And whence does this love of God flow? Only from that faith which is of the operation of God; which whoever has, has a direct evidence that "God was in Christ reconciling the world unto himself." When this is particularly applied to his heart, so that he can say, with humble boldness, "The life which I now live, I live by faith in the Son of God, who loved me, and gave himself for me"; then, and not till then, "the love of God is shed abroad in his heart." And this love sweetly constrains him to love every child of man with the love which is here spoken of; not with a love of esteem or of complacence; for this can have no place with regard to those who are (if not his personal enemies, yet) enemies to God and their own souls; but with a love of benevolence—of tender goodwill to all the souls that God has made.

The Meaning and Measure of Love

Though I bestow all my goods to feed the poor, and though I give my body to be burned, and have not charity [love], it profiteth me nothing.
1 Corinthians 13:3

Let us inquire what this love is—what is the true meaning of the word? We may consider it either as to its properties or effects: And that we may be under no possibility of mistake, we will not at all regard the judgment of men, but go to our Lord himself for an account of the nature of love; and, for the effects of it, to his inspired apostle.

The love which our Lord requires in all his followers, is the love of God and man—of God, for his own, and of man, for God's sake. Now, what is it to love God, but to delight in him, to rejoice in his will, to desire continually to please him, to seek and find our happiness in him, and to thirst day and night for a fuller enjoyment of him?

As to the measure of this love, our Lord has clearly told us, "Thou shalt love the Lord thy God with all thy heart." Not that we are to love or delight in none but him; for he has commanded us, not only to love our neighbor, that is, all men, as ourselves— to desire and pursue their happiness as sincerely and steadily as our own—but also to love any of his creatures in the strictest sense; to delight in them, to enjoy them: Only in such a manner and measure as we know and feel, not to indispose but to prepare us for the enjoyment of him. Thus, then, we are called to love God with all our heart.

Characteristics of Love

Charity [love] suffereth long, and is kind . . . envieth not . . . vaunteth not itself.
1 Corinthians 13:4

Love "vaunteth not itself"; which coincides with the very next words; but rather (as the word likewise properly imports)—*is not rash or hasty* in judging; it will not hastily condemn anyone. It does not pass a severe sentence on a slight or sudden view of things: it first weighs all the evidence, particularly that which is brought in favor of the accused. A true lover of his neighbor is not like the generality of men, who, even in cases of the nicest nature, "see a little, presume a great deal, and so jump to the conclusion." No: he proceeds with wariness and circumspection, taking heed to every step; willingly subscribing to the role of the ancient heathen (Oh, where will the modern Christian appear!), "I am so far from lightly believing what one man says against another, that I will not easily believe what a man says against himself. I will always allow him second thoughts, and many times counsel, too."

It follows, love "is not puffed up"; it does not incline or suffer any man "to think more highly of himself than he ought to think"; but rather to think soberly: yea, it humbles the soul unto the dust. It destroys all high conceits, engendering pride; and makes us rejoice to be as nothing, to be little and vile, the lowest of all, the servant of all. They who are "kindly affectioned one to another with brotherly love," cannot but "in honor prefer one another." Those who, having the same love, are of one accord, do in lowliness of mind "each esteem the other better than themselves."

"It doth not behave itself unseemly": it is not rude, or willingly offensive to any. It "renders to all their due; fear to whom fear, honor to whom honor"; courtesy, civility, humanity to all the world; in their several degrees "honoring all men." One writer defines good breeding, nay, the highest degree of it, politeness, as "a continual desire to please, appearing in all the behavior"; but if so, there is none so well bred as a Christian, a lover of all mankind. For he cannot but desire to "please all men for their good to edification": and this desire cannot be hid; it will necessarily appear in all his contacts with men. For his "love is without dissimulation"; it will appear in all his actions and conversation, yea, and will constrain him, though without guile, to "become all things to all men, if by any means he may save some."

And in becoming all things to all men, "love seeketh not her own." In striving to please all men, the lover of mankind has no eye at all to his own temporal advantage. He covets no man's silver, or gold, or apparel; he desires nothing but the salvation of their souls. Yea, in some sense, he may be said *not to seek his own* spiritual, any more than temporal advantage; for while he is on the full stretch to save their souls from death, he, as it were, forgets himself. No marvel that such love "is not provoked." The word *easily* is not in the original. Paul's words are absolute: "Love is not provoked" to unkindness toward anyone. It triumphs over all. In all trials it looks to Jesus and is more than conqueror in his love.

24. Of Love and Living

The Nature of Love

Charity [love] . . . is not puffed up.
1 Corinthians 13:4

"Love is not puffed up" (1 Cor. 13:4). It abases to the dust every soul wherein it dwells: accordingly, he was lowly of heart, little, mean, and vile in his own eyes. He neither sought, nor received, the praise of men, but that which comes of God only. He was meek and longsuffering, gentle to all, and easy to be entreated. Faithfulness and truth never forsook him; they were "bound about his neck, and written on the tablet of his heart." By the same Spirit he was enabled to be temperate in all things, refraining his soul even as a weaned child. He was "crucified to the world, and the world crucified to him"; superior to "the desire of the flesh, the desire of the eye, and the pride of life." By the same almighty love was he saved, both from passion and pride; from lust and vanity; from ambition and covetousness; and from every temper which was not in Christ.

It may easily be believed, he who had this love in his heart, would work no evil to his neighbor. It was impossible for him, knowingly and designedly, to do harm to any man. He was at the greatest distance from cruelty and wrong, from any unjust or unkind action. With the same care did he "set a watch before his mouth, and keep the door of his lips," lest he should offend in tongue, either against justice, or against mercy or truth. He put away all lying, falsehood, and fraud; neither was guile found in his mouth. He spake evil of no man; nor did an unkind word ever come out of his lips.

And, as he was deeply sensible of the truth of that word, "without me ye can do nothing," and, consequently, of the need he had to be watered of God every moment; so he continued daily in all the ordinances of God, the stated channels of his grace to man; "in the apostles' doctrine," or teaching, receiving that food of the soul with all readiness of heart; in "the breaking of bread," which he found to be the communion of the body of Christ; and "in the prayers" and praises offered up by the great congregation. And thus, he daily "grew in grace," increasing in strength, in the knowledge and love of God.

Love Believes . . . Hopes . . . Endures

[Love] believeth all things, hopeth all things, endureth all things.

1 Corinthians 13:7

Love "believeth all things." It is always willing to think the best; to put the most favorable construction on everything. It is ever ready to believe whatever may tend to the advantage of anyone's character. It is easily convinced of (what it earnestly desires) the innocence or integrity of any man; or, at least, of the sincerity of his repentance, if he had once erred from the way. It is glad to excuse whatever is amiss; to condemn the offender as little as possible; and to make all the allowance for human weakness, which can be done without betraying the truth of God.

And when it can no longer believe, then love "hopeth all things." Is any evil related of any man? Love hopes that the relation is not true, that the thing related was never done. Is it certain it was? "But perhaps it was not done with such circumstances as are related; so that allowing the fact, there is room to hope it was not as it is represented." Was the action apparently, undeniably evil? Love hopes the intention was not so. Is it clear the design was evil too? "Yet might it not spring from the settled temper of the heart, but from a start of passion, or from some vehement temptation, which hurried the man beyond himself?" And even when it cannot be doubted, but all the actions, designs, and tempers are equally evil; still love hopes that God will at last make bare his arm, and get himself the victory; and that there shall be "joy in heaven over [this] one sinner that repenteth, more than over ninety and nine just persons that need no repentance."

Last: It "endureth all things." This completes the character of him who is truly merciful. He endures not some, not many things only, not most, but absolutely *all things.* Whatever the injustice, the malice, the cruelty of men can inflict, he is able to suffer. He calls nothing intolerable; he never says of anything: "This is not to be borne." No; he cannot but suffer all things through Christ who strengthens him. And all he suffers does not destroy his love, nor impair it in the least. It is proof against all. It is a flame that burns even in the midst of the great deep. "Many waters cannot quench" his "love, neither can the floods drown it." It triumphs over all. It "never faileth," either in time or in eternity.

Make Love Your Aim

Make love your aim, and earnestly desire the spiritual gifts. . . .

1 Corinthians 14:1a (RSV)

The way of love—of loving all men for God's sake, of humble, gentle, patient love—is that which the apostle so admirably describes in the ensuing chapter. And without this he assures us, all eloquence, all knowledge, all faith, all works, and all sufferings are of no more value in the sight of God than sounding brass or a rumbling cymbal, and are not of the least avail toward our eternal salvation. Without this, all we know, all we believe, all we do, all we suffer, will profit us nothing in the great day of accounts.

But at present I would take a different view of the text and point out a "more excellent way" in another sense. It is the observation of an ancient writer, that there have been from the beginning two orders of Christians. The one loved an innocent life, conforming in all things not sinful, to the customs and fashions of the world; doing many good works, abstaining from gross evils, and attending the ordinances of God. They endeavored, in general, to have a conscience void of offense in their behavior, but did not aim at any particular strictness, being in most things like their neighbors. The other Christians not only abstained from all appearance of evil, were zealous of good works in every kind, and attended all the ordinances of God, but likewise used all diligence to attain the whole mind that was in Christ, and labored to walk, in every point, as their beloved Master. To do this, they walked in a constant course of universal self-denial, trampling on every pleasure which they were not divinely conscious prepared them for taking pleasure in God. They took up their cross daily. They strove, they agonized without intermission, to enter in at the straight gate. This one thing they did: they spared no pains to arrive at the summit of Christian holiness, "leaving the first principles of the doctrine of Christ, to go on to perfection," to "know all that love of God which passeth knowledge, and to be filled with all the fulness of God."

What Manner of Love?

For since by man came death, by man came also the resurrection of the dead.
1 Corinthians 15:21

We see, then, what unspeakable advantage we derive from the fall of our first parent with regard to faith—faith both in God the Father, who spared not his own Son, his only Son, but "wounded him for our transgressions," and "bruised him for our iniquities.". . . We see what advantage we derive therefrom with regard to the love of God; both of God the Father and God the Son. The chief ground of this love, as long as we remain in the body, is plainly declared by the apostle: "We love him, because he first loved us." But the greatest instance of his love had never been given if Adam had not fallen.

And as our faith both in God the Father and the Son receives an unspeakable increase, if not its very being, from this grand event, as does also our love both of the Father and the Son; so does the love of our neighbor also, our benevolence to all mankind, which cannot but increase in the same proportion with our faith and love of God. For who does not apprehend the force of that inference drawn by the loving apostle: "Beloved, if God so loved us, we ought also to love one another"? If God *so* loved us— observe, the stress of the argument lies on this very point: *so loved us*, as to deliver up his only Son to die a cursed death for our salvation. Beloved, what manner of love is this wherewith God has loved us; so as to give his *only Son*, in glory equal with the

Father, in Majesty co-eternal? What manner of love is this wherewith the only begotten Son of God has loved us so as to *empty himself,* as far as possible, of his eternal Godhead. . . . If God *so* loved us, how ought we to love one another! But this motive to brotherly love had been totally wanting if Adam had not fallen. Consequently, we could not then have loved one another in so high a degree as we may now. Nor could there have been that height and depth in the command of our blessed Lord, "As I have loved you, so love one another."

The Justice and Mercy of God

> *For as in Adam all die, even so in Christ shall all be made alive.*
> **1 Corinthians 15:22**

Behold then both the *justice* and mercy of God—his justice in punishing sin, the sin of him in whose loins we were then all contained, on Adam and his whole posterity—and his *mercy* in providing a universal remedy for a universal evil; in appointing the second Adam to die for all who had died in the first; that, "as in Adam all died, so in Christ all" might "be made alive"; that, "as by one man's offense, judgment came upon all men to condemnation, so by the righteousness of one, the free gift" might "come upon all unto justification of"—"justification of *life,*" as being connected with the new birth, the beginning of spiritual life, which leads us, through the life of holiness, to life eternal, to glory.

And it should be particularly observed, that "where sin abounded, grace does much more abound." For not as the condemnation, so is the free gift; but we may gain infinitely more than we have lost. We may now attain both higher degrees of holiness, and higher degrees of glory, than it would have been possible for us to attain. If Adam had not sinned, the Son of God had not died: consequently that amazing instance of the love of God to man had never existed, which has in all ages, excited the highest joy, and love, and gratitude from his children. We might have loved God the Creator, God the Preserver, God the Governor; but there would have been no place for love to God the Redeemer.

This could have had no being. The highest glory and joy of saints on earth, and saints in heaven, Christ crucified, had been wanting. We could not then have praised him who, thinking it no robbery to be equal with God, yet emptied himself, took upon him the form of a servant, and was obedient to death, even the death of the cross! This is now the noblest theme of all the children of God on earth; yea, we need not scruple to affirm, even of angels, and archangels, and all the company of heaven.

Our Bodies—Friend or Foe?

But some man will say, How are the dead raised up?
and with what body do they come?
1 Corinthians 15:35

Our bodies shall be raised spiritual bodies. Our spirits are now forced to serve our bodies, and to attend their leisure, and do greatly depend upon them for most of their actions. But our bodies shall then wholly serve our spirits, and minister to them, and depend upon them. So that, as by "a natural body" we understand one fitted for this lower, sensible world for this earthly state; so "a spiritual body" is one suited to a spiritual state, to an invisible world, to the life of angels. And, indeed, this is the principal difference between a mortal and a glorified body. This flesh is the most dangerous enemy we have; we therefore deny and renounce it in our baptism.

It constantly tempts us to evil. Every sense is a snare to us. All its lusts and appetites are inordinate. It is ungovernable and often rebels against reason. The law in our members wars against the law of our mind. When the spirit is willing, the flesh is weak; so that the best of men are forced to keep it under, and use it hardly, lest it should betray them into folly and misery. And how does it hinder us in all our devotions! How soon does it jade our minds when employed on holy things! How easily, by its enchanting pleasures, does it divert them from those noble exercises! But when we have obtained the resurrection unto life, our bodies will be spiritualized, purified, and refined from their earthly grossness; then they will be fit instruments for the soul in all its divine and heavenly employment; we shall not be weary of singing praises to God through infinite ages.

What Is a Conscience?

*For our rejoicing is this, the testimony of our
conscience, that in simplicity and godly sincerity, not
with fleshly wisdom, but by the grace of God, we have
had our conversation in the world, and more
abundantly to you-ward.*
2 Corinthians 1:12

What is conscience, in the Christian sense? It is that faculty of
the soul which, by the assistance of the grace of God, sees at
one and the same time: (1) our own tempers and lives—the real
nature and quality of our thoughts, words, and actions; (2) the
rule whereby we are to be directed; and, (3) the agreement or
disagreement therewith. To express this a little more largely; conscience implies, first, the faculty a man has of knowing himself—
of discerning, both in general and in particular, his own tempers,
thoughts, words, and actions. But this it is not possible for him
to do, without the assistance of the Spirit of God. Otherwise,
self-love, and indeed, every other irregular passion, would disguise
and wholly conceal him from himself. It implies, second, a knowledge of the rule whereby he is to be directed in every particular;
which is no other than the written Word of God. Conscience
implies, third, a knowledge that all his thoughts, and words, and
actions are conformable to that rule. In all the offices of conscience,
the "unction of the Holy One" is indispensably needful. Without
this, neither could we clearly discern our lives or tempers; nor
could we judge of the rule whereby we are to walk, or of our
conformity or disconformity to it.

25. Walking by Faith

A Good Conscience

For our boast is this, the testimony of our conscience that we have behaved in the world, and still more toward you, with holiness and godly sincerity. . . .
2 Corinthians 1:12a (RSV)

According to the meaning wherein it is generally used [in God's Word], particularly in the Epistles of St. Paul, we may understand, by conscience, a faculty or power, implanted by God in every soul that comes into the world, of perceiving what is right or wrong in his own heart or life, in his tempers, thoughts, words, and actions.

But what is the rule whereby men are to judge of right and wrong? . . . The rule of heathens, as the apostle teaches elsewhere, is "the law written in their hearts." . . . But the Christian rule of right and wrong is the Word of God, the writings of the Old and New Testament, all that the prophets and "holy men of old" wrote "as they were moved by the Holy Ghost," all that Scripture which was given by inspiration of God. . . . This is a lantern unto a Christian's feet, and a light in all his path. This alone he receives as his rule of right or wrong, of whatever is really good or evil. He esteems nothing good but what is here enjoined, either directly or by plain consequence, he accounts nothing evil but what is here forbidden, either in terms or by undeniable inference. Whatever the Scripture neither forbids nor enjoins, either directly or by plain consequence, he believes to be of an indifferent nature, to be in itself neither good nor evil; this being the whole and sole outward rule whereby his conscience is to be directed in all things. And if it be directed thereby, in fact, then hath he "the answer of a good conscience toward God."

The Spirit and Liberty

Now the Lord is that Spirit: and where the Spirit of the Lord is, there is liberty.
2 Corinthians 3:17

In him is laid up for us that supplement to our nature, which we shall find the need of sooner or later; and that cannot be countervailed by any assistance from the creatures, or any improvement of our own faculties: For we were made to be happy only in God; and all our labors and hopes, while we do not thirst after our deified state—to partake as truly of God as we do of flesh and blood, to be glorified in his nature, as we have been dishonored in our own—are the labors and hopes of these who utterly mistake themselves.

The divine wisdom knew what was our proper consolation, though we did not. What does more obviously present itself in the Savior of the world, than a union of man with God?—a union attended with all the propriety of behavior that *we* are called to, as candidates of the Spirit; such as walking with God in singleness of heart, perfect self-renunciation, and a life of sufferings—a union which submitted to the necessary stages of our progress; where the divine life was hid, for the most part, in the secret of the soul till death; in the state of separation, it comforted the soul, but did not raise it above the intermediate region of Paradise; at the resurrection, it clothed the body with heavenly qualities, and the powers of immortality; and at last raised it to the immediate presence and right hand of the Father.

Christ is not only God above us; which may keep us in awe, but cannot save; but he is Immanuel, God with us, and in us. As he is the Son of God, God must be where he is; and as he is the Son of man, he will be with mankind; the consequence of this is, that in the future age "the tabernacle of God will be with men," and he will show them his glory; and, at present, he will *dwell* in their hearts by faith in his Son.

A Treasure in Clay

But we have this treasure in earthen vessels, that the excellency of the power may be of God, and not of us.
2 Corinthians 4:7

Undoubtedly this was the main design of God in this wonderful dispensation; to humble man, to make and keep him little, and poor, and base, and vile, in his own eyes. And whatever we suffer hereby, we are well repaid, if it be a means of "hiding pride from man"; of laying us low in the dust; even then, when we are most in danger of being lifted up by the excellent gifts of God!

Nay, if we suffer hereby, from the mean habitation of the immortal spirit; if pain, sickness, and numberless other afflictions beside, to which we should not otherwise have been liable, assault us on every side, and at length bear us down into the dust of death; what are we losers by this? Losers! No, "In all these things we are more than conquerors, through him that loved us." Come on, then, disease, weakness, pain—afflictions, in the language of men. Shall we not be infinite gainers by them? Gainers forever and ever! seeing "these light afflictions, which are but for a moment, work out for us a far more exceeding and eternal weight of glory!"

And are we not, by the consciousness of our present weakness, effectually taught wherein our strength lies? How loud does it proclaim, "Trust in the Lord Jehovah; for in him is everlasting strength!" Trust in him who suffered a thousand times more than ever you can suffer! Has he not all power in heaven and in earth? Then, what though

> The heavenly treasure now we have
> In a vile house of clay!
> Yet He shall to the utmost save,
> And keep it to that day.

Faith Is Receiving Spiritual Sight

For we walk by faith, not by sight.
2 Corinthians 5:7

How wonderful it is that we Christians can "walk by faith"! God, having "opened the eyes of their understanding," pours divine light into their souls, whereby they are enabled to "see him that is invisible," to see God and the things of God. What their "eye had not seen, nor their ear heard, neither had it entered into their heart to conceive," God from time to time reveals to them by the "unction of the Holy One, which teacheth them of all things."

189

Having "entered into the holiest by the blood of Jesus," by that "new and living way," and being joined unto "the general assembly and church of the first-born, and unto God the Judge of all, and Jesus the Mediator of the New Covenant,"—each of these can say, "I live not, but Christ liveth in me"; I now live that life which "is hid with Christ in God"; "and when Christ, who is my life, shall appear, then I shall likewise appear with him in glory."

We Who Live by Faith

We live by faith, not by sight.
2 Corinthians 5:7 (NIV)

How short is this description of real Christians! And yet how exceeding full! It comprehends, it sums up, the whole experience of those who are truly such, from the time they are born of God till they remove into Abraham's bosom. For, who are the *we* here spoken of? All who are true Christian believers. . . . All who are not only *servants,* but *children,* of God. All who have "the Spirit of adoption, crying in their hearts, Abba, Father." All who have "the Spirit of God witnessing with their spirits, that they are the sons of God."

All these, and these alone, can say, "We walk by faith, not by sight" [KJV]. But before we can possibly "walk by faith," we must *live* by faith, and not by sight. And to all real Christians our Lord says, "Because I live, ye live also"; you live a life which the world, whether learned or unlearned, "knows not of." "You that," like the world, "were dead in trespasses and sins, hath he quickened," and made alive; given you new senses—spiritual senses—"senses exercised to discern spiritual good and evil."

How Love Works

For the love of Christ constraineth us; because we thus judge, that if one died for all, then were all dead.
2 Corinthians 5:14

Does the love of God constrain you to serve him with fear—to "rejoice unto him with reverence"? Are you more afraid of displeasing God, than either of death or hell? Is nothing so terrible to you as the thought of offending the eyes of his glory? Upon this ground do you "hate all evil ways," every transgression of his holy and perfect law; and herein "exercise thyself to have a conscience void of offense towards God, and towards man"?

Is your heart right toward your neighbor? Do you love, as yourself, all mankind without exception? "If you love those only that love you, what thank have ye?" Do you "love your enemies"? Is your soul full of goodwill, of tender affection toward them? Do you love even the enemies of God, the unthankful and unholy? Do you yearn over them? Could you "wish yourself temporally accursed" for their sake? And do you show this, by "blessing them that curse you, and praying for those that despitefully use you, and persecute you"?

Do you show your love by your works? While you have time, as you have opportunity, do you in fact "do good to all men," neighbors or strangers, friends or enemies, good or bad? Do you do them all the good you can; endeavoring to supply all their wants; assisting them both in body and soul, to the uttermost of your power? If you are thus minded, may every Christian say, yea, if you are but sincerely desirous of it, and following on till you attain, then "thy heart is right, as my heart is with thy heart" (2 Kings 10:15).

The Nature of Spiritual Life

Wherefore henceforth know we no man after the flesh: yea, though we have known Christ after the flesh, yet now henceforth know we him no more.
2 Corinthians 5:16

I have long desired to see something clearly and intelligibly written on these words. This is doubtless a point of no small importance; it enters deeply into the nature of religion; and yet what treatise have we in the English language which is written upon it? Possibly there may be such; but none of them has come to my notice; no, not so much as a single sermon.

This is here introduced by the apostle in a very solemn manner. The words, literally translated, run thus: "He died for all, that they who live," all who live upon the earth, "might not henceforth," from the moment they know him, "live unto themselves," seek their own honor, or profit, or pleasure, "but unto him," in righteousness and true holiness (v. 15). "So that we from this time," we that know him by faith, "know no one," either the rest of the apostles, or you, or any other person, "after the flesh." This uncommon expression, on which the whole doctrine depends, seems to mean: We regard no man according to his former state—his country, riches, power, or wisdom. We consider all men only in their spiritual state, and as they stand related to a better world. Yea, if we have known even Christ after the flesh (which undoubtedly they had done, beholding and loving him as a man, with a natural affection), yet now we know him so no more. We no more knew him as a man, by his face, shape, voice, or manner of conversation. We no more think of him as a man, or love him under that character.

The meaning, then, of this strongly figurative expression appears to be no other than this: From the time that we are created anew in Christ Jesus, we do not think, or speak, or act with regard to our blessed Lord as a mere man. We do not now use any expression with relation to Christ which may not be applied to him, not only as he is man, but as he is "God over all, blessed forever."

26. Walking in the Spirit

Trust in God

God was in Christ, reconciling the world unto himself, not imputing their trespasses unto them; and hath committed unto us the word of reconciliation.
2 Corinthians 5:19

We cannot serve God, unless we *believe* in him. This is the only true foundation of serving him. Therefore, the believing in God, as "reconciling the world to himself, through Christ Jesus," the believing in him, as a loving, pardoning God, is the first great branch of his service.

And thus to believe in God implies *to trust in him as our strength,* without whom we can do nothing, who every moment endues us with power from on high, without which it is impossible to please him; as our help, our only help in time of trouble, who compasses us about with songs of deliverance; as our shield, our defender, and the lifter up of our heads above all our enemies that are round about us.

It implies *to trust in God as our happiness;* as the center of our spirits; the only rest of our souls; the only good who is adequate to all our capacities, and sufficient to satisfy all the desires he has given us.

It implies (what is nearly allied to the other) *to trust in God as our end;* to have an eye to him in all things; to use all things only as means of enjoying him; wheresoever we are, or whatsoever we do, to see him that is invisible, looking on us well pleased, and to refer all things to him in Christ Jesus.

Crucified with Christ

I am crucified with Christ: nevertheless I live; yet not I, but Christ liveth in me: and the life which I now

193

live in the flesh I live by the faith of the Son of God,
who loved me, and gave himself for me.
Galatians 2:20

Whoever desires to have a conscience void of offense, let him see that he lay the right foundation. Let him remember, "other foundation" of this "can no man lay, than that which is laid, even Jesus Christ." And let him also be mindful, that no man builds on him but by a living faith; that no man is a partaker of Christ, until he can clearly testify, "The life which I now live, I live by faith in the Son of God"; in him who is now *revealed* in my heart; who "loved me, and gave himself for me." Faith alone is that evidence, that conviction, that demonstration of things invisible, whereby the eyes of our understanding being opened, and divine light poured in upon them, we "see the wondrous things of God's law," the excellency and purity of it; the height, and depth, and length, and breadth thereof, and of every commandment contained therein. It is by faith that, beholding "the light of the glory of God in the face of Jesus Christ," we perceive, as in a glass, all that is in ourselves, yea, the inmost motions of our souls. And by this alone can that blessed love of God be "shed abroad in our hearts," which enables us so to love one another as Christ loved us. By this is that gracious promise fulfilled unto all the Israel of God, "I will put my laws into their minds, and write [or engrave] them in their hearts" (Heb. 8:10), hereby producing in their souls an entire agreement with his holy and perfect law, and "bringing into captivity every thought to the obedience of Christ."

And, as an evil tree cannot bring forth good fruit, so a good tree cannot bring forth evil fruit. As the heart therefore of a believer, so likewise his life, is thoroughly conformed to the rule of God's commandments; in a consciousness whereof, he can give glory to God, and say with the apostle, "This is our rejoicing, the testimony of our conscience, that in simplicity and godly sincerity, not with fleshly wisdom, but by the grace of God, we have had our conversation in the world."

Walking After the Spirit

This I say then, Walk in the Spirit, and ye shall not
fulfil the lust of the flesh.
Galatians 5:16

They who "walk after the Spirit" are also led by him into all holiness of conversation. Their "speech is always in grace, seasoned with salt"; with the love and fear of God. "No corrupt communication comes out of their mouth, but only that which is good"; that which is "to the use of edifying"; which is "meet to minister grace to the hearers." And herein likewise do they exercise themselves day and night, to do only the things which please God; in all their outward behavior to follow him, "who left us an example that we might tread in his steps"; in all their intercourse with their neighbor to walk in justice, mercy, and truth; and "whatsoever they do," in every circumstance of life, to "do all to the glory of God."

These are they who indeed "walk after the Spirit." Being filled with faith and with the Holy Ghost, they possess in their hearts, and show forth in their lives, in the whole course of their words and actions, the genuine fruits of the Spirit of God, namely, "love, joy, peace, longsuffering, gentleness, goodness, fidelity, meekness, temperance," and whatsoever else is lovely or praiseworthy. They "adorn in all things the gospel of God our Savior"; and give full proof to all mankind, that they are indeed actuated by the same Spirit, "which raised up Jesus from the dead."

Happiness and Fruit

But the fruit of the Spirit is love, joy, peace, longsuffering, gentleness, goodness, faith.
Galatians 5:22

Had there been neither natural nor moral evil in the world, what must have become of patience, meekness, gentleness, longsuffering? It is manifest they could have had no being; seeing all these have evil for their object. If, therefore, evil had never entered into the world, neither could these have had any place in it. For who could have returned good for evil, had there been no evildoer in the universe? How had it been possible, on the supposition, to "overcome evil with good"? Will you say, "But all these graces might have been divinely infused into the hearts of men"? Undoubtedly they might; but if they had, there would have been no use or exercise for them. Whereas in the present state of things we can never long want occasion to exercise them; and the more they are exercised, the more all our graces are strengthened and increased. And in the same proportion as our resignation, our confidence in God, our patience and fortitude, our meekness, gentleness, and longsuffering, together with our faith, and love of God and man, increase, so must our happiness increase, even in the present world.

How to Spend

As we have therefore opportunity, let us do good unto all men, especially unto them who are of the household of faith.
Galatians 6:10

If then a doubt should at any time arise in your mind concerning what you are going to expend, either on yourself or any part of your family, you have an easy way to remove it. Calmly and seriously inquire, (1) In expending this, am I acting according to my character? Am I acting herein, not as a proprietor, but as a steward of my Lord's goods? (2) Am I doing this in obedience to his word? In what scripture does he require me so to do? (3) Can I offer up this action, this expense, as a sacrifice to God through Jesus Christ? (4) Have I reason to believe, that for this very work I shall have a reward at the resurrection of the just? You will seldom need anything more to remove any doubt which arises on this head; but, by this fourfold consideration, you will receive clear light as to the way wherein you should go.

If any doubt still remain, you may further examine yourself by prayer, according to those heads of inquiry. Try whether you can say to the Searcher of hearts, your conscience not condemning you, "Lord, you see I am going to expend this sum, on that food, apparel, furniture. And you know, I act therein with a single eye, as a steward of your goods, expending this portion of them thus, in pursuance of the design you had in entrusting me with them. You know I do this in obedience to your Word, as you command, and because you command it. Let this, I beseech you, be a holy sacrifice, acceptable through Jesus Christ! And give me a witness in myself, that for this labor of love, I shall have a recompense, when you reward every man according to his works." Now if your conscience bear you witness in the Holy Ghost, that this prayer is well pleasing to God, then have you no reason to doubt, but that expense is right and good, and such as will never make you ashamed.

The Seal of the Spirit

In whom ye also trusted, after that ye heard the word of truth, the gospel of your salvation: in whom also after that ye believed, ye were sealed with that holy Spirit of promise.

Ephesians 1:13

We are sealed by the Holy Spirit unto the day of redemption, as a sign of God's property in us, and as a mark that we belong to Christ. And this is, by his appointment, the condition and security of that future happiness, into which he will admit none but those who have received the Spirit of his Son into their hearts. But in whomsoever he finds this mark and character, when he shall come to judge the world, these will he take to himself, and will not suffer the destroyer to hurt them. To this very purpose the prophet Malachi, speaking of those who feared God, says, "They shall be mine, saith the Lord, in the day when I make up my jewels"— that is to say, when I set my seal and mark upon them—"and I will spare them, as a man spareth his own son that serveth him."

Now, if the Holy Spirit be the sign, the seal, and the security of our salvation, then, by grieving him by our sins, we break up this seal with our own hands, we cancel our firmest security, and, as much as in us lies, reverse our own title to eternal life.

Besides this, the Holy Spirit within us is the security of our salvation; he is likewise an earnest of it, and assures our spirits that we have a title to eternal happiness. "The Spirit of God beareth witness with our spirits that we are the children of God." And in order that this inward testimony may be lively and permanent, it is absolutely necessary to attend carefully to the secret operation of the Holy Spirit within us; who, by infusing his holy consolations into our souls, by enlivening our drooping spirits, and giving us a quick relish of his promises, raises bright and joyous sensations in us, and gives a man, beforehand, a taste of the bliss to which he is going. In this sense, God is said, by the apostle to the Corinthians, to have "sealed us, and to have given the earnest of his Spirit in our hearts"; and that earnest, not only by way of confirmation of our title to happiness, but as an actual part of that reward at present, the fullness of which we expect hereafter.

Justification and Sanctification

For by grace are ye saved through faith; and that not of yourselves: it is the gift of God.
Ephesians 2:8

We are at present concerned only with that salvation which the apostle is directly speaking of. And this consists of two general parts, justification and sanctification.

Justification is another word for pardon. It is the forgiveness of all our sins; and, what is necessarily implied therein, our acceptance with God. The price whereby this has been procured for us (commonly termed the meritorious cause of our justification) is the blood and righteousness of Christ; or, to express it a little more clearly, all that Christ has done and suffered for us, till he "poured out his soul for the transgressors." The immediate effects of justification are, the peace of God, a "peace that passeth all understanding," and a "rejoicing in hope of the glory of God," "with joy unspeakable and full of glory."

And at the same time that we are justified, yea, in that very moment, sanctification begins. In that instant we are born again, born from above, born of the Spirit: there is a *real* as well as a *relative* change. We are inwardly renewed by the power of God. We feel "the love of God shed abroad in our heart, by the Holy Ghost which is given unto us," producing love to all mankind, and more especially to the children of God; expelling the love of the world, the love of pleasure, of ease, of honor, of money; together with pride, anger, self-will, and every other evil temper; in a word, changing the earthly, sensual, devilish mind, into "the mind which was in Christ Jesus."

198

27. Walking in Love

The Nature of Grace

By grace you have been saved through faith; and this is not your own doing, it is the gift of God—not because of works, lest any man should boast.
Ephesians 2:8, 9 (RSV)

Grace is the free gift of God, which he bestows, not on those who are worthy of his favor, not on such as are previously holy, and so fit to be crowned with all the blessings of his goodness; but on the ungodly and unholy; on those who till that hour were fit only for everlasting destruction; those in whom was no good thing, and whose only plea was, "God be merciful to me, a sinner!" No merit, no goodness in man precedes the forgiving love of God. His pardoning mercy supposes nothing in us but a sense of mere sin and misery; and to all who see, and feel, and own their wants, and their utter inability to remove them, God freely gives faith, for the sake of him in whom he is always "well pleased."

Doing Good

For we are his workmanship, created in Christ Jesus unto good works, which God hath before ordained that we should walk in them.
Ephesians 2:10

God's permission of Adam's fall gave all his posterity a thousand opportunities of suffering, and thereby of exercising all those passive graces which increase both their holiness and happiness. It gives them opportunities of doing good in numberless instances; of exercising themselves in various good works, which otherwise could have had no being. And what exertions of benevolence, of compassion, of godlike mercy, had then been totally prevented! Who could then have said to the Lover of men—

> Thy mind throughout my life be shown;
> While listening to the wretch's cry,
> The widow's or the orphan's groan,
> On mercy's wings I swiftly fly,
> The poor and needy to relieve;
> Myself, my all for them to give?

It is the just observation of a benevolent man—

> All worldly joys are less
> Than that one joy of doing kindness.

Surely in "keeping this commandment," if no other, "there is great reward." "As we have time, let us do good unto all men"; good of every kind, and in every degree. Accordingly, the more good we do (other circumstances being equal), the happier we shall be. The more we deal our bread to the hungry, and cover the naked with garments—the more we relieve the stranger and visit them who are sick or in prison—the more kind offices we do to those who groan under the various evils of human life— the more comfort we give even in the present world, the greater the recompense we have in our own bosom.

Christians—Creatures Capable of God

> *That at that time ye were without Christ, being aliens from the commonwealth of Israel, and strangers from the covenants of promise, having no hope, and without God in the world.*
> ### Ephesians 2:12

If it is this which distinguishes men from beasts—that they are creatures capable of God, capable of knowing and loving and enjoying him; then whoever is "without God in the world," whoever does not know or love or enjoy God, and is not careful about the matter, does, in effect, disclaim the nature of man, and degrade himself into a beast. Let such vouchsafe a little attention to those remarkable words of Solomon: "I said in my heart concerning the estate of the sons of men, They might see that they themselves are beasts" (Eccles. 3:18.) These sons of men are undoubtedly beasts; and that by their own act and deed; for they deliberately and willfully disclaim the sole characteristic of human nature. It is true, they may have a share of reason; they have speech, and they walk erect; but they have not the mark, the only mark, which totally separates man from the brute creation. "That which befalleth beasts, the same thing befalleth them." They are equally without God in the world; "so that a man" of this kind "hath no preeminence above a beast."

So much more let all those who are of a nobler turn of mind assert the distinguishing dignity of their nature. Let all who are of a more generous spirit know and maintain their rank in the scale of beings. Rest not till you enjoy the privilege of humanity— the knowledge and love of God. Lift up your heads, ye creatures capable of God! Lift up your hearts to the Source of your being!

The Nature of Christian Faith

For through him we both have access by one Spirit unto the Father.
Ephesians 2:18

What faith is it then through which we are saved? It may be answered: first, in general, it is a faith in Christ; Christ, and God through Christ, are the proper objects of it. Herein, therefore, it is sufficiently, absolutely distinguished from the faith, either of ancient or modern heathens. And from the faith of a devil, it is fully distinguished by this: It is not barely a speculative, rational thing, a cold, lifeless assent, a train of ideas in the head; but also a disposition of the heart. For thus says the Scripture, "With the heart man believeth unto righteousness." And, "If thou shalt confess with thy mouth the Lord Jesus, and shalt believe with thy heart, that God hath raised him from the dead, thou shalt be saved."

And herein does it differ from that faith which the apostles themselves had while our Lord was on earth, that it acknowledges the necessity and merit of his death, and the power of his resurrection. It acknowledges his death as the only sufficient means of redeeming man from death eternal, and his resurrection as the restoration of us all to life and immortality; inasmuch as he "was delivered for our sins, and rose again for our justification." Christian faith is, then, not only an assent to the whole gospel of Christ, but also a full reliance on the blood of Christ; a trust in the merits of his life, death, and resurrection; a recumbency upon him as our atonement and our life, *as given for us,* and *living in us.* It is a sure confidence which a man has in God, that through the merits of Christ, *his* sins are forgiven, and *he* is reconciled to the favor of God.

The Manifold Wisdom of God

To the intent that now unto the principalities and powers in heavenly places might be known by the church the manifold wisdom of God, According to the eternal purpose which he purposed in Christ Jesus our Lord.
Ephesians 3:10, 11

The riches both of the wisdom and the knowledge of God are most eminently displayed in his church; in planting it like a grain of mustard seed, the least of all seeds; in preserving and continually increasing it, till it grew into a great tree, notwithstanding the uninterrupted opposition of all the powers of darkness. This the apostle justly terms *the manifold wisdom of God.* It is an uncommonly expressive word, intimating that his wisdom, in the manner of its operation, is diversified a thousand ways, and exerts itself with infinite varieties. . . .

But a little of this he has been pleased to reveal unto us; and by keeping close to what he has revealed, meantime comparing the Word and the work of God together, we may understand a part of his ways. We may in some measure trace this manifold wisdom from the beginning of the world; from Adam to Noah, from Noah to Moses, and from Moses to Christ. But I would now consider it (after just touching on the history of the church in past ages) only with regard to what he has wrought in the present age, during the last half century; yea, and in this little corner of the world, the British islands only.

202

In the fullness of time, just when it seemed best to his infinite wisdom, God brought his first-begotten into the world. He then laid the foundation of his church; though it hardly appeared till the day of Pentecost. And it was then a glorious church; all the members thereof being "filled with the Holy Ghost"; being "of one heart and of one mind, and continuing steadfastly in the apostles' doctrine, and in fellowship, in the breaking of bread, and in the prayers." In *fellowship;* that is, having all things in common; no man counting anything he had his own—

> Meek, simple followers of the Lamb
> They lived, and thought, and spake the same:
> They all were of one heart and soul,
> And only love inspired the whole.

The Worthy Walk

I therefore, the prisoner of the Lord, beseech you that ye walk worthy of the vocation wherewith ye are called.

Ephesians 4:1

What is it to "walk worthy of the vocation wherewith we are called"? It should always be remembered that the word *walk,* in the language of the apostle, is of a very extensive significance. It includes all our inward and outward motions; all our thoughts, and words, and actions. It takes in, not only everything we do, but everything we either speak or think. It is, therefore, no small thing "to walk," in this sense of the word, "worthy of the vocation wherewith we are called"; to think, speak, and act in every instance, in a manner worthy of our Christian calling.

We are called to walk "with all lowliness": to have the mind in us which was also in Christ Jesus; not to think of ourselves more highly than we ought to think. . . . And suppose this is done—suppose he has now quickened us, infusing life into our dead souls; yet how much of the carnal mind remains! How prone is our heart still to depart from the living God! . . . Who can be duly sensible how much remains in him of his natural enmity to God, or how far he is still alienated from God by the ignorance that is in him?

Yea, suppose God has now thoroughly cleansed our heart, and scattered the last remains of sin; yet how can we be sensible enough of our own helplessness, our utter inability to all good, unless we are every hour, yea, every moment, endued with power from on high? Who is able to think one good thought, or to form one good desire, unless by that almighty power which works in us both to will and to do of his good pleasure? We have need, even in this state of grace, to be thoroughly and continually penetrated with a sense of this. Otherwise we shall be in perpetual danger of robbing God of his honor, by glorying in something we have received, as though we had not received it.

Walking in Love

Walk . . . with all lowliness and meekness, with longsuffering, forbearing one another in love.
Ephesians 4:1, 2

Walk with all "longsuffering." This is nearly related to meekness, but implies something more. It carries on the victory already gained over all your turbulent passions; notwithstanding all the powers of darkness, all the assaults of evil men or evil spirits. It is patiently triumphant over all opposition, and unmoved though all the waves and storms thereof go over you. Though provoked ever so often, it is still the same—quiet and unshaken; never being "overcome of evil," but overcoming evil with good.

The "forbearing one another in love" seems to mean not only not resenting anything, and not avenging yourselves; not only not injuring, hurting, or grieving each other, either by word or deed; but also bearing one another's burdens; yea, and lessening them by every means in our power. It implies sympathizing with them in their sorrows, afflictions, and infirmities; bearing them up when, without our help, they would be liable to sink under their burdens; endeavoring to lift their sinking heads, and to strengthen their feeble knees.

The true members of the church of Christ "endeavor," with all possible diligence, with all care and pains, with unwearied patience (and all will be little enough), to "keep the unity of the Spirit in the bond of peace"; to preserve inviolate the same spirit of lowliness and meekness, of longsuffering, mutual forbearance, and love; and all these cemented and knit together by that sacred tie—the peace of God filling the heart. Thus only can we be and continue living members of that church which is the body of Christ.

28. Of Faith and Joy

Faith Is Assurance

There is one body, and one Spirit, even as ye are called in one hope of your calling.
Ephesians 4:4

Taking the word in a more particular sense, faith is a divine *evidence* and *conviction,* not only that "God was in Christ, reconciling the world unto himself," but also that Christ loved *me,* and gave himself for *me.* It is by this faith (whether we term it the *essence,* or rather a *property* thereof) that we *receive Christ;* that we receive him in all his offices, as our Prophet, Priest, and King. It is by this that he is "made of God unto us wisdom, and righteousness, and sanctification, and redemption."

"But is this *the faith of assurance,* or *faith of adherence?*" The Scripture mentions no such distinction. The apostle says, "There is one faith, and one hope of our calling"; one Christian, saving faith; "as there is one Lord," in whom we believe, and "one God and Father of us all." And it is certain, this faith necessarily implies an *assurance* (which is here only another word for *evidence,* it being hard to tell the difference between them) that Christ loved me, and gave himself for me. For "he that believeth," with the true living faith, "hath the witness in himself"; "The Spirit witnesseth with his spirit, that he is a child of God." "Because he is a son, God hath sent forth the Spirit of his Son into his heart, crying, Abba, Father"; giving him an assurance that he is so, and a childlike confidence in him. But let it be observed that, in the very nature of the thing, the assurance goes before the confidence. For a man cannot have a childlike confidence in God till he knows he is a child of God. Therefore confidence, trust, reliance, adherence, or whatever else it be called, is not the first, as some have supposed, but the second branch or act of faith.

206

The New Man

And that ye put on the new man, which after God is created in righteousness and true holiness. . . . And have put on the new man, which is renewed in knowledge after the image of him that created him.
**Ephesians 4:24;
Colossians 3:10**

[St. Paul] writes to the Christians at Ephesus, of "putting on the new man, which is created after God, in righteousness and true holiness"; and to the Colossians, of "the new man renewed after the image of him that created him"; plainly referring to the words in Genesis (1:27), "So God created man in his own image." Now, the moral image of God consists (as the apostle observes) "in righteousness and true holiness." By sin this is totally destroyed. And we never can recover it, till we are "created anew in Christ Jesus." And this is perfection.

St. Peter expresses it in a still different manner, though to the same effect: "As he which hath called you is holy, so be ye holy in all manner of conversation" (1 Peter 1:15). According to this apostle, then, perfection is another name for universal holiness: inward and outward righteousness—holiness of life, arising from holiness of heart.

If any expressions can be stronger than these, they are those of St. Paul to the Thessalonians (1 Thess. 5:23): "The God of peace himself sanctify you wholly; and may the whole of you, the spirit, the soul, and the body" (this is the literal translation) "be preserved blameless unto the coming of our Lord Jesus Christ."

God Is Light

Wherefore he saith, Awake thou that sleepest, and arise from the dead, and Christ shall give thee light.
Ephesians 5:14

How encouraging a consideration is this, that whosoever you are who obey his call, you cannot seek his face in vain! If you even now awake and arise from the dead, he has bound himself to give you light. The Lord shall give you grace and glory; the light of his grace here, and the light of his glory when you receive the crown that fades not away. "The light shall break forth as the morning, and thy darkness be as the noonday." "God, who commands the light to shine out of darkness, shall shine in your heart; to give the knowledge of the glory of God in the face of Jesus Christ." "On them that fear the Lord shall the Sun of righteousness arise, with healing in his wings." And in that day it shall be said unto you, "Arise, shine; for thy light is come, and the glory of the Lord is risen upon thee." For Christ shall reveal himself in you, and he is the true light.

God is light, and will give himself to every awakened sinner who waits for him; and you shall then be a temple of the living God, and Christ shall "dwell in thy heart by faith"; and, "being rooted and grounded in love, thou shalt be able to comprehend with all saints, what is the breadth, and length, and depth, and height of that love of Christ which passeth knowledge, that thou mayest be filled with all the fullness of God."

You see your calling, brethren. We are called to be "a habitation of God through his Spirit"; and through his Spirit dwelling in us, to be saints here, and partakers of the inheritance of the saints in light. So exceeding great are the promises which are given unto us, actually given unto us who believe! For by faith we "receive, not the spirit of the world, but the Spirit which is of God," the sum of all the promises, "that we may know the things that are freely given to us of God."

The Mind of Christ

Let this mind be in you, which was also in Christ Jesus.
Philippians 2:5

He to whom this character belongs, and he alone, is a Christian. To him the one eternal, omnipresent, all-perfect Spirit, is the "Alpha and Omega, the first and the last," not his Creator only, but his Sustainer, his Preserver, his Governor; yea, his Father, his Savior, Sanctifier, and Comforter. This God is his God, and his All, in time and in eternity. It is the benevolence springing from this root which is pure and undefiled religion. But if it be built on any other foundation, as it is of no avail in the sight of

God, so it brings no real, solid, permanent happiness to man, but leaves him still a poor, dry, indigent, and dissatisfied creature.

Let all therefore who desire to please God condescend to be taught of God, and take care to walk in that path which God himself has appointed. Beware of taking half of this religion for the whole; but take both parts of it together. And see that you begin where God himself begins: "Thou shalt have no other gods before me." Is not this the first, our Lord himself being the Judge, as well as the great, commandment? First, therefore, see that you love God; next, your neighbor—every child of man. From this fountain let every temper, every affection, every passion flow. So shall that "mind be in you which was also in Christ Jesus." Let all your thoughts, words, and actions spring from this! So shall you "inherit the kingdom prepared for you from the beginning of the world."

Working Out Your Salvation

And that every tongue should confess that Jesus Christ is Lord, to the glory of God the Father.
Philippians 2:11

What are the steps which the Scriptures direct us to take, in the working out of our own salvation? The prophet Isaiah gives us a general answer, touching the first steps which we are to take: "Cease to do evil; learn to do well." If ever you desire that God should work in you that faith, from which comes both present and eternal salvation, by the grace already given flee all sin as from the face of a serpent; carefully avoid every evil word and work; yea, abstain from all appearance of evil. And "learn to do well"; be zealous of good works, of works of piety, as well as works of mercy; family prayer, and crying to God in secret. Fast in secret, and "your Father which seeth in secret, he will reward you openly." "Search the Scriptures"; hear them in public, read them in private, and meditate therein. At every opportunity, be a partaker of the Lord's Supper. "Do this in remembrance" of him; and he will meet you at his own table. Let your conversation be with the children of God; and see that it "be in grace, seasoned with salt." As you have time, do good unto all men; to their souls and to their bodies. And herein "be ye steadfast, unmovable, always abounding in the work of the Lord." It then only remains, that you deny yourselves and take up your cross daily. Deny yourselves every pleasure which does not prepare you for taking pleasure in God, and willingly embrace every means of drawing near to God, though it be a cross, though it be grievous to flesh and blood. Thus when you have redemption in the blood of Christ, you will "go on to perfection"; till "walking in the light as he is in the light," you are enabled to testify that "he is faithful and just," not only to "forgive" your sins," but to "cleanse" you "from all unrighteousness."

God's Work and Our Work

Wherefore, my beloved, as ye have always obeyed, not as in my presence only, but now much more in my absence, work out your own salvation with fear and trembling. For it is God which worketh in you both to will and to do of his good pleasure.
Philippians 2:12, 13

If God works in you, then *work out* your own salvation. The original word, rendered work out, implies the doing a thing thoroughly. *Your own;* for you yourselves must do this, or it will be left undone forever. Your *own salvation:* Salvation begins with what is usually termed (and very properly) *preventing grace;* including the first wish to please God, the first dawn of light concerning his will, and the first slight transient conviction of having sinned against him. All these imply some tendency toward life; some degree of salvation; the beginning of a deliverance from a blind, unfeeling heart, quite insensible of God and the things of God. Salvation is carried on by *convincing grace,* usually in Scripture termed *repentance;* which brings a larger measure of self-knowledge, and a further deliverance from the heart of stone. Afterward we experience the proper Christian salvation: whereby, "through grace," we "are saved by faith"; consisting of those two grand branches, justification and sanctification. By justification we are saved from the guilt of sin, and restored to the favor of God; by sanctification we are saved from the power and root of sin, and restored to the image of God. All experience, as well as Scripture,

210

shows this salvation to be both instantaneous and gradual. It begins the moment we are justified, in the holy, humble, gentle, patient love of God and man. It gradually increases from that moment, as "a grain of mustard-seed, which, at first, is the least of all seeds," but afterward puts forth large branches, and becomes a great tree; till, in another instant, the heart is cleansed from all sin, and filled with pure love to God and man. But even that love increases more and more, till we "grow up in all things into him that is our Head"; till we attain "the measure of the stature of the fullness of Christ."

Grace and the Ground of the Christian's Joy

But what things were gain to me, those I counted loss for Christ. Yea doubtless, and I count all things but loss for the excellency of the knowledge of Christ Jesus my Lord: for whom I have suffered the loss of all things, and do count them but dung, that I may win Christ.
Philippians 3:7, 8

It could not be that ever he should attain to this, but by "excellent knowledge of Jesus Christ" our Lord; or "by the grace of God"— another expression of nearly the same import. By "the grace of God" is sometimes to be understood that free love, that unmerited mercy, by which I a sinner, through the merits of Christ, am now reconciled to God. But in this place it rather means that power of God, the Holy Ghost, which "worketh in us both to will and to do of his good pleasure." As soon as ever the grace of God in the former sense, his pardoning love, is manifested to our souls, the grace of God in the latter sense, the power of his Spirit, takes place therein. And now we can perform, through God, what to man was impossible. Now we can order our conversation aright. We can do all things in the light and power of that love, through Christ who strengthens us. . . .

This is properly the ground of a Christian's joy. We may now therefore readily conceive, how he that has this testimony in himself rejoices evermore. "My soul," may he say, "doth magnify the Lord and my spirit rejoiceth in God my Savior.". . . I rejoice, because his Spirit bears witness to my spirit, that I am bought with the blood of the Lamb; and that, believing in him, "I am a member of Christ, a child of God, and an inheritor of the kingdom of heaven." I rejoice, because the sense of God's love to me has, by the same Spirit, wrought in me to love him, and to love for his sake every soul he has made. I rejoice because he gives me to feel in myself "the mind that was in Christ."

29. *Faith Is Growing*

Perfection and Growing in Grace

Not as though I had already attained, either were already perfect: but I follow after, if that I may apprehend that for which also I am apprehended of Christ Jesus.

Philippians 3:12

Nor can we expect till then to be wholly free from temptation. Such perfection doesn't belong to this life. It is true, there are those who, being given up to work all uncleanness with greediness, scarce perceive the temptations which they resist not; and so seem to be without temptation. There are also many, whom the wise enemy of souls, seeing to be fast asleep in the dead form of godliness, will not tempt to gross sin, lest they should awake before they drop into everlasting burnings. I know there are also children of God, who, being now justified freely, having found redemption in the blood of Christ, for the present feel no temptation. God has said to their enemies, "Touch not mine anointed, and do my children no harm." And for this season, it may be for weeks or months, he causes them to ride on high places, he bears them as on eagles' wings, above all the fiery darts of the wicked one. But this state will not last always, as we may learn from that single consideration, that the Son of God himself, in the days of his flesh, was tempted even to the end of his life. Therefore, so let his servant expect to be; for "it is enough that he be as his Master."

Christian perfection, therefore, does not imply (as some men seem to have imagined) an exemption either from ignorance, or mistake, or infirmities, or temptations. Indeed, it is only another term for holiness. They are two names for the same thing. Thus, every one who is holy is, in the Scripture sense, perfect. Yet we may, lastly, observe that neither in this respect is there any absolute perfection on earth. There is *no perfection of degrees* as it is termed;

none which does not admit of a continual improvement. So that however much any man has attained, or in however high a degree he is perfect, he still needs to "grow in grace," and daily to advance in the knowledge and love of God his Savior.

Walking and Living by Faith

I press toward the mark for the prize of the high calling of God in Jesus Christ. Let us therefore, as many as be perfect, be thus minded: and if in any thing ye be otherwise minded, God shall reveal even this unto you. Nevertheless, whereto we have already attained, let us walk by the same rule, let us mind the same thing.
Philippians 3:14–16

Brethren, are you of this number? . . . Do you see "him that is invisible?" Have you faith, living faith, the faith of a child? Can you say, "The life that I now live, I live by faith in the Son of God, who loved me, and gave himself for me?" Do you "walk by faith?"

Observe the question. I do not ask whether you curse, or swear, or profane the Sabbath, or live in any outward sin. I do not ask whether you do good, more or less, or attend all the ordinances of God. But, suppose you are blameless in all these respects, I ask, in the name of God, by what standard do you judge of the value of things—by the visible or the invisible world? Bring the matter to an issue in a single instance. Which do you judge best— that your son should be a pious cobbler, or a profane lord? Which appears in you most eligible—that your daughter should be a child of God, and walk on foot, or a child of the devil, and ride in a coach-and-six? When the question is concerning marrying your daughter, if you consider her body more than her soul, take knowledge of yourself: you are in the way to hell, and not to heaven, for you walk by sight, and not by faith. I do not ask whether you live in any outward sin or neglect; but, do you seek, in the general tenor of your life, "the things that are above," or the things that are below? Do you "set your affection on things above," or on "things of the earth"? . . . My dear friends, let every man, every woman among you deal honestly with yourselves. Ask your own heart, "What am I seeking day by day? What am I desiring? What am I pursuing—earth or heaven? The things that are seen, or the things that are not seen?" What is your object, God or the world? As the Lord liveth, if the world is your object, still all your religion is in vain.

Putting God First

For this cause we also, since the day we heard it, do not cease to pray for you, and to desire that ye might be filled with the knowledge of his will in all wisdom and spiritual understanding.
Colossians 1:9

Agreeable to this his one desire, is the one design of St. Paul's life, namely, "not to do his own will, but the will of him that sent him." His one intention at all times and in all things is, not to please himself, but him whom his soul loves. He has a single eye. And because "his eye is single, his whole body is full of light." Indeed, where the loving eye of the soul is continually fixed upon God, there can be no darkness at all, "but the whole is light; as when the bright shining of a candle doth enlighten the house." God then reigns alone. All that is in the soul is holiness to the Lord. There is not a motion in his heart, but is according to his will. Every thought that arises points to him, and is in obedience to the law of Christ.

The God of Motion

And he is before all things, and by him all things consist.
Colossians 1:17

I would particularly remark (what perhaps has not been sufficiently observed), that God is the true Author of all the *motion* that is in the universe. To spirits, indeed he has given a small degree of self-moving power, but not to matter. All matter, of whatever kind it be, is absolutely and totally inert. It does not—cannot, in any case—move itself; and whenever any part of it seems to move, it is in reality moved by something else. See that log, which, vulgarly speaking, *moves* on the sea! It is in reality *moved* by the water. The water is moved by the wind; that is, a current of air. And the air itself owes all its motion to the ethereal fire, a particle of which is attached to every particle of it. Deprive it of that fire, and it moves no longer; it is fixed; it is as inert as sand. Remove fluidity (owing to the ethereal fire intermixed with it) from water, and it has no more motion than the log. Impact fire into iron, by hammering it when red hot, and it has no more motion than fixed air, or frozen water. But when it is unfixed, when it is in its most active state, what gives motion to fire? The very heathen will tell you. It is,

> Making your souls his loved abode,
> The temples of indwelling God.

The Christian's Business

Whatsoever ye do in word or deed, do all in the name of the Lord Jesus, giving thanks to God and the Father by him.
Colossians 3:17

The generality of Christians, after using some prayer, usually apply themselves to the *business* of their day. Every man who has any pretense to be a Christian will not fail to do this; seeing it is impossible that an idle man can be a good man—sloth being inconsistent with religion. But with what view, for what end, do you undertake and follow your worldly business? "To provide things necessary for myself and my family." It is a good answer, as far as it goes; but it does not go far enough. For a Turk or a heathen goes so far—does his work for the very same ends. But a Christian may go abundantly farther: his end in all his labor is to please God; to do, not his own will, but the will of him who sent him into the world—for this very purpose, to do the will of God on earth as angels do in heaven. He works for eternity. He "labors not for the meat that perisheth," (this is the smallest part of his motive,) "but for that which endureth to everlasting life."

Thanksgiving and Prayer

Continue in prayer, and watch in the same with thanksgiving.

Colossians 4:2

What thankfulness becomes those who have escaped the corruption that is in the world; whom God has chosen out of the world, to be holy and unblamable. "Who is it that maketh thee to differ?" "And what hast thou which thou has not received?" Is it not God alone "who worketh in thee both to will and to do of his good pleasure"? "And let those give thanks whom the Lord hath redeemed and delivered from the hand of the enemy." Let us praise him, that he has given us to see the deplorable state of all that are round about us, to see the wickedness which overflows the earth, and yet not be borne away by the torrent! We see the general, the almost universal contagion; and yet it cannot approach to hurt us! Thanks be unto him "who hath delivered us from so great a death, and doth still deliver"! And have we not further ground for thankfulness, yea, and strong consolation, in the blessed hope which God has given us, that the time is at hand, when righteousness shall be as universal as unrighteousness is now? Allowing that "the whole creation now groaneth together" under the sin of man, our comfort is, it will not always groan. God will arise and maintain his own cause; and the whole creation shall then be delivered both from moral and natural corruption. Sin, and its consequence, pain, shall be no more. Holiness and happiness will cover the earth. Then shall all the ends of the world see the salvation of our God; and the whole race of mankind shall know, and love, and serve God, and reign with him forever and ever!

Zeal Is Fervent Love

Epaphras, who is one of you, a servant of Christ, saluteth you, always labouring fervently for you in prayers, that ye may stand perfect and complete in all the will of God. For I bear him record, that he hath a great zeal for you, and them that are in Laodicea, and them in Hierapolis.

Colossians 4:12, 13

217

When any of our passions are strongly moved on a religious account, whether for anything good, or against anything which we conceive to be evil, this we term *religious zeal*.

But it is not all that is called religious zeal which is worthy of that name. It is not properly religious or Christian zeal, if it be not joined with charity. A fine writer (Bishop Sprat) carries the matter further still. "It has been affirmed," says that great man, "no zeal is right, which is not charitable, but is mostly so. Charity, or love, is not only one ingredient, but the chief ingredient in its composition." May we not go further still? May we not say, that true zeal is not mostly charitable, but wholly so? That is, if we take charity, in St. Paul's sense, for love; the love of God and our neighbor. For it is a certain truth (although little understood in the world), that Christian zeal is all love. It is nothing else. The love of God and man fills up its whole nature.

Yet it is not every degree of that love to which this appellation is given. There may be some love, a small degree of it, where there is not zeal. But it is, properly, love in a higher degree. It is *fervent love*. True Christian zeal is not other than the flame of love. This is the nature, the inmost essence, of it. Epaphras was this kind of man.

30. A Creed for Christians

Pray Without Ceasing

Pray without ceasing.
1 Thessalonians 5:17

What does it mean to "pray without ceasing"? It is given him "always to pray, and not to faint." Not that he is always in the house of prayer; though he neglects no opportunity of being there. Neither is he always on his knees, although he often is, or on his face, before the Lord his God. Nor yet is he always crying aloud to God, or calling upon him in words; for many times "the Spirit maketh intercession for him with groans that cannot be uttered." But at all times the language of his heart is this: "Thou brightness of the eternal glory, unto thee is my heart, though without a voice, and my silence speaketh unto thee." And this is true prayer, and this alone. But his heart is ever lifted up to God, at all times and in all places. In this he is never hindered, much less interrupted, by any person or thing. In retirement or company, in leisure, business, or conversation, his heart is ever with the Lord. Whether he lie down or rise up, God is in all his thoughts; he walks with God continually, having the loving eye of his mind still fixed upon him, and everywhere "seeing him that is invisible."

Created for Good Works

And the very God of peace sanctify you wholly; and I pray God your whole spirit and soul and body be preserved blameless unto the coming of our Lord Jesus Christ.
1 Thessalonians 5:23

To this confidence, that God is both able and willing to sanctify us now, there needs to be added one thing more, a divine evidence and conviction that he does it. In that hour it is done. God says to the inmost soul, "According to thy faith be it unto thee!" Then the soul is pure from every spot of sin; it is clean "from all unrighteousness." The believer then experiences the deep meaning of those solemn words, "If we walk in the light as he is in the light, we have fellowship one with another, and the blood of Jesus Christ his Son cleanseth us from all sin."

"But does God work this great work in the soul gradually or instantaneously?" Perhaps it may be gradually wrought in some; I mean in this sense, they do not advert to the particular moment wherein sin ceases to be. But it is infinitely desirable, were it the will of God that it should be done instantaneously; that the Lord should destroy sin "by the breath of his mouth," in a moment, in the twinkling of an eye. And so he generally does; a plain fact, of which there is evidence enough to satisfy any unprejudiced person. Therefore look for it every moment! Look for it in the way above described; in all those *good works* whereunto you are "created anew in Christ Jesus." There is then no danger: you can be no worse, if you are no better for that expectation. For were you to be disappointed of your hope, still you lose nothing. But you shall not be disappointed of your hope: it will come, and will not tarry. Look for it then every day, every hour, every moment! Why not this hour, this moment? Certainly you may look for it *now,* if you believe it is by faith. And by this token you may surely know whether you seek it by faith or by works. If by works, you want something to be done *first,* before you are sanctified. You think, I must first be or do thus or thus. Then you are seeking it by works unto this day. If you seek it by faith, you may expect it as you are; and if as you are; then expect it now. It is of importance to observe, that there is an inseparable connection between these three points: expect it by faith, expect it as you are, and expect it now! To deny one of them is to deny them all. . . . Stay for nothing; why should you? Christ is ready; and he is all you want. He is waiting for you; he is at the door! Let your inmost soul cry out,

> Come in, come in, thou heavenly guest!
>   Nor hence again remove;
> But sup with me, and let the feast
>   Be everlasting love.

A Mystery Revealed

For the mystery of iniquity doth already work: only he who now letteth will let, until he be taken out of the way.

2 Thessalonians 2:7

In the fullness of time, when iniquity of every kind, when ungodliness and unrighteousness had spread over all nations and covered the earth as a flood, it pleased God to lift up a standard against it by "bringing his first-begotten into the world" (Heb. 1:6). Now, then, one would expect "the mystery of godliness" would totally prevail over "the mystery of iniquity"; that the Son of God would be "a light to lighten the Gentiles," as well as "salvation to his people Israel." All Israel, one would think, yea, and all the earth would soon be filled with the glory of the Lord. . . . How exceeding small was the number of those whose souls were healed by the Son of God himself! . . . And even these were but imperfectly healed; the chief of them being a little before so weak in faith that, though they did not, like Peter, forswear their Master, yet "they all forsook him and fled"—a plain proof that the sanctifying "Spirit was not" then "given, because Jesus was not glorified."

It was then, when he had "ascended up on high, and led captivity captive," that "the promise of the Father" was fulfilled, which they had heard from him. . . . "When the day of Pentecost was fully come, suddenly there came a sound from heaven, as of a rushing mighty wind, and there appeared tongues as of fire: and they were all filled with the Holy Ghost." In consequence of this, three thousand souls received medicine to heal their sickness, were restored to the favor and the image of God under one sermon of St. Peter's (Acts 2:1ff). "And the Lord added to them daily," not *such as should be saved;* a manifest perversion of the text; but "such as were saved." The expression is peculiar; and so indeed is the position of the words, which run thus: "And the Lord added those that were saved daily to the church." First, they "were saved" from the power of sin; then they "were added" to the assembly of the faithful.

How the Holy Spirit Acts

God hath from the beginning chosen you to salvation through sanctification of the Spirit and belief of the truth.

2 Thessalonians 2:13b

The author of faith and salvation is God alone; it is he that works in us both to will and to do. He is the sole Giver of every good gift, and the sole Author of every good work. There is not more of power than of merit in man; but as all merit is in the Son of God, in what he has done and suffered for us, so all power is in the Spirit of God. And therefore every man, in order to believe unto salvation, must receive the Holy Ghost. This is essentially necessary to every Christian, not in order to his working miracles, but in order to faith, peace, joy, and love—the ordinary fruits of the Spirit.

Although no man on earth can explain the particular manner wherein the Spirit of God works on the soul, yet whosoever has these fruits, cannot but know and *feel* that God has wrought them in his heart.

Sometimes he acts more particularly on the understanding, opening or enlightening it (as the Scripture speaks), and revealing, unveiling, discovering to us "the deep things of God."

Sometimes he acts on the wills and affections of men—withdrawing them from evil, inclining them to good, inspiring (breathing, as it were) good thoughts into them through his Holy Spirit. But however it be expressed, it is certain all true faith, and the whole work of salvation, every good thought, word, and work, is altogether by the operation of the Spirit of God.

Goods and Talents

But godliness with contentment is great gain. For we brought nothing into this world, and it is certain we can carry nothing out. And having food and raiment let us therewith be content.

1 Timothy 6:6–8

God has entrusted us with a portion of worldly goods; with food to eat, raiment to put on, and a place where to lay our head; with not only the necessaries but the conveniences of life. Above all, he has committed to our charge that precious talent, which contains all the rest, money; indeed it is unspeakably precious, if we are wise and faithful stewards of it, if we employ every part of it for such purposes as our blessed Lord has commanded us to do.

God has also entrusted us with several talents, which do not properly come under any of these heads. Such is bodily strength; such are health, a pleasing person, an agreeable address; such are learning and knowledge in their various degrees, with all the other advantages of education. Such is the influence which we have over others, whether by their love and esteem of us, or by power; power to do them good or hurt, to help or hinder them in the circumstances of life. Add to these that invaluable talent of time, with which God entrusts us from moment to moment. Add, lastly, that on which all the rest depend, and without which they would all be curses, not blessings: namely, the grace of God, the power of his Holy Spirit, which alone works in us all that is acceptable in his sight.

John Wesley's Creed

But they that will be rich fall into temptation and a snare, and into many foolish and hurtful lusts, which drown men in destruction and perdition.
1 Timothy 6:9

Lay not up for yourselves treasures upon earth. . . . But lay up for yourselves treasures in heaven, where neither moth nor rust doth corrupt, and where thieves do not break through nor steal.
Matthew 6:19, 20

Permit me to speak as freely of myself as I would of another man. I *gain all I can* (namely, by writing) without hurting either my soul or body. I *save all I can,* not willingly wasting anything, not a sheet of paper, not a cup of water. I do not lay out anything, not a shilling, unless as a sacrifice to God. Yet by *giving all I can,* I am effectually secured from "laying up treasures upon earth." Yea, and I am secured from either desiring or endeavoring it, as long as I give all I can. And that I do this, I call all who know me, both friends and foes, to testify.

But some may say, "Whether you endeavor it or no, you are undeniably *rich*. You have more than the necessaries of life." I have. But the apostle does not fix the charge barely on *possessing* any quantity of goods, but on possessing more than we employ according to the will of the Donor.

Words to Rich Men

For the love of money is the root of all evil. . . .
1 Timothy 6:10

Herein, my brethren, let you who are rich be even as I am. Do you that possess more than food and raiment ask, "What shall we do? Shall we throw into the sea what God has given us?" God forbid that you should! It is an excellent talent; it may be employed much to the glory of God. Your way lies plain before your face; if you have courage, walk in it. Having *gained,* in a right sense, *all you can,* and *saved all you can;* in spite of nature, and custom and worldly prudence, *give all you can.* I do not say, "Be a good Jew—giving a tenth of all you possess." I do not say, "Be a good Pharisee; giving a fifth of all your substance." I dare not advise you to give half of what you have; no, nor three-quarters; but all! Lift up your hearts, and you will see clearly, in what sense this is to be done. . . .

O Methodists, hear the word of the Lord! I have a message from God to all men, but to *you* above all. For above forty years I have been a servant to you and to your fathers. And I have not been as a reed shaken with the wind: I have not varied my testimony. I have testified to you the very same thing, from the first day even until now. But "who hath believed our report?" I fear, not many rich. I fear there is need to apply to some of you those terrible words of the apostle, "Go to now, ye rich men! Weep and howl for the miseries which shall come upon you. Your gold and silver is cankered, and the rust of them shall witness against you, and shall eat your flesh, as it were fire." Certainly it will, unless ye both save all you can, and give all you can. But who of you has considered this, since you first heard the will of the Lord concerning it? Who is now determined to consider and practice it? By the grace of God, begin today!

31. Admonitions For Living

Meekness and Faith

> *But thou, O man of God, flee these things; and follow after righteousness, godliness, faith, love, patience, meekness.*
>
> **1 Timothy 6:11**

Very nearly related to patience is *meekness*, if it be not rather a species of it. For may it not be defined, patience of injuries; particularly affronts, reproach, or unjust censure? This teaches us not to return evil for evil, or railing for railing: but contrariwise blessing. Our blessed Lord himself seems to place a peculiar value upon this temper. This he peculiarly calls us to learn of him, if we would find rest for our souls.

But what may we understand by the *work of patience?* "Let patience have its perfect work." It seems to mean, let it have its full fruit or effect. And what is the fruit which the Spirit of God is accustomed to produce hereby, in the heart of a believer? One immediate fruit of patience is peace: a sweet tranquillity of mind; a serenity of spirit, which can never be found, unless where patience reigns. And this peace often rises into joy. Even in the midst of various temptations, those who are enabled "in patience to possess their souls," can witness, not only quietness of spirit, but triumph and exultation. This both

> Lays the rough paths of peevish nature even,
> And opens in each breast a little heaven.

Freedom from Sin

> *For God hath not given us the spirit of fear; but of power, and of love, and of a sound mind.*
>
> **2 Timothy 1:7**

An immediate and constant fruit of this faith whereby we are born of God, a fruit which can in no wise be separated from it, no, not for an hour, is power over sin—power over outward sin of every kind; over every evil word and work; for wheresoever the blood of Christ is thus applied, it "purgeth the conscience from dead works"—and over inward sin; for it purifies the heart from every unholy desire and temper. This fruit of faith St. Paul has largely described in the sixth chapter of his epistle to the Romans. "How shall we," says he, "who [by faith] are dead to sin, live any longer therein?" "Our old man is crucified with Christ, that the body of sin might be destroyed, that henceforth we should not serve sin." "Likewise, reckon ye yourselves to be dead unto sin, but alive unto God, through Jesus Christ our Lord. Let not sin therefore reign [even] in your mortal body," "but yield yourselves into God, as those that are alive from the dead." "For sin shall not have dominion over you. God be thanked, that ye were the servants of sin, but being made free"—the plain meaning is, God be thanked, that though ye were, in time past, the servants of sin, yet now—"being free from sin, ye are become the servants of righteousness."

Preach the Whole Truth

You then, my son, be strong in the grace that is in Christ Jesus, and what you have heard from me before many witnesses entrust to faithful men who will be able to teach others also.
2 Timothy 2:1, 2 (RSV)

Not everyone who talks largely and earnestly on those precious subjects—the righteousness and the blood of Christ—is a gospel minister. . . . If he stops there, if he does not show man's duty, as well as Christ's sufferings; if he does not apply all to the conscience of his hearers; he will never lead them to life, either here or hereafter. . . . Not every one who preaches justification by faith is a gospel minister. He who goes no further than this, who does not insist upon sanctification also, upon all the fruits of faith, upon universal holiness, does not declare the counsel of God, and consequently is not a gospel minister. Who then is a gospel minister in the full Scriptural sense of the word? . . . He that does not put asunder what God has joined, but publishes alike, "Christ dying for us and Christ living in us."

On Riches and Happiness

This know also, that in the last days perilous times shall come. For men shall be lovers of their own selves, covetous . . . lovers of pleasures more than lovers of God.
2 Timothy 3:1–4

O ye lovers of money, hear the word of the Lord. Do you suppose that money, though multiplied as the sand of the sea, can give happiness? Then you are "given up to a strong delusion to believe a lie"—a palpable lie, confuted daily by a thousand experiments. Open your eyes! Look all around you! Are the richest men the happiest? Have those the largest share of contentment who have the largest possessions? Is not the very reverse true? Is it not a common observation that the richest of men are, in general, the most discontented, the most miserable? Had not the far greater part of them more content, when they had less money? Look inside yourselves. If you are increased in goods, are you proportionably increased in happiness? You have more substance; but have you more content? You know that in seeking happiness from riches, you are only striving to drink out of empty cups. And let them be painted and gilded ever so finely, they are empty still.

On Searching the Scriptures

And that from a child thou hast known the holy scriptures, which are able to make thee wise unto salvation through faith which is in Christ Jesus.
2 Timothy 3:15

It should be observed that this is spoken primarily and directly of the Scriptures which Timothy had known from a child; which must have been those of the Old Testament, for the New was not then written. How far then was St. Paul (though he was "not a whit behind the very chief of the apostles," nor, therefore, I presume, behind any man now upon earth) from making light of the Old Testament! Behold this, lest you one day "wonder and perish," you who make so small account of one half the oracles of God! Yea, and that half of which the Holy Ghost expressly declares, that it is "profitable," as a means ordained of God, for this very thing, "for doctrine, for reproof, for correction, for instruction in righteousness"; to the end, "the man of God may be perfect, throughly furnished unto all good works."

Nor is this profitable only for the men of God, for those who walk already in the light of his countenance; but also for those who are yet in darkness, seeking him whom they know not. Thus St. Peter, "We have also a more sure word of prophecy": literally, "And we have the prophetic word more sure"; confirmed by our being "eyewitnesses of his majesty," and "hearing the voice which came from the excellent glory"; unto which (prophetic word: so he styles the holy Scriptures) "ye do well that ye take heed, as unto a light that shineth in a dark place, until the day dawn, and the day star arise in your hearts" (2 Pet. 1:19). Let all therefore, who desire that day to dawn upon their hearts, wait for it in searching the Scriptures.

The Hope of the Resurrection

In hope of eternal life, which God, that cannot lie, promised before the world began.
Titus 1:2

Let the hope of the resurrection engage us patiently to bear whatever troubles we may be exercised with in the present life. The time of our eternal redemption draws near. Let us hold out a little longer, and all tears shall be wiped from our eyes, and we shall never sigh nor sorrow any more. And how soon shall we forget all we endured in this earthly tabernacle, when once we are clothed with the house which is from above! We are now but on our journey toward home, and so must expect to struggle with many difficulties; but it will not be long before we come to our journey's end, and that will make amends for all. We shall then be in a quiet and safe harbor, out of the reach of all storms and dangers. We shall then be at home in our Father's house, no longer exposed to the inconveniences which, so long as we abide abroad in these tents, we are subject to. And let us not forfeit all this happiness, for want of a little more patience. Only let us hold out to the end, and we shall receive an abundant recompense for all the trouble and uneasiness of our passage, which shall be endless rest and peace.

Let this, especially, fortify us against the fear of death: It is now disarmed, and can do us no hurt. It divides us, indeed, from this body awhile; but it is only that we may receive it again more glorious. As God, therefore, said once to Jacob, "Fear not to go down into Egypt, for I will go down with thee, and will surely bring thee up again"; so may I say to all who are born of God, "Fear not to go down into the grave; lay down your heads in the dust; for God will certainly bring you up again, and that in a much more glorious manner."

Love on the Throne

Looking for that blessed hope, and the glorious appearing of the great God and our Savior Jesus Christ; who gave himself for us, that he might redeem us from all iniquity, and purify unto himself a peculiar people, zealous of good works.
Titus 2:13, 14

In a Christian believer *love* sits upon the throne which is erected in the inmost soul; namely, love of God and man, which fills the whole heart, and reigns without a rival. In a circle near the throne are all holy tempers—longsuffering, gentleness, meekness, fidelity, temperance. . . . In an exterior circle are all the *works of mercy,* whether to the souls or bodies of men. By these we exercise all holy tempers; by these we continually improve them, so that all these are real means of grace, although this is not commonly adverted to.

Next to these are those that are usually termed works of piety— reading and hearing the Word; public, family, private prayer, receiving the Lord's Supper; fasting or abstinence. Lastly, that his followers may the more effectually provoke one another to love, holy tempers, and good works, our blessed Lord has united them together in one body, the church, dispersed all over the earth; a little emblem of which, of the church universal, we have in every particular Christian congregation.

This is that religion which our Lord has established upon earth, ever since the descent of the Holy Spirit on the day of Pentecost. This is the entire, connected system of Christianity. And thus the several parts of it rise one above another, from that lowest point, the assembling ourselves together, to the highest—love enthroned in the heart. And hence it is easy to learn the comparative value of every branch of religion. An important property of true zeal is that it is always exercised *in that which is good,* so it is always *proportioned* to that good, to the degree of goodness that is in its object.

32. The Nature of Real Religion

On the Speaking of Evil

To speak evil of no man, to be no brawlers, but gentle, shewing all meekness unto all men.

Titus 3:2

"Speak evil of no man," says the great apostle—as plain a command as, "Thou shalt do no murder." But who, even among Christians, regards this command? Yea, how few are there, that so much as understand it? What is evil speaking? It is not, as some suppose, the same with lying or slandering. All a man says may be as true as the Bible; and yet the saying of it is evil speaking. For evil speaking is neither more nor less than speaking evil of an absent person; relating something evil, which was really done or said by one that is not present when it is related. Suppose having seen a man drunk, or heard him curse or swear, I tell this when he is absent; it is evil speaking. In our language, this is also, by an extremely proper name, termed backbiting. Nor is there any material difference between this and what we usually style talebearing. If the tale be delivered in a soft and quiet manner (perhaps with expressions of goodwill to the person, and of hope that things may not be quite so bad), then we call it whispering. But in whatever manner it be done, the thing is the same; the same in substance, if not in circumstance. Still it is evil speaking; still this command, "Speak evil of no man," is trampled under foot; if we relate to another the fault of a third person, when he is not present to answer for himself. The antidote is found in these words of Jesus:

If thy brother shall trespass against thee, go and tell him his fault between thee and him alone: if he shall hear thee, thou hast gained thy brother.
But if he will not hear thee, then take with thee one or two more, that in the mouth of two or three witnesses every word may be established.

And if he shall neglect to hear them, tell it unto the church: but if he neglect to hear the church, let him be unto thee as a heathen man and a publican (Matt. 18:15–17).

On Serving Others

Are they not all ministering spirits, sent forth to minister for them who shall be heirs of salvation?
Hebrews 1:14

Does not the Scripture teach, "The help which is done upon earth, God doeth it himself"? Most certainly he does. And he is able to do it by his own immediate power. He has no need of using any instruments at all, either in heaven or earth. He wants not either angels or men, to fulfill the whole counsel of his will. But it is not his pleasure so to work. He never did; and we may reasonably suppose he never will. He has always wrought by such instruments as he pleases; but still it is God himself who does the work. Whatever help, therefore, we have either by angels or men, is as much the work of God, as if he were to put forth his almighty arm, and work without any means at all. But he has used them from the beginning of the world; in all ages he has used the ministry both of men and angels. And hereby, especially, is seen "the manifold wisdom of God in the church." Meantime the same glory redounds to him, as if he used no instruments at all.

The grand reason why God is pleased to assist men by men, rather than immediately by himself, is undoubtedly to endear us to each other by these mutual good offices, in order to increase our happiness both in time and eternity. And is it not for the same reason that God is pleased to give his angels charge over us? namely, that he may endear us and them to each other; that by the increase of our love and gratitude to them, we may find a proportionate increase of happiness, when we meet in our Father's kingdom. In the meantime, though we may not worship them (worship is due only to our common Creator), yet we may "esteem them very highly in love for their works' sake." And we may imitate them in all holiness; suiting our lives to the prayer our Lord himself has taught us; laboring to do his will on earth, as angels do it in heaven.

God Omnipotent and Omnipresent

Neither is there any creature that is not manifest in his sight: but all things are naked and opened unto the eyes of him with whom we have to do.
Hebrews 4:13

Nearly allied to the eternity of God, is his omnipresence. As he exists through infinite duration, so he cannot but exist through infinite space; according to his own question, equivalent to the strongest assertion, "Do not I fill heaven and earth, saith the Lord" (heaven and earth, in the Hebrew idiom, implying the whole universe); which, therefore, according to his own declaration, is filled with his presence.

This one, eternal, omnipresent Being is likewise all-perfect. He has, from eternity to eternity, all the perfections and infinitely more than it ever did or ever can enter into the heart of man to conceive; yea, infinitely more than the angels in heaven can conceive. These perfections we usually term the attributes of God.

And he is omnipotent, as well as omnipresent; there can be no more bounds to his power, than to his presence. He "hath a mighty arm; strong is his hand, and high is his right hand." He does whatsoever pleases him, in the heavens, the earth, the sea, and in all deep places. With men we know many things are impossible, but not with God—with him "all things are possible." Whensoever he wills, to do is present with him.

Comparing the Temporal with the Eternal

And being made perfect, he became the author of eternal salvation unto all them that obey him.
Hebrews 5:9

What then is he—how foolish, how mad, in how unutterable a degree of distraction—who, seeming to have the understanding of a man, deliberately prefers temporal things to eternal? Who (allowing that absurd, impossible supposition, that wickedness is happiness—a supposition utterly contrary to all reason, as well as to matter of fact) prefers the happiness of a year, say a thousand years, to the happiness of eternity, in comparison of which, a thousand ages are infinitely less than a year, a day, a moment? especially when we take this into the consideration (which, indeed, should never be forgotten), that refusing a happy eternity implies the choosing of a miserable eternity. For there is not, cannot be, any medium area between everlasting joy and everlasting pain. It is a vain thought which some have entertained, that death will put an end to the soul as well as the body. It will put an end to neither the one nor the other; it will only alter the manner of their existence. But when the body "returns to the dust as it was, the spirit will return to God that gave it." Therefore, at the moment of death, it must be unspeakably happy, or unspeakably miserable; and that misery will *never* end. . . .

And so it must be; such is the constitution of our nature; till nature is changed by almighty grace. But this is no manner of excuse for those who continue in their natural blindness to futurity; because a remedy for it is provided, which is found by all who seek it; yea, it is freely given to all who sincerely ask it. This remedy is faith. . . .

> Faith lends its realizing light,
> The clouds disperse, the shadows fly;
> The invisible appears in sight,
> And God is seen by mortal eye.

The Sum of Christian Perfection

Therefore leaving the principles of the doctrine of Christ, let us go on unto perfection; not laying again the foundation of repentance from dead works, and of faith toward God.
Hebrews 6:1

What is then the perfection of which man is capable while he dwells in a corruptible body? It is complying with that kind command, "My son, give me thy heart." It is "loving the Lord his God with all his heart, and with all his soul, and with all his mind." This is the sum of Christian perfection: it is all comprised in that one word, *love*. The first branch of it is the love of God. And as he who loves God loves his brother also, it is inseparably connected with the second: "Thou shalt love thy neighbor as thy-

234

self." You shall love every man as your own soul, as Christ loved us. "On these two commandments hang all the Law and the Prophets." These contain the whole of Christian perfection.

Another view of this is given us in those words of the great apostle: "Let this mind be in you which was also in Christ Jesus." For although this immediately and directly refers to the humility of our Lord, yet it may be taken in a far more extensive sense, so as to include the whole disposition of his mind, all his affections, all his tempers, both toward God and man. Now, it is certain that as there was no evil affection in him, so no good affection or temper was wanting. So that "whatsoever things are holy, whatsoever things are lovely," are all included in "the mind that was in Christ Jesus."

Going On to Perfection

Therefore let us leave the elementary doctrines of Christ and go on to maturity [perfection].
Hebrews 6:1a (RSV)

I propose to answer some objections to this scriptural account of perfection:

One common objection to it is that there is no promise of it in the Word of God. If this were so, we must give it up; we should have no foundation to build upon. For the promises of God are the only sure foundation of our hope. But surely there is a very clear and full promise that we shall all love the Lord our God with all our hearts. So we read (Deut. 30:6), "Then will I circumcise thy heart, and the heart of thy seed, to love the Lord thy God with all thy heart, and with all thy soul." Equally express is the Word of our Lord, which is no less a promise, though in the form of a command: "Thou shalt love the Lord thy God with all thy heart, and with all thy soul, and with all thy mind" (Matt. 22:37). No words can be stronger than these; no promise can be more express. In like manner, "Thou shalt love thy neighbor as thyself," is as express a promise as a command.

And indeed that general and unlimited promise which runs through the whole gospel dispensation, "I will put my laws in their minds, and write them in their hearts," turns all the com-

235

mands into promises; and, consequently, that among the rest, "Let this mind be in you which was also in Christ Jesus." The command here is equivalent to a promise, and gives us full reason to expect that he will work in us what he requires of us.

With regard to the fruit of the Spirit, the apostle, in affirming, "the fruit of the Spirit is love, joy, peace, longsuffering, gentleness, goodness, fidelity, meekness, temperance," does, in effect, affirm that the Holy Spirit actually works love, and these other tempers, in those that are led by him. So that here also, we have firm ground to tread upon; this Scripture likewise being equivalent to a promise, and assuring us that all these shall be wrought in us, provided we are led by the Spirit.

The Nature of Real Religion

Wherefore he is able also to save them to the uttermost that come unto God by him, seeing he ever liveth to make intercession for them.
Hebrews 7:25

Here then we see in the clearest, strongest light, what is real religion: a restoration of man by him who bruises the serpent's head, to all that the old serpent deprived him of; a restoration, not only to the favor but likewise to the image of God, implying not barely deliverance from sin, but the being filled with the fullness of God. It is plain, if we attend to the preceding considerations, that nothing short of this is Christian religion. Everything else, whether negative or external, is utterly wide of the mark. But what a paradox is this! How little is it understood in the Christian world; yea, in this enlightened age, wherein it is taken for granted, the world is wiser than ever it was from the beginning!

Among all our discoveries, who has discovered this? How few either among the learned or unlearned! And yet, if we believe the Bible, who can deny it? Who can doubt of it? It runs through the Bible from the beginning to the end, in one connected chain; and the agreement of every part of it, with every other, is, properly, the analogy of faith. Beware of taking *anything else:* Do not imagine an outward form, a round of duties, both in public and private, is religion! Do not suppose that honesty, justice, and whatever is called *morality* (though excellent in its place), is religion! And least of all dream that orthodoxy, right opinion (vulgarly called *faith*), is religion. Of all religious dreams, this is the vainest; which takes hay and stubble for gold tried in the fire!

O do not take *anything less than this* for the religion of Jesus Christ! Do not take part of it for the whole! . . . Take no less for his religion, than the "faith that worketh by love"; all inward and outward holiness. Be not content with any religion which does not imply the destruction of all the works of the devil; that is, of all sin. We know weakness of understanding and a thousand infirmities will remain, while this corruptible body remains; but sin need not remain. This is that work of the devil, eminently so called, which the Son of God was manifested to destroy in this present life. He is able, he is willing, to destroy it now, in all that believe in him. . . . He has spoken; and is he not ready likewise to perform? Only "come boldly to the throne of grace," trusting in his mercy; and you shall find, "He saveth to the uttermost all those that come to God through him!"

33. The Path of Patience

Faith—the Evidence of Things Not Seen

Now faith is the substance of things hoped for, the
evidence of things not seen.
Hebrews 11:1

In particular, faith is an evidence to me of the existence of that unseen thing, my own soul. Without this I should be in utter uncertainty concerning it. I should be constrained to ask that melancholy question—

> Hear'st thou submissive, but a lowly birth,
> Some separate particles of finer earth?

But by faith I know it is an immortal spirit, made in the image of God; in his natural and moral image; "an incorruptible picture of the God of glory." By the same evidence I know that I am now fallen short of the glorious image of God; yea, that I, as well as all mankind, am "dead in trespasses and sins." So utterly dead, that "in me dwelleth no good thing"; that I am inclined to all evil, and totally unable to quicken my own soul.

By faith I know that, besides the souls of men, there are other orders of spirits; yea, I believe that

> Millions of creatures walk the earth
> Unseen, whether we wake, or if we sleep.

These I term angels; and I believe part of them are holy and happy, and the other part wicked and miserable. I believe the former of these, the good angels, are continually sent of God "to minister to the heirs of salvation"; who will be "equal to angels" by and by, although they are now a little inferior to them. I believe the latter, the evil angels, called in Scripture, devils, united under one head (termed in Scripture, Satan—emphatically the enemy, the adversary, both of God and man), either range the upper regions; whence they are called "princes of the power of the air"; or, like him, walk about the earth as "roaring lions, seeking whom they may devour."

But I know by faith that, above all these, is the Lord Jehovah . . . and he governs all things in heaven above, in earth beneath, and under the earth. By faith I know "there are Three that bear record in heaven, the Father, the Word, and the Holy Spirit, and that these Three are One"; that the Word, God the Son, "was made flesh," lived and died for our salvation, rose again, ascended into heaven, and now sits on the right hand of the Father. By faith I know that the Holy Spirit is the giver of all spiritual life; of righteousness, peace, and joy in the Holy Ghost; of holiness and happiness, by the restoration of that image of God wherein we are created. Of all these things, faith is the evidence, the sole evidence, to the children of men.

Faith—the Witness of the Spirit

But without faith it is impossible to please him: for he that cometh to God must believe that he is, and that he is a rewarder of them that diligently seek him.
Hebrews 11:6

Unless the servants of God halt by the way, they will receive the adoption of sons. They will receive the faith of the children of God, by his revealing his only begotten Son in their hearts. Thus, the faith of a child is, properly and directly, a divine conviction, whereby every child of God is enabled to testify, "The life that I now live, I live by faith in the Son of God, who loved me, and gave himself for me." And whosoever has this, the Spirit of God witnesses with his spirit, that he is a child of God. So the apostle writes to the Galatians: "Ye are the sons of God by faith. And because ye are sons, God hath sent forth the Spirit of his Son into your hearts, crying, Abba, Father"; that is, giving you a childlike confidence in him, together with a kind affection toward him. This then it is, that (if St. Paul was taught of God, and wrote as he was moved by the Holy Ghost) properly constitutes the difference between a servant of God, and a child of God. "He that believeth," as a child of God, "hath the witness in himself." This the servant does not have. Yet let no man discourage him; rather, lovingly exhort him to expect it every moment.

It is easy to observe that all the sorts of faith which we can conceive are reducible to one or other of the preceding. But let us covet the best gifts and follow the most excellent way. There is no reason why you should be satisfied with the faith of a materialist, a heathen, or a deist; nor, indeed, with that of a servant. I do not know that God requires it at your hands. Indeed, if you have received this, you ought not to cast it away; you ought not in anywise to undervalue it; but to be truly thankful for it. Yet, in the meantime, beware how you rest here; press on till you receive the Spirit of adoption; rest not, till that Spirit clearly witnesses with your spirit that you are a child of God.

Laying Aside the Weights

Let us lay aside every weight, and the sin which doth so easily beset us, and let us run with patience the race that is set before us.
Hebrews 12:1b

In running "the race that is set before us," according to the will of God, there is often a cross lying in the way; that is, something which is not only not joyous, but grievous; something which is contrary to our will, which is displeasing to our nature. What then is to be done? The choice is plain: either we must take up our cross, or we must turn aside from the way of God, "from the holy commandment delivered to us"; if we do not stop altogether, or turn back to everlasting perdition!

In order to heal that corruption, that evil disease, which every man brings with him into the world, it is often needful to pluck out, as it were, a right eye, to cut off a right hand—so painful is either the thing itself, which must be done, or the only means of doing it; the parting, suppose, with a foolish desire, with an inordinate affection; or a separation from the object of it, without which it can never be extinguished. In the former kind, the tearing away such a desire or affection, when it is deeply rooted in the soul, is often like the piercing of a sword, yea, like "the dividing asunder of the soul and spirit, the joints and marrow." The Lord then sits upon the soul as a refiner's fire, to burn up all the dross thereof. And this is a cross indeed; it is essentially painful; it must be so, in the very nature of the thing. The soul cannot be thus torn asunder, it cannot pass through the fire, without pain.

In the latter kind, the means to heal a sin-sick soul, to cure a foolish desire, an inordinate affection, are often painful, not in the nature of the thing, but from the nature of the disease. So when our Lord said to the rich young man, "Go, sell that thou hast, and give to the poor" (as well knowing, this was the only means of healing his covetousness), the very thought of it gave him so much pain, that "he went away sorrowful"; choosing rather to part with his hope of heaven, than his possessions on earth. This was a burden he could not consent to lift, a cross he would not take up. And in the one kind or the other, every follower of Christ will surely have need to "take up his cross daily."

On Temptation and Joy

My brethren, count it all joy when ye fall into divers temptations.
James 1:2

We are liable to a thousand temptations, from the corruptible body variously affecting the soul. The soul itself, encompassed as it is with infirmities, exposes us to ten thousand more. And how many are the temptations which we meet with even from the good men (such, at least, they are in part, in their general character) with whom we are called to converse from day to day! Yet what are these to the temptations we may expect to meet with from an evil world? seeing we all, in effect, "dwell with Mesech, and have our habitation in the tents of Kedar." Add to this, that the most dangerous of our enemies are not those that assault us openly. No:

> Angels our march oppose,
> Who still in strength excel:
> Our secret, sworn, eternal foes,
> Countless, invisible!

For is not our "adversary the devil, as a roaring lion," with all his infernal legions, still going "about seeking whom he may devour"? This is the case with all the children of men; yea, and with all the children of God, as long as they sojourn in this strange land. Therefore, if we do not willfully and carelessly rush into them, yet we shall surely "fall into divers temptations"; temptations innumerable as the stars of heaven; and those varied and complicated a thousand ways. But, instead of counting this a loss, as unbelievers would do, "count it all joy; knowing that the trial of your faith," even when it is "tried as by fire," "worketh patience." But "let patience have its perfect work, and ye shall be perfect and entire, wanting nothing."

On Faith and Patience

Knowing this, that the trying of your faith worketh patience.
James 1:3

"My brethren," says the apostle in the preceding verse, "count it all joy when ye fall into divers temptations." At first view, this may appear a strange direction; seeing most temptations are "for the present not joyous, but grievous." Nevertheless you know by your own experience, that "the trial of your faith worketh patience"; and if "patience have its perfect work, ye shall be perfect and entire, wanting nothing."

It is not to any particular person, or church, that the apostle gives this instruction; but to all who are partakers of like precious faith, and are seeking after that common salvation. For as long as any of us are upon earth, we are in the region of temptation. He who came into the world to save his people from their sins, did not come to save them from temptation. He himself "knew no sin"; yet while he was in this vale of tears, "he suffered being tempted"; and herein also "left us an example, that we should tread in his steps."

The Perfect Work of Patience

But let patience have her perfect work, that ye may be perfect and entire, wanting nothing.
James 1:4

What is the *perfect work* of patience? Is it anything less than the "perfect love of God," constraining us to love every soul of man, "even as Christ loved us"? Is it not the whole of religion, the whole "mind which was also in Christ Jesus?" Is it not "the renewal of our soul in the image of God, after the likeness of him that created us"? And is not the fruit of this, the constant resignation of ourselves, body and spirit, to God; entirely giving up all we are, all we have, and all we love, as a holy sacrifice, acceptable unto God through the Son of his love? It seems this is "the perfect work of patience," consequent upon the trial of our faith.

Patience Purified and Perfected

But let patience have her perfect work. . . .
James 1:4

Everyone that is born of God, though he be as yet only a "babe in Christ," has the love of God in his heart; the love of his neighbor; together with lowliness, meekness, and resignation. But all of these are then in a low degree, in proportion to the degree of his faith. The faith of a babe in Christ is weak, generally mingled with doubts or fears; with doubts, whether he has not deceived himself; or fear, that he shall not endure to the end. And if, in order to prevent those perplexing doubts, or to remove those tormenting fears, he catches hold of the opinion that a true believer cannot make shipwreck of the faith, experience will sooner or later show that it is merely the staff of a broken reed, which will be so far from sustaining him, that it will only enter into his hand and pierce it. But to return: In the same proportion as he grows in holiness; he increases in love, lowliness, meekness, in every part of the image of God; till it pleases God, after he is thoroughly convinced of inbred sin, of the total corruption of his nature, to take it all away; to purify his heart and cleanse him from all unrighteousness; to fulfill that promise which he made first to his ancient people, and in them to the Israel of God in all ages: "I will circumcise thy heart, and the heart of thy seed, to love the Lord thy God with all thy heart, and with all thy soul."

34. Of Hope and Faith

On Losing Love

For the sun is no sooner risen . . . but it withereth the grass, and the flower thereof falleth, and the grace of the fashion of it perisheth: so also shall the rich man fade away in his ways. Blessed is the man that endureth temptation: for when he is tried, he shall receive the crown of life, which the Lord hath promised to them that love him.

James 1:11, 12

O you that desire or endeavor to be rich, hear the word of the Lord! Why should you be stricken anymore? Will not even experience teach you wisdom? Will you leap into a pit with your eyes open? Why should you any more "fall into temptation"? It cannot be but temptation will beset you, as long as you are in the body. But though it should beset you on every side, why will you *enter into it?* There is no necessity for this: It is your own voluntary act and deed. Why should you any more plunge yourselves *into a snare*, into the trap Satan has laid for you, that is ready to break your bones in pieces, to crush your soul to death? After fair warning, why should you sink any more into "foolish and hurtful desires", desires as inconsistent with wisdom as they are with religion itself; desires that have done you more hurt already than all the treasures upon earth can countervail?

Have they not hurt you already, have they not wounded you in the tenderest part, by slackening, if not utterly destroying, your "hunger and thirst after righteousness"? Have you now the same longing that you had once, for the whole image of God? Have you the same vehement desire as you formerly had, of "going on unto perfection"? Have they not hurt you by weakening your *faith?* Have you now faith's "abiding impression, realizing things to come"? Do you endure, in all temptations, from pleasure or pain, "seeing him that is invisible"? Have you every day, and every hour, an uninterrupted sense of his presence? Have they not hurt you with regard to your *hope?* Have you now a hope full of immortality? Are you still big with earnest expectation of all the great and precious promises? Do you not "taste the powers of the world to come"? Do you "sit in heavenly places with Christ Jesus"?

Have they not so hurt you, as to stab your religion to the heart? Have they not cooled (if not quenched) your *love to God?* This is easily determined. Have you the same delight in God which you once had? Can you now say,

> I nothing want beneath, above;
> Happy, happy in Thy love?

I fear, not. And if your love of God is in anywise decayed, so is also your love of your neighbor. You are then hurt in the very life and spirit of your religion! If you lose love, you lose all.

On Asking and Receiving

Ye have not, because ye ask not.
James 4:2b

"He spake also another parable, to this end, that men ought always to pray, and not to faint," till through this means they should receive of God whatsoever petition they asked of him. "There was in a city a judge which feared not God, neither regarded man. And there was a widow in that city, and she came unto him, saying, Avenge me of my adversary. And he would not for a while; but afterwards he said within himself, Though I fear not God, nor regard man, yet because this widow troubleth me, I will avenge her, lest by her continual coming, she weary me" (Luke 28:1–5). The application of this our Lord himself has made: "Hear what the unjust judge saith!" Because she continues to ask, because she will take no denial, therefore I will avenge her. "And shall not God avenge his own elect which cry day and night unto him? I tell you he will avenge them speedily," if they pray and faint not.

He has given us a direction, equally full and express, to wait for the blessings of God in private prayer, together with a positive promise, that, by this means, we shall obtain the request of our lips. The command comes in those well-known words: "Enter into thy closet; and when thou hast shut thy door, pray to thy Father which is in secret; and thy Father, which seeth in secret, shall reward thee openly" (Matt. 6:6).

If it be possible for any direction to be more clear, it is that which God has given us by the apostle, with regard to prayer of every kind, public or private, and the blessing annexed thereto. "If any of you lack wisdom, let him ask of God, that giveth to all men liberally" (if they ask; otherwise "ye have not, because ye ask not," James 4:2) "and upbraideth not; and it shall be given him" (James 1:5).

If it be objected: but this is no direction to unbelievers, to them who know not the pardoning grace of God, for the apostle adds, "But let him ask in faith," otherwise "let him not think that he shall receive anything of the Lord"; I answer: the meaning of the word *faith,* in this place, is fixed by the apostle himself, as if it were on purpose to obviate this objection, in the words immediately following; "Let him ask in faith, nothing wavering," nothing *doubting,* not doubting but God heareth his prayer, and will fulfill the desire of his heart.

Words about the World

> *Ye adulterers and adulteresses, know ye not that the friendship of the world is enmity with God? whosoever therefore will be a friend of the world is the enemy of God.*
>
> **James 4:4**

What is it which the apostle here means by *the world?* He does not here refer to this outward frame of things, termed in Scripture, heaven and earth; but to the inhabitants of the earth, the children of men, or, at least, the greater part of them. But what part? This is fully determined both by our Lord himself, and by his beloved disciple. First, by our Lord himself. His words are, "If the world hate you, ye know that it hated me before it hated you. If ye were of the world, the world would love its own; but because ye are not of the world, but I have chosen you out of the world, therefore the world hateth you. If they have persecuted me, they will also persecute you. And all these things will they do unto you, because they know not him that sent me" (John 15:18ff.). You see here *"the world"* is placed on one side, and *those who "are not of the world"* on the other. They whom God has "chosen out of the world," namely, by "sanctification of the Spirit, and belief of the truth," are set in direct opposition to those whom he has not so chosen. Yet again: Those "who know not him that sent me," says our Lord, who know not God, they are *"the world."*

Equally express are the words of the beloved disciple. "Marvel not, my brethren, if the world hate you. We know that we have passed from death unto life, because we love the brethren" (1 John 3:13, 17.) As if he had said, "You must not expect any should love you, but those that have 'passed from death unto life.'" It follows, those who are not passed from death unto life, who are not alive to God, are *"the world."* The same we may learn from those words in the fifth chapter, verse 19, "We know that we are of God, and the whole world lieth in the wicked one." Here *"the world"* plainly means, those who are not of God, and who, consequently, "lie in the wicked one."

God Gives More Grace

But he giveth more grace. Wherefore he saith, God resisteth the proud, but giveth grace unto the humble.
James 4:6

It is not easy to conceive what a difference there is between that which the new Christian experiences now, and that which he experienced earlier in his Christian life. Till this spiritual growth was wrought in his soul, all his holiness was *mixed*. He was humble, but not entirely; his humility was mixed with pride. He was meek; but his meekness was frequently interrupted by anger, or some uneasy and turbulent passion. His love of God was frequently damped by the love of some creature; the love of his neighbor, by evil surmising, or some thought, if not temper, contrary to love. His will was not wholly melted down into the will of God.

247

But although in general he could say, "I come 'not to do my own will, but the will of him that sent me' ", yet now and then nature rebelled, and he could not clearly say—"Lord, not as I will, but as thou wilt." His whole soul is now consistent with itself; there is no jarring string. All his passions flow in a continual stream, with an even tenor to God. To him who is entered into this rest, you may truly say,

> Calm thou ever art within,
> All unruffled, all serene!

A Lively Hope

Blessed be the God and Father of our Lord Jesus Christ, which according to his abundant mercy hath begotten us again unto a lively hope by the resurrection of Jesus Christ from the dead.
1 Peter 1:3

Another scriptural mark of those who are born of God is hope. Thus St. Peter, speaking to all the children of God who were then scattered abroad, saith, "Blessed be the God and Father of our Lord Jesus Christ, which according to his abundant mercy, hath begotten us again unto a lively hope" (1 Pet. 1:3). A *lively* or *living* hope, says the apostle; because there is also a *dead* hope, as well as a dead faith; a hope which is not from God, but from the enemy of God and man—as evidently appears by its fruits; for as it is the offspring of pride, so it is the parent of every evil word and work; whereas, every man that has in him this living hope, is "holy as he that calleth him is holy." Every man that can truly say to his brethren in Christ, "Beloved, now are we the sons of God, and we shall see him as he is," "purifieth himself, even as he is pure."

This hope is "the full assurance of faith, and the full assurance of hope," expressions the best which our language could afford (although far weaker than those in the original)—as described in Scripture, implies, first, the testimony of our own spirit or conscience, that we walk "in simplicity and godly sincerity"; but second, and chiefly, the testimony of the Spirit of God, "bearing witness with," or to, "our spirit, that we are the children of God," "and if children, then heirs, heirs of God, and joint heirs with Christ."

Faith That Lives and Rejoices

Wherein ye greatly rejoice, though now for a season, if need be, ye are in heaviness through manifold temptations.

1 Peter 1:6

At the same time that they were "in heaviness," they were possessed of living faith. Their heaviness did not destroy their faith: they still "endured, as seeing him that is invisible."

Neither did their heaviness destroy their peace; the "peace which passeth all understanding"; which is inseparable from true living faith. This we may easily gather from the second verse, wherein the apostle prays, not that grace and *peace* may be *given* them, but only, that it may "be *multiplied* unto them"; that the blessing, which they already enjoyed, might be more abundantly bestowed upon them.

The persons to whom the apostle here speaks were also full of a living hope. For thus he speaks, verse 3, "Blessed be the God and Father of our Lord Jesus Christ, who, according to his abundant mercy, hath begotten us again"—me and you, all of us who are "sanctified by the Spirit," and enjoy the "sprinkling of the blood of Jesus Christ"—"unto a living hope, unto an inheritance"—that is, unto a living hope of an inheritance, "incorruptible, undefiled, and that fadeth not away." So that, notwithstanding their heaviness, they still retained a hope full of immortality.

And they still "rejoiced in hope of the glory of God." They were filled with joy in the Holy Ghost. So, verse 8, the apostle having just mentioned the final "revelation of Jesus Christ," (namely, when he comes to judge the world) immediately adds, "in whom, though now ye see him not [not with your bodily eyes], yet believing, ye rejoice with joy unspeakable and full of glory." Their heaviness, therefore, was not only consistent with living hope, but also with joy unspeakable; at the same time they were thus heavy, they nevertheless rejoiced with joy full of glory. In the midst of their heaviness, they likewise still enjoyed the love of God, which had been shed abroad in their hearts—"whom," says the apostle, "having not seen, ye love." Though ye have not yet seen him face to face; yet, knowing him by faith, ye have obeyed his word, "My son, give me thy heart." He is your God, and your love, the desire of your eyes, and your "exceeding great reward." You have sought and found happiness in him; ye "delight in the Lord," and he has given you your "hearts' desire."

Faith on Trial

That the trial of your faith, being much more precious than of gold that perisheth, though it be tried with fire, might be found unto praise and honour and glory at the appearing of Jesus Christ.
1 Peter 1:7

For what ends then does God permit heaviness to befall so many of his children? The apostle gives us a plain and direct answer to this important question: "That the trial of their faith, which is much more precious than gold that perisheth, though it be tried by fire, may be found unto praise, and honor, and glory, at the revelation of Jesus Christ." There may be an allusion to this in that well-known passage of the fourth chapter (although it primarily relates to quite another thing) "Think it not strange concerning the fiery trial which is to try you: but rejoice that ye are partakers of the sufferings of Christ; that, when his glory shall be revealed, ye may likewise rejoice with exceeding great joy" (v. 12ff.).

Hence we learn that the first and great end of God's permitting the temptations which bring heaviness on his children, is the trial of their faith, which is tried by these, even as gold by the fire. Now we know, gold tried in the fire is purified thereby; is separated from its dross. And so is faith in the fire of temptation; the more it is tried, the more it is purified; yea, and not only purified, but also strengthened, confirmed, increased abundantly, by so many more proofs of the wisdom and power, the love and faithfulness of God. This, then—to increase our faith—is one gracious end of God's permitting those manifold temptations.

They serve to try, to purify, to confirm, and increase that living hope also, whereunto "the God and Father of our Lord Jesus Christ hath begotten us again of his abundant mercy." Indeed our hope cannot but increase, in the same proportion with our faith. On this foundation it stands: Believing in his name, living by faith in the Son of God, we hope for, we have a confident expectation of, the glory which shall be revealed; and, consequently, whatever strengthens our faith, increases our hope also. At the same time it increases our joy in the Lord, which cannot but attend a hope full of immortality. In this view the apostle exhorts believers in the other chapter; "Rejoice, that ye are partakers of the sufferings of Christ." On this very account, "happy are you; for the spirit of glory and of God resteth upon you"; and hereby ye are enabled, even in the midst of sufferings, to "rejoice with joy unspeakable, and full of glory."

35. Christ Is the Example

Be Ye Holy As He Is Holy

But as he which hath called you is holy, so be ye holy in all manner of conversation; Because it is written, Be ye holy; for I am holy.

1 Peter 1:15, 16

The command of God, given by St. Peter, "Be ye holy, as he that hath called you is holy, in all manner of conversation," implies a promise that we shall be thus holy, if we are not wanting to ourselves. Nothing can be wanting on God's part: As he has called us to holiness, he is undoubtedly willing, as well as able, to work this holiness in us. For he cannot mock his helpless creatures, calling us to receive what he never intends to give. That he does call us thereto is undeniable; therefore he will give it if we are not disobedient to the heavenly calling.

The prayer of St. Paul for the Thessalonians, that God would "sanctify" them throughout, and "that the whole of them, the spirit, the soul, and the body, might be preserved blameless," will undoubtedly be heard in behalf of all the children of God, as well as of those at Thessalonica. Hereby, therefore, all Christians are encouraged to expect the same blessing from "the God of peace"; namely, that they also shall be "sanctified throughout, in spirit, soul, and body"; and that "the whole of them shall be preserved blameless unto the coming of our Lord Jesus Christ."

The Glorious Body of Christ

Who by him do believe in God, that raised him up from the dead, and gave him glory; that your faith and hope might be in God.

1 Peter 1:21

Our bodies shall be raised in glory. "Then shall the righteous shine as the sun in the kingdom of their Father." A resemblance of this we have in the luster of Moses's face, when he had conversed with God on the mount. His face shone so bright that the children of Israel were afraid to come near him, till he threw a veil over it. And that extraordinary majesty of Stephen's face seemed to be an earnest of his glory. "All that sat in the council, looking steadfastly on him, saw his face as it had been the face of an angel."

How then, if it shone so gloriously even on earth, will it shine in the other world, when his, and the bodies of all the saints, are made like unto Christ's glorious body! How glorious the body of Christ is, we may guess from his transfiguration. St. Peter, when he saw this as our Lord's face shone like the sun, and his raiment became shining and white as snow, was so transported with joy and admiration, that he knew not what he said. When our Savior discovered but a little of that glory which he now possesses, and which in due time he will impart to his followers, yet that little of it made the place seem a paradise; and the disciples thought that they could wish for nothing better than always to live in such pure light, and enjoy so beautiful a sight. "It is good for us to be here. Let us make three tabernacles"—here let us fix our abode forever. And if they thought it so happy only to be present with such heavenly bodies and to behold them with their eyes, how much happier must it be to dwell in such glorious mansions, and to be themselves clothed with so much brightness!

Salvation and Sacrifice

[Ye are] an holy priesthood, to offer up spiritual sacrifices, acceptable to God by Jesus Christ.
1 Peter 2:5

But what sacrifices shall we offer now, seeing the Jewish dispensation is at an end? If you have truly presented yourselves to God, you offer up to him continually all your thoughts, and words, and actions, through the Son of his love, as a sacrifice of praise and thanksgiving.

Thus you experience that he whose name is called Jesus does

253

not bear that name in vain. He does, in fact, "save his people from their sins," the root as well as the branches. And this salvation from sin, from all sin, is another description of perfection; though indeed it expresses only the least, the lowest branch of it, only the negative part of the great salvation.

Courage Can Come from Trials

> *But sanctify the Lord God in your hearts: and be ready always to give an answer to every man that asketh you a reason of the hope that is in you with meekness and fear.*
>
> **1 Peter 3:15**

How lively is the account which the apostle Peter gives not only of the peace and joy, but of the hope and love, which God works in those patient sufferers "who are kept by the power of God through faith unto salvation." Indeed he appears herein to have an eye to this very passage of St. James: "Though ye are grieved for a season, with manifold temptations that the trial of your faith" (the same expression which was used by St. James) "may be found to praise, and honor, and glory, at the revelation of Jesus Christ; whom, having not seen, ye love; in whom, though now ye see him not, yet believing, ye rejoice with joy unspeakable and full of glory." See here the peace, the joy, and the love, which, through the mighty power of God, are the fruit or "work of patience"!

And as peace, hope, joy, and love are the fruits of patience, both springing from, and confirmed by it, so is also rational, genuine *courage,* which indeed cannot subsist without patience. The brutal courage, or rather fierceness, of a lion may probably spring from impatience; but true fortitude, the courage of a man, springs from just the contrary temper. Christian *zeal* is likewise confirmed and increased by patience, and so is *activity* in every good work.

The Minister As Shepherd

> *Tend the flock of God that is your charge, not by constraint but willingly, not for shameful gain but*

eagerly, not as domineering over those in your charge but being examples to the flock. And when the chief Shepherd is manifested you will obtain the unfading crown of glory.

1 Peter 5:2–4 (RSV)

What is a minister of Christ, a shepherd of souls, unless he is all devoted to God? Unless he abstain, with the utmost care and diligence, from every evil word and work; from all appearance of evil; yea, from the most innocent things, whereby any might be offended or made weak? Is he not called, above others, to be an example to the flock, in his private as well as public character? An example of all holy and heavenly tempers, filling the heart so as to shine through the life? Consequently, is not his whole life, if he walks worthy of his calling, one incessant labor of love; one continued tract of praising God, and helping man; one series of thankfulness and beneficence? Is he not always humble, always serious, though rejoicing evermore; mild, gentle, patient, abstinent? May you not resemble him to a guardian angel, ministering to those "who shall be heirs of salvation"? Is he not one sent forth from God, to stand between God and man, to guard and assist the poor, helpless children of men, to supply them both with light and strength, to guide them through a thousand known and unknown dangers, till at the appointed time he returns, with those committed to his charge, to his and their Father who is in heaven?

Clothed with Humility

All of you be subject one to another, and be clothed with humility: for God resisteth the proud, and giveth grace to the humble. Humble yourselves therefore under the mighty hand of God, that he may exalt you in due time.

1 Peter 5:5b, 6

When our inmost soul is thoroughly tinctured therewith, it remains that we "be clothed with humility." The word used by St. Peter seems to imply that we be covered with it as with a surcoat; that we be all humility, both within and without; tincturing all we think, speak, and do. Let all our actions spring from this fountain; let all our words breathe this spirit; that all men may know we have been with Jesus, and have learned of him to be lowly in heart.

And being taught of him who was meek as well as lowly in heart, we shall then be enabled to "walk with all meekness," being taught of him who teaches as never man taught, to be meek as well as lowly in heart. This implies not only a power over anger, but over all violent and turbulent passions. It implies having all our passions in due proportion; none of them either too strong or too weak; but all duly balanced with each other; all subordinate to reason; and reason directed by the Spirit of God. Let this equanimity govern your whole souls; that your thoughts may all flow in an even stream, and the uniform tenor of your words and actions be suitable thereto. In this "patience" you will then "possess your souls"; which are not our own while we are tossed by unruly passions. And by this all men may know that we are indeed followers of the meek and lowly Jesus.

Watch and Pray

But the God of all grace, who hath called us unto his eternal glory by Christ Jesus, after that ye have suffered a while, make you perfect, stablish, strengthen, settle you.
1 Peter 5:10

We ought always to watch and pray, and use our utmost endeavors to avoid falling into darkness. But we need not be solicitous how to avoid, so much as how to improve by heaviness. Our great care should be so to behave ourselves under it, so to wait upon the Lord therein, that it may fully answer all the design of his love in permitting it to come upon us; that it may be a means of increasing our faith, of confirming our hope, of perfecting us in all holiness. Whenever it comes, let us have an eye to these gracious ends for which it is permitted, and use all diligence, that we may not "make void the counsel of God against ourselves." Let us earnestly work together with him, by the grace of our Lord Jesus Christ, till we are received into his everlasting kingdom!

36. Love Is the Way

The Love of God Perfected in the Christian

But whoso keepeth his word, in him verily is the love of God perfected: hereby know we that we are in him.
1 John 2:5

A true Methodist is one who has "the love of God shed abroad in his heart by the Holy Ghost given unto him," one who "loves the Lord his God with all his heart, and with all his soul, and with all his mind, and with all his strength." God is the joy of his heart, and the desire of his soul; which is constantly crying out, "Whom have I in heaven but thee? and there is none upon earth that I desire beside thee! My God and my all! Thou art the strength of my heart, and my portion forever!"

He is therefore happy in God, yea, always happy, as having in him "a well of water springing up into everlasting life," and overflowing his soul with peace and joy. "Perfect love" having now "cast out fear," he "rejoices evermore." He rejoices "in the Lord always," even "in God his Savior"; and in the Father, "through our Lord Jesus Christ, by whom he hath now received the atonement." "Having" found "redemption through his blood, the forgiveness of his sins," he cannot but rejoice, whenever he looks back on the horrible pit out of which he is delivered; when he sees "all his transgressions blotted out as a cloud, and his iniquities as a thick cloud."

He cannot but rejoice whenever he looks on the state wherein he now is; "being justified freely, and having peace with God through our Lord Jesus Christ." For "he that believeth, hath the witness" of this "in himself"; being now the son of God by faith. "Because he is a son, God hath sent forth the Spirit of his Son into his heart, crying, Abba, Father!" And "the Spirit itself beareth witness with his spirit, that he is a child of God." He rejoices also, whenever he looks forward, "in hope of the glory that shall be revealed"; yea, his joy is full, and all his bones cry out, "Blessed be the God and Father of our Lord Jesus Christ, who, according to his abundant mercy, hath begotten me again to a living hope—of an inheritance incorruptible, undefiled, and that fadeth not away, reserved in heaven for me!"

Love Is Living in the Light

He that loveth his brother abideth in the light, and there is none occasion of stumbling in him.
1 John 2:10

While one always exercises his love to God, by praying without ceasing, rejoicing evermore, and in everything giving thanks, this commandment is written in his heart, "That he who loveth God, loveth his brother also." And he accordingly loves his neighbor as himself; he loves every man as his own soul. His heart is full of love to all mankind, to every child of "the Father of the spirits of all flesh." That a man is not personally known to him, is no bar to his love; no, nor that he is known to be such as he approves not, that he repays hatred for his goodwill. For he "loves his enemies"; yea, and the enemies of God, "the evil and the unthankful." And if it be not in his power to "do good to them that hate him," yet he ceases not to pray for them, though they continue to spurn his love, and still "despitefully use him and persecute him."

For he is "pure in heart." The love of God has purified his heart from all revengeful passions, from envy, malice, and wrath, from every unkind temper or malign affection. It has cleansed him from pride and haughtiness of spirit, whereof alone comes contention. And he has now "put on bowels of mercies, kindness, humbleness of mind, meekness, longsuffering": so that he "forbears and forgives, if he had a quarrel against any; even as God in Christ hath forgiven him." And indeed all possible ground for contention, on his part, is utterly cut off. For none can take from him what he desires; seeing he "loves not the world, nor" any of "the things of the world"; being now "crucified to the world,

258

and the world crucified to him"; being dead to all that is in the world, both to "the lust of the flesh, the lust of the eye, and the pride of life." For "all his desire is unto God, and to the remembrance of his name."

Abiding in Christ

And the world passeth away, and the lust thereof: but he that doeth the will of God abideth forever.
1 John 2:17

They who are of Christ, who abide in him, "have crucified the flesh with its affections and lusts." They abstain from all those works of the flesh; from "adultery and fornication"; from "uncleanness and lasciviousness"; from "idolatry, witchcraft, hatred, variance"; from "emulations, wrath, strife, sedition, heresies, envyings, murders, drunkenness, revellings"; from every design, and word, and work, to which the corruption of nature leads. Although they feel the root of bitterness in themselves, yet are they endued with power from on high, to trample it continually under foot, so that it cannot "spring up to trouble them"; insomuch, that every fresh assault which they undergo, only gives them fresh occasion of praise, of crying out, "Thanks be unto God, who giveth us the victory, through Jesus Christ our Lord."

They now "walk after the Spirit," both in their hearts and lives. They are taught of him to love God and their neighbor, with a love which is as "a well of water, springing up into everlasting life." And by him they are led into every holy desire, into every divine and heavenly temper, till every thought which arises in their heart is holiness unto the Lord.

Our Heavenly Bodies

Beloved, we are God's children now; it does not yet appear what we shall be, but we know that when he appears we shall be like him, for we shall see him as he is.
1 John 3:2 (RSV)

259

This excellency of our heavenly bodies will probably arise, in great measure from the happiness of our souls. The unspeakable joy that we then shall feel will break through our bodies, and shine forth in our countenances; as the joy of the soul, even in this life, has some influence upon the countenance, by rendering it more open and cheerful: So Solomon tells us, "A man's wisdom makes his face to shine." Virtue, as it refines a man's heart, so it makes his very looks more cheerful and lively.

Our bodies shall be raised in power. This expresses the sprightliness of our heavenly bodies, the nimbleness of their motion, by which they shall be obedient and able instruments of the soul. In this state, our bodies are no better than clogs and fetters, which confine and restrain the freedom of the soul. The corruptible body presses down the soul, and the earthly tabernacle weighs down the mind. Our dull, sluggish, inactive bodies are often unable, or too backward, to obey the commands of the soul. But in the other life, "they that wait upon the Lord shall renew their strength; they shall mount up with wings as eagles; they shall run, and not be weary: they shall walk, and not faint." Or, as another expresses it, "they shall run to and fro like sparks among the stubble." The speed of their motion shall be like that of devouring fire in stubble; and the height of it, above the towering of an eagle; for they shall meet the Lord in the air when he comes to judgment, and mount up with him into the highest heaven. This earthly body is slow and heavy in all its motions, listless and soon tired with action. But our heavenly bodies shall be as fire; as active and as nimble as our thoughts are.

The Road to Purity

And every man that hath this hope in him purifieth himself, even as he is pure.
1 John 3:3

And he who has this hope, thus "full of immortality, in everything giveth thanks"; as knowing that this (whatsoever it is) "is the will of God in Christ Jesus concerning him." From him, therefore, he cheerfully receives all, saying, "Good is the will of the Lord"; and whether the Lord gives or takes away, equally "blessing the name of the Lord." For he has "learned, in whatsoever state he is, therewith to be content." He knows "both how to be abased, and how to abound. Everywhere and in all things he is instructed both to be full and to be hungry, both to abound and suffer need." Whether in ease or pain, whether in sickness or health, whether in life or death, he gives thanks from the ground of his heart to him who orders it for good; knowing that as "every good gift cometh from above," so none but good can come from the Father of lights, into whose hand he has wholly committed his body and soul, as into the hands of a faithful Creator. He is therefore "careful" (anxious or uneasy) "for nothing"; as having "cast all his care on him that careth for him," and "in all things" resting on him, after "making his request known to him with thanksgiving."

Destroying the Devil

He that committeth sin is of the devil; for the devil sinneth from the beginning. For this purpose the Son of God was manifested, that he might destroy the works of the devil.

1 John 3:8

How he does this, in what manner and by what steps he does actually destroy them, we are now to consider. First, as Satan began his first work in Eve by tainting her with unbelief, so the Son of God begins his work in man by enabling us to believe in him. He both opens and enlightens the eyes of our understanding. Out of darkness he commands light to shine, and takes away the veil which the "god of this world" had spread over our hearts. And we then see not by a chain of *reasoning,* but by a kind of *intuition,* by a direct view, that "God was in Christ, reconciling the world to himself, not imputing to them their former trespasses"; not imputing them to me. In that day "we know that we are of God," children of God by faith; "having redemption through the blood of Christ, even the forgiveness of sins." "Being justified by faith, we have peace with God through our Lord Jesus Christ"— that peace which enables us in every state therewith to be content; which delivers us from all perplexing doubts, from all tormenting fears; and, in particular, from the "fear of death whereby we were all our lifetime subject to bondage."

At the same time the Son of God strikes at the root of that grand work of the devil—pride—causing the sinner to humble himself before the Lord, to abhor himself, as it were, in dust and ashes. He strikes at the root of self-will; enabling the humbled sinner to say in all things, "Not as I will, but as thou wilt." He destroys the love of the world; delivering them that believe in him from "every foolish and hurtful desire"; from the "desire of the flesh, the desire of the eyes, and the pride of life." He saves them from seeking, or expecting to find, happiness in any creature. As Satan turned the heart of man from the Creator to the creature, so the Son of God turns his heart back again from the creature to the Creator. Thus it is by manifesting himself, he destroys the works of the devil; restoring the guilty outcast from God, to his favor, to pardon and peace; the sinner in whom dwells no good thing, to love and holiness; the burdened, miserable sinner, to joy unspeakable, to real, substantial happiness.

The Quickening Power of God

Whosoever is born of God doth not commit sin; for his seed remaineth in him: and he cannot sin, because he is born of God.

1 John 3:9

The Scriptures describe being born of God, which must precede the witness that we are his children, as a vast and mighty change; a change "from darkness to light," as well as "from the power of Satan unto God"; as a "passing from death unto life," a resurrection from the dead. Thus the apostle to the Ephesians; "You hath he quickened who were dead in trespasses and sins" (2:1). And again, "When we were dead in sins, he hath quickened us together in heavenly places in Christ Jesus" (2:5, 6). But what knows he, concerning whom we now speak, of any such change as this? He is altogether unacquainted with this whole matter. This is a language which he does not understand. He tells you, "He always was a Christian. He knows no time when he had need of such a change." By this also, if he give himself leave to think, may he know, that he is not born of the Spirit; that he has never yet known God; but has mistaken the voice of nature for the voice of God.

But waiving the consideration of whatever he has or has not experienced in time past; by the present marks may we easily distinguish a child of God from a presumptuous self-deceiver. The Scriptures describe that joy in the Lord which accompanies the witness of his Spirit as an humble joy, a joy that abases to the dust; that makes a pardoned sinner cry out, "I am vile! What am I, or my father's house? Now mine eye seeth thee, I abhor myself in dust and ashes!" And wherever lowliness is, there is meekness, patience, gentleness, longsuffering. There is a soft, yielding spirit; a mildness and sweetness, a tenderness of soul, which words cannot express.

But do these fruits attend that *supposed* testimony of the Spirit, in a presumptuous man? Just the reverse. The more confident he is of the favor of God, the more is he lifted up; the more does he exalt himself; the more haughty and assuming is his whole behavior. The stronger witness he imagines himself to have, the more overbearing is he to all around him; the more incapable of receiving any reproof; the more impatient of contradiction. Instead of being more meek, and gentle, and teachable, more "swift to hear, and slow to speak," he is more slow to hear, and swift to speak; more unready to learn of anyone; more fiery and vehement in his temper, and eager in his conversation, his whole deportment, as if he were just going to take the matter out of God's hands, and himself to "devour the adversaries."

While you behold what manner of love the Father has given you, that you should be called a child of God, cleanse yourself "from all filthiness of flesh and spirit, perfecting holiness in the fear of God"; and let all your thoughts, words, and works be a spiritual sacrifice, holy, acceptable to God through Jesus Christ!

37. Thoughts on the True

Obedience Observed

And he that keepeth his commandments dwelleth in him, and he in him. And hereby we know that he abideth in us, by the Spirit which he hath given us.
1 John 3:24

"Hereby we know that he abideth in us by the [obedient] Spirit which he hath given us."

It is highly probable, there never were any children of God, from the beginning of the world unto this day, who were further advanced in the grace of God, and the knowledge of our Lord Jesus Christ, than the apostle John at the time when he wrote these words, and the fathers in Christ to whom he wrote. Notwithstanding which, it is evident, both the apostle himself, and all those pillars in God's temple, were very far from despising these marks of their being the children of God; and that they applied them to their own souls for the confirmation of their faith. Yet all this is no other than rational evidence, the witness of our spirit, our reason or understanding. It all revolves into this: Those who have these marks are the children of God. But we have these marks; therefore we are children of God (Rom. 8:16).

But how does it appear that we have these marks? This is a question which still remains. How does it appear that we do love God and our neighbor, and that we keep his commandments? Observe that the meaning of the question is, How does it appear to *ourselves* (not to *others*)? I would ask him, then, who proposes this question, How does it appear to you, that you are alive? And that you are now in ease, and not in pain? Are you not immediately conscious of it? By the same immediate consciousness, you will know if your soul is alive to God; if you are saved from the pain of proud wrath, and have the ease of a meek and quiet spirit. By the same means you cannot but perceive if you love, rejoice, and delight in God. By the same you must be directly assured, if you love your neighbor as yourself, if you are kindly affectioned to all mankind, and full of gentleness and longsuffering. And with regard to the outward mark of the children of God, which is, according to St. John, the keeping his commandments, you undoubtedly know in your own breast, if, by the grace of God, it belongs to you.

Love Is . . . Happiness

If we love one another, God dwelleth in us, and his love is perfected in us.
1 John 4:12b

Now, will anyone be so hardy as to say that love is misery? Is it misery to love God, to give him my heart who alone is worthy of it? Nay, it is the truest happiness; indeed, the only true happiness which is to be found under the sun. So does all experience prove the justness of that reflection which was made long ago, "Thou hast made us for thyself; and our heart cannot rest, until it resteth in thee." Or does anyone imagine, the love of our neighbor is misery; even the loving every man as our own soul? So far from it, that, next to the love of God, this affords the greatest happiness of which we are capable. Therefore,

> Let not the Stoic boast his mind unmoved,
> The brute philosopher, who ne'er has proved
> The joy of loving, or of being loved.

Love Leads to Fullness

No man has ever seen God; if we love one another, God abides in us and his love is perfected in us.
1 John 4:12 (RSV)*

When you thus love God and all mankind, and are transformed into his likeness, then the commandments of God will not be

---

* The concluding reading in the book is also based on 1 John 4 (vv. 2, 13)

grievous; you will no more complain that they destroy the comforts of life. So far from it, that they will be the very joy of your heart—ways of pleasantness, paths of peace! You will experience here that solid happiness which you had elsewhere sought in vain. Without servile fear or anxious care, so long as you continue on earth, you will gladly do the will of God here as the angels do it in heaven; and when the time is come that you should depart hence, when God says, "Arise, and come away," you will pass with joy unspeakable out of the body, into all the fullness of God.

Three in One

For there are three that bear record in heaven, the Father, the Word, and the Holy Ghost: and these three are one.

1 John 5:7

As strange as it may seem, in requiring you to believe, "there are three that bear record in heaven, the Father, the Word, and the Holy Ghost: and these three are one," you are not required to believe any mystery. Nay, that great and good man, Dr. Peter Browne, sometime Bishop of Cork, has proved at large that the Bible does not require you to believe any mystery at all. The Bible barely requires you to believe such facts; not the manner of them. Now the mystery does not lie in the *fact*, but altogether in the *manner*.

For instance: "God said, Let there be light: And there was light." I believe it: I believe the plain *fact*: There is no mystery at all in this. The mystery lies in the *manner* of it. But of this I believe nothing at all; nor does God require it of me.

Again: "The Word was made flesh." I believe this fact also. There is no mystery in it; but as to the *manner how* he was made flesh, wherein the mystery lies, I know nothing about it; I believe nothing about it; it is no more the object of my faith, than it is of my understanding.

To apply this to the case before us: "There are three that bear record in heaven: and these three are one." I believe this *fact* also (if I may use the expression), that God is Three and One. But the *manner how* I do not comprehend; and I do not believe

266

it. Now in this, in the *manner,* lies the mystery; and so it may; I have no concern with it. It is no object of my faith: I believe just so much as God has revealed, and no more. But this, the *manner,* he has not revealed; therefore, I believe nothing about it. But would it not be absurd in me to deny the fact, because I do not understand the manner? That is, to reject *what God has revealed,* because I do not comprehend *what he has not revealed?*

Loving and Living

> *And this is the record, that God hath given to us*
> *eternal life, and this life is in his Son.*
> **1 John 5:11**

This eternal life then commences when it pleases the Father to reveal his Son in our hearts; when we first know Christ, being enabled to "call him Lord by the Holy Ghost"; when we can testify, our conscience bearing us witness in the Holy Ghost, "The life which I now live, I live by faith in the Son of God, who loved me, and gave himself for me." And then it is that happiness begins; happiness real, solid, substantial. Then it is that heaven is opened in the soul, that the proper heavenly state commences, while the love of God, as loving us, is shed abroad in the heart, instantly producing love to all mankind; general, pure benevolence, together with its genuine fruits: lowliness, meekness, patience, contentedness in every state; an entire, clear, full acquiescence and in everything to give thanks.

As our knowledge and our love of him increase, by the same degrees and in the same proportion, the kingdom of an inward heaven must necessarily increase also; while we "grow up in all things into him who is our head." And when we are *complete in him,* as our translators render it; but more properly when we are *filled with him;* when "Christ in us, the hope of glory," is our God and our all; when he has taken the full possession of our heart; when he reigns therein without a rival, the Lord of every motion there; when we dwell in Christ, and Christ in us, we are one with Christ, and Christ with us; then we are completely happy; then we live "all the life that is hid with Christ in God"; then, and not till then, we properly experience what that word means, "God is love: and whosoever dwelleth in love, dwelleth in God, and God in him."

Dwelling in God

We know that whosoever is born of God sinneth not; but he that is begotten of God keepeth himself, and that wicked one toucheth him not.
1 John 5:18

No sooner is the child born into the world, than he exists in a quite different manner than he did in his mother's womb. He now *feels* the air with which he is surrounded, and which pours into him from every side, as fast as he alternately breathes it back, to sustain the flame of life, and hence springs a continual increase of strength, of motion, and of sensation; all the bodily senses being now awakened, and furnished with their proper objects.

His eyes are now opened to perceive the light, which, silently flowing in upon them, discovers not only itself, but an infinite variety of things, with which before he was wholly unacquainted. His ears are unclosed, and sounds rush in with endless diversity. Every sense is employed upon such objects as are peculiarly suitable to it; and by these inlets the soul, having an open intercourse with the visible world, acquires more and more knowledge of sensible things, of all the things which are under the sun.

So it is with him who is born of God. Before that great change is wrought, although he subsists by him, in whom all that have life "live, and move, and have their being," yet he is not *sensible* of God; he does not *feel,* he has no inward consciousness of his presence. He does not perceive that divine breath of life, without which he cannot subsist a moment: nor is he sensible of any of the things of God; they make no impression upon his soul. God is continually calling to him from on high, but he hears not; his ears are shut, so that the "voice of the charmer" is lost in him, "charm he never so wisely." He sees not the things of the Spirit of God; the eyes of his understanding being closed, and utter darkness covering his whole soul, surrounding him on every side. It is true he may have some faint dawnings of life, some small beginnings of spiritual motion; but as yet he has no spiritual senses

268

capable of discerning spiritual objects; consequently he "discerneth not the things of the Spirit of God; he cannot know them, because they are spiritually discerned."

Hence he has scarce any knowledge of the invisible world, as he has scarce any contact with it. Not that it is afar off; no, he is in the midst of it; it encompasses him round about. The *other world,* as we usually term it, is not far from every one of us: it is above, and beneath, and on every side. Only the natural man discerns it not; partly, because he has not spiritual senses, whereby alone we can discern. But when he is born of God, born of the Spirit, how he is changed. His soul is now sensible to God. The eyes of his understanding are now open. He clearly perceives and hears the voice of God: He "dwelleth in God, and God in him."

The Breath of the Spirit

We know that any one born of God does not sin, but He who was born of God keeps him, and the evil one does not touch him.
1 John 5:18 (RSV)

Being born of God immediately and necessarily implies the continual inspiration of God's Holy Spirit—God's breathing into the soul and the soul's breathing back what it first receives from God; a continual action of God upon the soul, and a reaction of the soul upon God; an unceasing presence of God, the loving, pardoning God, manifested to the heart, and perceived by faith; and an unceasing return of love, praise, and prayer, offering up all the thoughts of our hearts, all the words of our tongues, all the works of our hands, all our body, soul, and spirit, to be a holy sacrifice, acceptable unto God in Christ Jesus.

Thus we may infer the absolute necessity of this reaction of the soul (whatsoever it be called), in order to the continuance of the divine life therein. For it plainly appears, God does not continue to act upon the soul, unless the soul reacts upon God. He goes before us indeed with the blessings of his goodness. He first loves us, and manifests himself unto us. While we are yet afar off, he calls us to himself, and shines upon our hearts. But if we do not then love him who first loved us; if we will not hearken to his voice; if we turn our eye away from him, and will not attend to the light which he pours in upon us, his Spirit will not always strive; he will gradually withdraw and leave us to the darkness of our own hearts. He will not continue to breathe into our soul, unless our soul breathes toward him again; unless our love, and prayer, and thanksgiving, return to him, a sacrifice wherewith he is well pleased.

Let us learn then to follow that direction of the great apostle, "Be not high minded, but fear." Let us fear sin, more than death or hell. Let us have a jealous (though not painful) fear, lest we should succumb to our own deceitful hearts. "Let him that standeth take heed lest he fall." Even he who now stands fast in the grace of God, in the faith that overcomes the world, may nevertheless fall into inward sin, and thereby "make shipwreck of his faith." And how easily then will outward sin regain its dominion over him! You, therefore, oh, man of God! Watch always; that you may always hear the voice of God! Watch, that you may pray without ceasing, at all times, and in all places, pouring out our heart before him! So shall you always believe, and always love, and never commit sin.

38. Some Conclusions

Circles Inner and Outer

And we know that we are of God. . . .
1 John 5:19

There is a difference in his providential government over the children of men. A pious writer observes, "There is a threefold circle of divine providence." The *outermost circle* includes all the sons of men, Heathens, Mohammedans, Jews, and Christians. He causeth his sun to rise upon all. He giveth them rain and fruitful seasons. He pours ten thousand benefits upon them, and fills their hearts with food and gladness. With an *interior circle* he encompasses the whole visible Christian church, all that name the name of Christ. He has an additional regard to these, and a nearer attention to their welfare. But the *innermost circle* of his providence encloses only the invisible church of Christ, all real Christians, wherever dispersed in all corners of the earth; all that worship God (whatever denomination they are of) in spirit and in truth. He keeps these as the apple of an eye; he hides them under the shadow of his wings. And it is to these in particular that our Lord says, "Even the hairs of your head are all numbered."

The True God

And we know that the son of God is come, and hath given us an understanding, that we may know him that is true, and we are in him that is true, even in his Son Jesus Christ. This is the true God, and eternal life.

1 John 5:20

He is the true God, the only Cause, the sole Creator of all things. "By him," says the apostle Paul, "were created all things that

271

are in heaven, and that are on earth" yea, earth and heaven themselves; but the inhabitants are named, because more noble than the house—"visible and invisible." The several species of which are subjoined. "Whether they be thrones, or dominions, or principalities, or powers." So St. John: "All things were made by him, and without him was not anything made that was made." And, accordingly, St. Paul applies to him those strong words of the psalmist: "Thou, Lord, in the beginning hast laid the foundation of the earth, and the heavens are the work of thy hands."

And as the true God, he is also the Supporter of all the things that he has made. He bears, upholds, sustains all created things by the word of his power, by the same powerful word which brought them out of nothing. As this was absolutely necessary for the beginning of their existence, it is equally so for the continuance of it. Were his almighty influence withdrawn, they could not subsist a moment longer. Hold up a stone in the air; the moment you withdraw your hand, it naturally falls to the ground. In like manner, were he to withdraw his hand for a moment, the creation would fall into nothing.

As the true God, he is likewise the Preserver of all things. He not only keeps them in being, but preserves them in that degree of well-being which is suitable to their several natures. He preserves them in their several relations, connections, and dependencies, so as to compose one system of beings, to form one entire universe, according to the counsel of his will. How strongly and beautifully is this expressed:

"By whom all things consist." Or, more literally, "By and in him are all things compacted into one system." He is not only the support, but also the cement, of the whole universe.

True Religion

And we know that the Son of God has come and has given us understanding, to know him who is true; and we are in him who is true, in his Son Jesus Christ. This is the true God and eternal life.
1 John 5:20 (RSV)

True religion is right tempers toward God and man. It is, in two words, gratitude and benevolence; gratitude to our Creator and supreme Benefactor, and benevolence to our fellow-creatures. In other words, it is loving God with all our heart, and our neighbor as ourselves.

It is in consequence of our knowing God loves us, that we love him, and love our neighbor as ourselves. Gratitude toward our Creator cannot but produce benevolence to our fellow-creatures. The love of Christ constrains us, not only to be harmless, to do no ill to our neighbor, but to be useful, to be "zealous of good works"; "as we have time, to do good unto all men"; and to be patterns to all of true, genuine morality; of justice, mercy, and truth. This is religion, and this is happiness; the happiness for which we were made. This begins when we begin to know God, by the teaching of his own Spirit. As soon as the Father of spirits reveals his Son in our hearts, and the Son reveals his Father, the love of God is shed abroad in our hearts; then, and not till then, we are happy.

Doing Good Is of God

He that doeth good is of God: but he that doeth evil hath not seen God.
3 John 11b

We *are of God* who love God, or at least "fear him, and keep his commandments." This is the lowest character of those who "are of God"; who are not properly sons, but servants; who depart from evil, and study to do good, and walk in all his ordinances, because they have the fear of God in their hearts, and a sincere desire to please him. Fix in your heart this plain meaning of the term, *"the world";* those who do not thus fear God. Let no man deceive you with vain words; it means neither more nor less than this.

But understanding the term in this sense, what kind of friendship may we have with the world? We may, we ought to love them as ourselves (for they also are included in the word *neighbor*); to bear them real goodwill; to desire their happiness, as sincerely as we desire the happiness of our own souls; yea, we are in a sense to honor them (seeing we are directed by the apostle to "honor all men"), as the creatures of God; nay, as immortal spirits, who are capable of knowing, of loving, and of enjoying him to all eternity. We are to honor them as redeemed by his blood who "tasted death for every man." We are to bear them tender compassion when we see them forsaking their own mercies, wandering from the path of life, and hastening to everlasting destruction. We are never willingly to grieve their spirits, or give them any pain; but, on the contrary, to give them all the pleasure we innocently can; seeing we are to "please all men for their good." We are never to aggravate their faults; but willingly to allow all the good that is in them.

A Positive Religion

But ye, beloved, building up yourselves on your most holy faith, praying in the Holy Ghost, Keep yourselves in the love of God, looking for the mercy of our Lord Jesus Christ unto eternal life.
                                    Jude 20, 21

Religion does not consist in negatives, in bare harmlessness of any kind; nor merely in externals, in doing good, or using the means of grace, in works of piety (so-called) or of charity. It is nothing short of, or different from "the mind that was in Christ"; the image of God stamped upon the heart; inward righteousness, attended with the peace of God; and "joy in the Holy Ghost." The only way under heaven to true religion is, to "repent and believe the gospel"; or, (as the apostle words it,) "repentance towards God, and faith in our Lord Jesus Christ." By this faith, "he that worketh not, but believeth on him that justifieth the ungodly, is justified freely by his grace, through the redemption which is in Jesus Christ." And, lastly, that "being justified by faith," we taste of the heaven to which we are going; we are holy and happy; we tread down sin and fear, and "sit in heavenly places with Christ Jesus."

How We Should Walk

And when I saw him, I fell at his feet as dead. And he laid his right hand upon me, saying unto me, Fear not; I am the first and the last.
                                Revelation 1:17

We may learn from this short view of the providence of God, first, to put our whole trust in him who has never failed those who seek him. Our blessed Lord himself makes this very use of the great truth now before us. "Fear not, therefore." If you truly fear God, you need fear none beside. He will be a strong tower to all who trust in him from the face of your enemies. What is there either in heaven or in earth that can harm you, while you are under the care of the Creator and Governor of heaven and earth! Let all earth and all hell combine against you; yea, the whole animate and inanimate creation; they cannot harm while God is on your side. His favorable kindness covers you as a shield.

Nearly allied to this confidence in God is the thankfulness we owe for his kind protection. Let those give thanks whom the Lord thus delivers from the hand of all their enemies. What an unspeakable blessing it is to be the peculiar care of him who has all power in heaven and earth! How can we sufficiently praise him, while we are under his wings, and his faithfulness and truth are our shield and buckler!

But meantime we should take the utmost care to walk humbly and closely with our God. Walk *humbly*. For if you in anywise rob God of his honor, if you ascribe anything to yourself, the things which should have been for your wealth will prove to you an "occasion of falling." And walk *closely*. See that you have a conscience void of offense toward God and toward man. It is so long as you do this that you are the peculiar care of your Father which is in heaven. But let not the consciousness of his caring for you make you careless, indolent, or slothful: On the contrary, while you are penetrated with that deep truth, "The help that is done upon earth, he doeth it himself," be as earnest and diligent in the use of all the means as if you were your own protector.

A Concluding Note

Hereby know ye the Spirit of God: Every spirit that confesseth that Jesus Christ is come in the flesh is of God. . . . Hereby know we that we dwell in him, and he in us, because he hath given us of his Spirit.
1 John 4:2, 13

Let a man descend calmly into his heart, and see if there be no root of bitterness springing up; whether, at least, his thoughts, which are ever in motion, do not sometimes sally out into projects suggested by pride, or sink into indolent trifling, or be entangled in mean anxiety. Does not he find a motion of anger, or of gaiety, leavening him in an instant throughout; depriving him of the meekness and steady discernment he labored after? Or, let him but conceive at any time, that unfeigned obedience, and watchful zeal, and dignity of behavior, which is suitable, I do not say to an angel, but to a sinner that has "a good hope through grace," and endeavor to work himself up to it; and if he find no sort of obstacle to this within him, he has indeed then no opportunity of suffering. In short, if he is such an abject sort of creature, as will, unless grace should do him a perpetual violence, relapse frequently into a course of thinking and acting entirely without God; then he can never want occasions of suffering, but will find his own nature to be the same burden to him, as that "faithless and perverse generation" was to our Savior, of whom he said, "How long shall I be with you?"

I will conclude well with that excellent collect of our church—"O God, who in all ages hast taught the hearts of thy faithful people, by sending to them the light of the Holy Spirit; grant us by the same Spirit to have a right judgment in all things, and evermore to rejoice in his holy comfort, through the merits of Jesus Christ our Savior; who liveth and reigneth with thee, in the unity of the same Spirit, one God, world without end. Amen."